The Mid-

GARI
GUII

Proceeds from the sale of this book are distributed for community botanical needs.

Cover picture was taken July 8, 1982, Memphis, Tennessee. The following flowers are included in arrangement: Liatris, Roses, Daisies, Globe Thistle, Queen Anne's Lace, Daylilies, Cleome, Phlox, Butterfly Weed, Balloon Flower, Trumpet Vine, Gloriosa Daisy, Montbretia, Zinnias, Goose Neck, Double Daylily, Ageratum, Petunia, Crape Myrtle, Bee Balm

The Mid-South
GARDEN GUIDE

Completely Revised and Enlarged Edition

Compiled and Edited by
THE MEMPHIS GARDEN CLUB

Published for the
MEMPHIS GARDEN CLUB
1984

Manufactured in the United States of America

Library of Congress Cataloging in Publication Data
Main entry under title:

The Mid-south garden guide.

Bibliography: p.
Includes index.
1. Gardening. I. Memphis Garden Club
SB451.34.S68M53 1984 635.9'0975 83-23552
ISBN 0-87805-213-5

First Edition — 1954
Second Edition — 1958
Revised Edition — 1968
Revised Fourth Edition — 1972
Fifth Edition — 1975
Sixth Edition Completely Revised
First Printing — 1984
Second Printing — 1986
Third Printing — 1988
Fourth Printing — 1992
Fifth Printing – 1996

Contents

Charts

Acknowledgments

The new *Mid-South Garden Guide* would not be possible without the inspiration and expertise provided by the authors of the original volume. This committee wishes to thank those who led the way and in whose footsteps we follow.

Garden Guide Committee

Editor	Mrs. G. Blair Macdonald
Horticultural Editor	Mr. Edwin J. Toth
Assistant Editors	Mrs. Richard D. Harwood
	Mrs. J. Peter Norfleet
	Mrs. G. Carroll Todd
	Mrs. R. Dale Woodall
Business Managers	Mrs. Wm. Fitzgerald Fay
	Mrs. E. Alan Catmur
	Mrs. G. Blair Macdonald
Photography	Mr. Elvin McDonald
Illustrations	Mrs. Robert E. Norcross

Contributors

Mrs. Albert M. Austin
Mrs. Richard D. Austin
Mrs. B. Snowden Boyle, Jr.
Mrs. John D. Canale, Jr.
Mrs. George A. Coors
Mrs. Crittenden Currie
Mrs. W. Jeter Eason
Mr. and Mrs. Guy Erb
Mrs. Edward F. Falls
Mrs. Sidney Feuerstein
Mr. Andrew J. Hays, Jr.
Mr. Ferd Heckle
Mr. Karl Kaestle
Mrs. Peggy Smith Latham
Ms. Sylvia Leatherman
Mrs. William A. Leatherman
Mrs. Ross M. Lynn
Mrs. David B. Martin
Mrs. Michael McDonnell
Mrs. Clifford Merrin
Mr. and Mrs. Wilbur Olson
Mrs. J. Folsom Paul
Mr. Thomas D. Pellett
Mr. John Pierce
Mrs. Cooper Y. Robinson
Mrs. Robert G. Snowden
Mrs. Thomas H. Todd, Jr.
Mr. Plato Touliatos
Mrs. Richard A. Trippeer, Jr.
Mr. Dan West
Mrs. Hugh R. Wynne

Although adjustments should be made for varying climatic conditions, the horticultural information in the book will prove of great value and service to gardeners throughout the United States.

The AMERICAN HORTICULTURAL SOCIETY is the headquarters for all plant societies. For further information write the society at Mount Vernon, Virginia 22121.

The Mid-South

GARDEN GUIDE

Month by Month Gardening

The garden hints given in this section are aimed at average conditions in an average garden. Since gardening is not an exact science, there will always be some variation. Time of bloom may vary two or even three weeks, depending upon the weather, time of planting, depth of planting, and location in the garden. The period of bloom listed for each plant represents not its full cycle of bloom but the time when the plant can be depended upon for its main display. References cited are to special articles found elsewhere in the book.

JANUARY

January is usually a quiet month in the garden and is a good time to prepare for spring.

Planning

Plan on paper a new garden or changes in the old.
Order seed for early planting.
Order seed for some new and different plants.
Order new rose plants early.
Order ferns and wild flower plants.

Equipment

Get lawn mowers and pruning tools repaired and sharpened.
Make needed replenishments of flats, stakes, and labels.
Check condition of spraying equipment.
Be sure to have two separate sprayers, one for poison and one for fertilizer.

Plant

Perennials, trees, and *shrubs*—May be moved any time the soil is friable.

Sweet Peas—The latter part of this month is the ideal time for planting.

Poppies, larkspur—Sow after a shower or in light snow.

Fertilize

Trees & shrubs—The period of January, February, March is the proper time to fertilize. *See* "Trees."

Lawns—Apply lime if needed and not done in December. *See* "Lawns."

Spread sand in low areas.

Spray

Spray *broad-leaved evergreens,* especially *camellia, holly, photinia* and *euonymus* if infested with scale. Use a dormant oil spray if temperature is above 40° and below 80°.

Mulch

Mulch *lilies* with compost. Provide winter protection for tender plants.

Miscellaneous

Roses—Watch for holes at roots where plants have been loosened in ground by wind and rodents. Firm plants in ground and mound up. Sometimes it may be necessary to fasten large plants to stakes to hold them firmly.

After every freeze watch to see if any plants, especially *pansies*, have been heaved out of the ground.

See that *birds* are provided with suet, crumbs, wild bird seed, and a mixture of peanut butter, corn meal, and bacon grease. Peanut butter alone will choke the birds. Water is essential.

Winter greenery and plants for house

Aucuba will root in water; as light is needed, use glass container.

Mahonia will bloom and last a long time.

A tablespoon of sugar added to the water will help hold berries on *holly*.

House Plants

Wash and dust off leaves.

Water only when soil surface is dry; mist often. Do not mist geraniums or gesneriads.

Inspect for insects and disease.

January Bloom

Camellia, winter honeysuckle, winter jasmine, and in mild winters, flowering quince.

FEBRUARY

In many locations the sap begins to rise and days become longer. By February the Mid-South is usually past zero weather. The last two weeks of the month are tremendously important for planting. Plants which have had this extra time to make good root systems before hot weather will be more vigorous.

Spray

The first big job of the month is to get a *dormant spray* on the garden. The most effective time for this is just before the leaf buds pop. This is usually during the first or second week of the month. Not only *trees* and *shrubs* but also *roses* and the *perennial border* should be included in this spray. This is the most important spray of the year. *See* "Sprays."

Plant

Dogwood—February is the ideal time. The important thing in planting dogwood is good drainage and shallow planting. Dogwood thrives best in acid soil. Plant high. For best results start with small trees.

Broad-leaved evergreens—February is also an ideal time to plant broad-leaved evergreens, especially *magnolia, holly,* and *photinia.*

Perennials—Most perennials may be divided and transplanted.

Trees and *Shrubs*

Roses—Plant as soon after February 15th as possible. This applies to planting of new roses and moving of old ones. *See* "Roses."

Seed—Sow seed outdoors of annual *candytuft, cornflowers, larkspur,* and *phlox drummondi.*

Fertilize

Roses—Apply top-dressing of cottonseed meal or milorganite under generous layer of compost or rotted manure. Dehydrated manure (obtainable at seed and garden stores) eliminates danger of nut grass and weed seeds. Keep manure away from stems.

Lawns—Apply lime if needed and not done in December or January. *See* "Lawns."

Trees and all but *spring flowering Shrubs*—If not done in January. *See* "Trees."

Prune

Evergreens—One of the big projects for the latter part of the month is to get the evergreens pruned for size and shape control. It is important to get this done before the new growth comes out. This seems to be the phase of gardening that is most often badly done. Prune off holly berries to promote blooming for new berries. *See* "Pruning."

Flowering shrubs—Cut out only dead wood. Many borers can be pruned out at this time. Dispose of clippings.

Prune *hydrangeas* the last week in the month. *See* "Pruning."

Roses—*See* "Roses."

Cold Frame

Seeds—For early bloom, plant seeds of blue salvia, feverfew, lupine, nicotiana, scabiosa, snapdragon, verbena.

Cuttings—Plant cuttings of *shrubs*. Make cuttings about 8 inches long, putting at least two buds underground. Use ⅓ perlite, ⅓ sand, and ⅓ soil. *See* "Propagation."

Vegetables—Plant seeds of brussels sprouts, spring cabbage plants, kale, lettuce, onion sets, English and snap peas, radishes, spring spinach. Plant *asparagus* in already prepared beds.

February Bloom

Indoors—As soon as buds begin to swell, force into bloom in water, sprays of *forsythia, fruit trees, Japanese quince, Oriental magnolia*. Place in sunny window.

In the Garden—Crocus, early daffodils, helleborus (Christmas rose and Lenten rose), hyacinth, pansy, scilla, snowdrop, snowflake, violet; camellia, flowering quince, forsythia, loropetalum, pussy willow, spirea, thunbergia, winter jasmine.

MARCH

March, with its lavish display of daffodils and flowering trees, is one of the most beautiful months of the year. It is also one of the busiest.

Roses

If not pruned in February, do so immediately. Watch for borers while pruning and be sure to cut them out. Dispose of all trimmings.

After pruning, give final dormant spray of lime-sulphur or a dormant oil spray. After new leaves appear, give weekly treatment for black spot. *See* "Sprays." It is suggested that roses should be sprayed twice a week for the first two or three weeks after leafing out since the best way to deal with black spot is to prevent its getting started.

Plant new roses now. Try to get them in the ground before March 15th. Excellent field grown two-year-old roses may be obtained locally at this time. Buy plants in containers, or plants whose roots have been "heeled in" to protect them from drying. This is the time to plant tree roses.

Plant

Roses—*See* "Roses."

Evergreens—Plant *magnolia, holly*, etc. Balls should be handled carefully. Plants should be watered, then mulched to conserve moisture.

Flowering shrubs—May be moved with ball of dirt, small plants barerooted. Dig or cut away sprouts of *lilac* and other flowering shrubs and transplant. This is an inexpensive way to increase stock of plants. This is the best month to move *crape myrtle.*

Perennials—Divide and replant.

Gladiolus—Put out first planting early in month and continue at two week intervals for succession of bloom. Before planting, soak corms for three hours in solution of Lysol, 1½ tablespoons to gallon of water.

Lawns—Lawns may be sodded. Treat lawns with a preemergence weed killer to control crabgrass.

Summer flowering bulbs

Clematis—See "Vines."

Pansy Seedlings—May still be moved into border.

Lilies—Some may still be planted if good bulbs are available. *See* "Lilies."

Hosta

Tuberoses—Soak in water two or three hours beforehand.

Ferns and wild flowers—See "Ferns" and "Wild Flowers."

Fall flowering bulbs

Zephyranthes lily—both the pink and the white. Plant or transplant.

Outdoor containers—Weather permitting. Start caladium tubers indoors, do not put outside until both soil and temperature are warm day and night.

Fertilize

All the garden except acid-loving plants and iris. *See* "Iris."

Trees if not done in January or February. *See* "Trees."

Tulips and Daffodils—Small amount of superphosphate, bone meal or 0–20–20 early in month to increase size of flowers.

Gardenias—Scatter aluminum sulphate or powdered sulfur around, a handful to each plant.

Peonies—Scatter wood ashes or superphosphate around plants.

Clematis—Apply 1 cupful lime per plant.

Boxwood—Fertilize and lime. *See* "Boxwood."

Camellias—Top-dress with prepared azalea-camellia fertilizer. Do not overfertilize. Follow directions.

Roses—See "Roses."

Prune

Crape Myrtles and *altheas—See* "Pruning."

Evergreens—If this pruning was not completed in February, finish as early in this month as possible. *See* "Pruning."

Ivy—Cut back hard, whether on wall or used as a ground cover. It will look bare at first but will soon come out. It will kill trees if allowed to climb. Ivy likes lime.

Liriope—Cut back with a lawn mower. Raise blade above it and lower on top of plant.

Spray

See "Sprays."

Peonies, lilies, and *clematis*—as they emerge. If they had blight last season, spray with a fungicide. Repeat twice at ten-day intervals.

Lilacs, ivy, vinca minor, and other plants that suffer from leaf spot with a fungicide such as Manzate.

Camellias—for scale with a dormant oil spray.

Azaleas—for blight with a fungicide such as Zineb.

Roses—as soon as leaves emerge. *See* "Roses."

Mulch

Replenish mulch on *azaleas* and *camellias* if needed. Avoid a deep mulch as it will injure feeder roots. Remove leaf covering from the garden gradually. Too-heavy covering will smother plants just coming up. Too-sudden removal may expose them to frost.

Cold Frame

Start seeds of *scabiosa, snapdragon, nicotiana,* and *verbena.* Seeds of *perennials* may also be started.

Slips of many perennials may be rooted: *carnations, pinks, shasta daisies,* etc.

Root cuttings of *azaleas, camellias, hollies,* and *shrubs.* Still time for *rose* cuttings. Place under glass jar in the garden.

Miscellaneous

As soon as soil dries out enough begin to cultivate by hand weeding to avoid injuring shallow roots.

Rake up bird seed hulls from under bird feeders as they will kill anything under them.

Sweet peas must be supported by cane brush, twine, or chicken wire.

Pick dead flowers from *tulips* and *daffodils* because seed production weakens next year's bulbs. To assure next year's bloom do not cut bulb foliage before it turns yellow and dies.

Vegetables

See "Vegetables."

Plant beets, broccoli plants, brussels sprouts, cabbage plants, carrot seeds, cauliflower plants, English peas, Irish potatoes, lettuce, onion sets, radish seeds, snap peas, and turnip greens.

Houseplants

Divide or at least repot any overgrown houseplant. After repotting, cut back weak, leggy portions to encourage new growth. Now increase fertilizer. Apply an application every two weeks. To start cuttings, *see* "Propagation."

March bloom

Bluebells, chionodoxa, daffodil, hyacinth, early iris, pansy, violet, Carolina jasmine; azalea, camellia, forsythia, pearl bush, photinia, quince, spirea, viburnum burkwoodii; and flowering trees, fruit trees (crabapple, cherry, peach, and pear) early magnolia, and redbud.

APRIL

This is the biggest month for most gardens as they are ablaze with color.

Dahlia

The first project of the month is to bring dahlias out of storage. *See "Dahlia."*

Plant

Roses—Dormant roses should not be planted after April 15th. Container roses may be planted until May 15. It is very important to mulch newly planted roses. It is also advisable to cover each rose with a basket for a week or so after planting to protect from drying out. *See* "Roses."

Tuberoses—Late-planted bulbs should be soaked a couple of hours in water before planting.

Gladiolus—Make additional planting.

Violets—Divide and replant.

Vegetables—Bush snap beans, pole snap beans, sweet corn, radishes, tomato plants, lettuce. *See* "Vegetables."

Perennial Phlox

Transplant seedlings of early planted perennials from cold frame into garden. Transplanted early, they get a good start before it gets hot.

Do not put tender bedding plants out too soon. Check frost date with local nursery or garden center.

Fertilize

Lawns—*See* "Lawns"

Roses—*See* "Roses"

Camellias—after they bloom with azalea-camellia fertilizer.

Epsom Salts may be applied to the garden, especially all berried plants, for healthier plants.

Pot Up Plants for Terraces and Garden Urns

For plants on a shady terrace nothing flourishes and blooms better than the angel wing *begonia*, a variety with silver-spotted leaves. Other choice selections are *caladium, impatiens, fibrous begonia, geranium,* and *pandanus.* Caladiums are available in red, pink, or white with green veins—the latter shows up particularly well at night. Since caladiums are very tender, they should not be put out until the soil is warm. If plants or planted urns are to be placed in full sun, select plant material that will survive hot sun and drying out. *Periwinkle (vinca rosea)* and *pandanus* are recommended for such spots. *Geraniums* need partial shade. Paint porch and garden furniture, bird bath, urns, and mailbox.

Spray

See "Sprays."

Spray *perennials, peonies, clematis,* and *vinca minor* with a fungicide.
Spray *holly* and *boxwood* for leaf miner.
Spray *azaleas* immediately after blooming for lace bug.
Use same spray on *pyracantha*.
Spray *roses*.
Spray *gladioli* for thrips.

Mulch

It is very important that every newly-planted flower, shrub, or tree should be mulched at time of planting. Do it as a part of the planting routine, like watering. It will add a great deal to the plant's chance of success and keep the ground around it from caking on top. *See* "Materials to Use For Mulch."

Prune

Azaleas—Prune during and immediately after blooming. Kurumes hold onto faded flowers which should be picked off to avoid unsightliness.

Flowering shrubs—Prune as soon as they have finished blooming or while in bloom for arrangements.

Peonies and roses—Disbud for specimen blooms.

Propagate

Shrubs, especially *azalea* and *winter jasmine, climbing rose, magnolia,* and many vines, may be propagated by layering. Continue to make cuttings of houseplants. *See* "Propagation," and "Layering" (under "Azaleas").

Start cuttings of chrysanthemums in cold frame. *See* "Chrysanthemums." Stock of many bedding plants may be increased by cuttings, especially dwarf ageratum, torenia, and verbena.

Cold Frame

Plant seeds of perennials and biennials—columbine, canterbury bells, foxglove, sweet william. These seedlings should be transplanted into a partially shaded place for the summer, then put into permanent places in fall.

Plant seeds of many annuals, including early flowering aster and petunia. For spikes of bloom, plant celosia in many forms and colors.

Zinnia—Wait until May for planting zinnia seeds. They get a better start in hot weather and soon catch up with greenhouse-grown plants.

Order

Place orders for *daffodil, hyacinth,* and *tulip bulbs.* There is usually a discount on orders received by growers before May 1st.

April Bloom

Ajuga, alyssum, bleeding-heart, candytuft, columbine, daffodil, daisy, daylily, forget-me-not, grass pinks, iris, Jacob's ladder, lily-of-the-valley, pansy, phlox divaricata, primrose, ranunculus, scilla, shooting star, sweet william, thrift, tulip, vinca, violet; azalea, beauty bush, deutzia, lilac, some spireas, tamarisk, viburnum, weigela, yellow jasmine, dogwood, and most flowering trees.

MAY

May is the month of the iris, peony, and rose.

Plant

Annuals and Perennials—plant early in the month. Keep well watered.

Bermuda Seed—Best time to sow; *see* "Lawns."

Chrysanthemum—Transplant rooted cuttings into garden; *see* "Chrysanthemums."

Dahlia—Cut, divide, and plant; *see* "Dahlias."

Gladiolus—Make additional plantings.

Roses—Container-grown roses may be planted until May 15.

Vegetables—Bush and pole snapbeans, bush and pole lima beans, cantaloupes, sweet corn, cucumbers, eggplants, okra, parsley, peppers, squash, tomatoes, watermelons. *See* "Vegetables."

Fertilize

Azaleas—See "Azaleas."

Roses—See "Roses."

Lawns—If not done in April. *See* "Lawns."

Spring Bulbs—After blooming. *See* "Bulbs."

Spray

See "Spray."

Arborvitae and junipers—Watch for bagworm. If infested spray with insecticide such as Malathion, Diazinon, or Cygon. Follow directions carefully. Picking off "bags" is often sufficient.

Azaleas—Spray for lace bug if not done in April.

Gladiolus—Spray for thrips.
Mimosa—Spray at end of the month for worms.
Rose—Continue to spray

Prune

Climbing roses—Prune as soon as they have finished blooming. Cut some of the oldest wood back to the ground or to a strong new shoot. New canes will soon come out which will produce next year's flowers. Climbers need no other pruning except removal of dead of diseased wood.

Bulbs and bearded iris—Cut seed pods as soon as they form because they sap the plant's strength.

Stake

Stake tall plants early before the weather beats them down.

May Bloom

Azalea, baptisia, bugloss, canterbury-bells, clematis, columbine, coreopsis, cornflower, early daisy, foxglove, iris, lily, pansy, peony, pinks, phlox, poppy, rose, salvia, sweet william, veronica; abelia, azalea, deutzia, golden-chain tree, honeysuckle, Japanese snowball, mock orange, pomegranate, weigela.

JUNE

June is the transition time from spring to summer. Now is the time to remove faded flowers and foliage of perennials and fill the gaps with bedding plants.

Mulch

The time of heat and shortage of rain is almost at hand. The important job of the month is to finish working out the garden and protect it with a generous mulching. *See* "Mulch." *Azaleas, camellias,* and other acid-loving plants need a special mulch. *See* "Azaleas."

Spray

Spray *roses*—*See* "Sprays."

Plant

Gladiolus—Late plantings give spikes of bloom in fall to arrange with dahlias.

Daylily—May be seen in bloom and planted at this time.

Iris—Good time to divide and replant bearded type. Cut foliage back to about 6″ after moving. *See* "Iris."

Naked Lady and *spider lily*

Seeds—Still time to plant seeds of *zinnia, marigold,* and *balsam* for second crop.

Vegetables—Bush & pole snap beans, bush & pole lima beans, cucumbers, eggplants, peppers, squash, tomato plants.

Water

Water during dry spells.

Fertilize

Camellia—Fertilize early in month if not done in April. Use special azalea-camellia fertilizer. Follow directions.

Bermuda and *Zoysia*—Fertilize and water in.

Roses—*See* "Roses."

Prune

Chrysanthemums—Pinch out tips when plants are 6″ to 8″ high. For more compact plants, pinch once or twice more later in season until July 15th before the buds form.

Hardy candytufts and *golden alyssum*—Shear after blooming to remove seed pods and make plants neat and compact.

June Bloom

Balloon flower, bee balm, blackberry lily, butterfly weed, coreopsis, cornflower, daylily, feverfew, funkia, gladiolus, hollyhock, Japanese iris, lily, nicotiana, petunia, phlox, rose scabiosa, shasta daisy, sweet pea, verbena; butterfly bush, golden-rain tree, hydrangea, hypericum, mimosa, stewartia, sourwood, vitex, yucca.

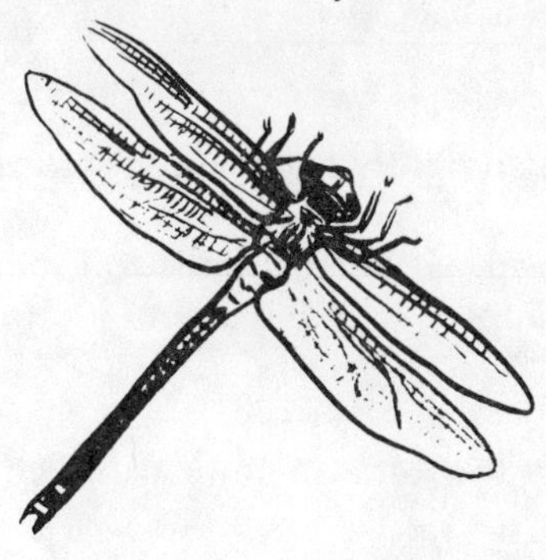

JULY

The key to getting through the month successfully is mulch and water.

Plant

Daylily—Still may be planted.
Gladiolus—Last planting July 1st.
Seedlings—Transplant second crop.
Biennial seeds—Such as canterbury bells, foxglove and sweet william.
Perennial phlox—Start root cuttings.
Ivy, wandering Jew, philodendron, and *begonia*—Start cuttings for houseplants.
Vegetables—Fall cabbage, parsley seeds, collards.

Fertilize

Camellias—Do not fertilize after July 1st.
Chrysanthemums—Fertilize about July 15th and water well. *See* "Chrysanthemums."
Dahlias—For extra special blooms, *see* "Dahlia."
Roses—*See* "Roses."

Spray

See "Sprays."
Roses—Continue to spray.
Gladiolus—Spray for thrips.
Azalea, camellia, boxwood—Spray for lace bug and spider mite.
Evergreen—Scale.
Mimosa—Fresh hatching of worms.
Arborvitae and *juniper*—Check for bagworm, pick off, and dispose; spray if infestation is bad.

Prune

Roses—Prune bush lightly about July 1st to encourage new growth for fall bloom.
Ferns—Cut broken, withered fronds to ground at the end of July. Fresh fronds will appear for fall garden.

Mulch

Azaleas and *Camellias*—Check mulch. Mulch should never be less than 2 inches deep, but do not smother plants.

Zinnias and *Chrysanthemums*—Mulch is a necessity. Plants not mulched need to be cultivated frequently. Overhead sprinkling causes mildew.

Miscellaneous—*Important*—

Soak garden thoroughly at least once a week during dry weather.

Raise blades on lawn mowers. Grass should not be closely cut in hot, dry weather.

July Bloom

Balsam, butterfly weed, canna, cleome, cosmos, dahlia, daylily, funkia, gladiolus, hibiscus, lily, lycoris, lythrum, marigold, petunia, phlox, portulaca, rudbeckia, salvia, scabiosa, shasta daisy, snapdragon, snow-on-the-mountain, tuberose, verbena, veronica, zinnia; althaea, buddleia, crape myrtle, montbretia.

AUGUST

Annuals are at their peak of bloom. Work in the garden pretty much follows the pattern of July.

Plant

Madonna Lily

Seeds—Calendula, columbine, English daisy, forget-me-not, pansy, sweet william, violet.

Boxwood—Root cuttings. *See* "Boxwood."

Phlox—Root cuttings.

Shasta Daisy—Root cuttings.

Vegetables—Fall cabbage, kale, turnip greens.

Fertilize

Roses—Last feeding early in the month; *see* "Roses."

Chrysanthemums—Last feeding for special blooms; *see* "Chrysanthemums."

Azaleas and *camellias*—Add acid to soil if the leaves show signs of chlorosis. *See* "pH Factor in Soil." Do not confuse this yellowing of leaves with the whitish, speckled condition of leaves caused by lace bug. Epsom salts will also green up a plant.

Spray

See "Sprays."

Azalea, camellia, boxwood—For spider mite and lace bug.
Roses—*See* "Roses."
Gladiolus—Thrips.
Perennial phlox and *zinnia*—With a fungicide at first sign of mildew. Follow this with frequent use of an all-purpose spray which includes control for red spider.
Dahlia—Red spider and chewing insects; *see* "Sprays."

Prune

Chrysanthemums and *dahlias*—Disbud for specimen flowers. Do not disbud the pompom mum.
Torenia, browallia, verbena—Shear for fresh crop of bloom.
Native fern—Cut shaggy and broken fronds at ground level.

Water

Continue to water garden, especially *azaleas* and *camellias*, which are forming buds for next year. Water early in the morning or late afternoon as sun will burn leaves.

Mulch

Weed and mulch garden. *See* "Materials to Use for Mulch."

August Bloom

Ageratum, angel's-trumpet, balsam, browallia, canna, celosia, cleome, clematis, dahlia, four-o-clock, funkia, gladiolus, lily, marigold, phlox, portulaca, rattle box, salvia, snow-on-the-mountain, torenia, vinca, pink zephyranthes lily, zinnia; althaea, butterfly bush, crape myrtle, Pee Gee hydrangea, tamarisk.

SEPTEMBER

This is the month to weed, water, and mulch again.

Plant

Madonna Lily—if not done in August
Peony and *phlox*—divide and plant
Daylily
Phlox—root cutting
Shasta Daisy—root cutting
Vegetables—Lettuce, all spinach, and turnip greens
Winter grass—Sow rye grass early in the month for winter lawn. In

bare places seed comes up much better if dirt is loosened before planting. Otherwise it is apt to float away when watered.

Fertilize

Lawns—See "Lawns."

Chrysanthemum—Stop feeding when buds show color.

Azaleas and *camellias*—May need to have acid added to the soil. The long-continued summer watering tends to bring soil back to neutral. *See* "pH Factor in Soil."

Water

Begin to slow down on the watering of *azaleas* toward end of this month to harden them off for winter. Do not let dry out.

Camellias—Spray foliage often on camellias which are about to burst into bloom. Frequent foliage spraying as well as the weekly soaking is what they like at this time.

Spray

See "Sprays."

Azalea and *pyracantha*—Lace bug.

Rose—Continue to spray.

Dahlia—Continue to spray. Try to avoid spray on blooms.

Prune

Dahlia and large flowered *chrysanthemums*—disbud. Keep faded blooms cut off of all plants to prolong bloom.

Mulch

Azaleas and *camellias* may need more mulch.

September Bloom

Ageratum, aster, perennial aster, begonia, canna, celosia, chrysanthemum, coral vine, ginger lily, gladiolus, jacobinia, liriope, marigold, morning glory, petunia, phlox, rattle box, rose, spider lily, torenia, vinca, white zephyranthes lily, zinnia; althaea, buddleia, crape myrtle, Franklin tree.

OCTOBER

October is a rewarding month in the garden. The light frosts seem only to stimulate all the plants to an extra spurt of bloom and an

added intensification of color. The garden this month is choice for the flower arranger because of the great variety of form and color. This is the month when the dahlias and chrysanthemums come into their own, when the rose puts out its most perfect long-stemmed flowers.

Plant

Camellias—See "Camellias."

Perennials—Plant *daylilies* early in the month. Plant *shasta daisies, Siberian iris, peonies,* and *phlox.*

Biennials—Transplant into their permanent locations husky seedlings of *canterbury bells, English daisy, forget-me-nots, foxglove,* and *pansy.*

Bulbs—Plant after soil has cooled, *chionodoxa, crocus, daffodil, scilla,* and other small bulbs of spring. Caution: Do not plant *lilies* til mid-November; do not plant *tulips* before November 15th, preferably December 1st. *See* "Bulbs."

Annuals—Broadcast seeds of *cornflower, larkspur,* and *Queen Anne's lace* where they are to bloom, mixing seeds with sand to insure even distribution.

Herbs—Pot up *basil, chives, parsley, rosemary, sage,* and *sweet marjoram* for the sunny window.

Evergreens—Most evergreens may be planted this month. *See* "Evergreens." Small plants grown in cans are recommended for varieties hard to transplant, especially pyracantha.

Evergreen Propagation—Dip cuttings in a hormone powder, such as Rootone. Place in the compost pile with lots of sand. Water well. Cuttings should be rooted by spring.

Fertilize

Lawns—If not done in September; *see* "Lawns."

Spray

Azaleas—Lace bug; *see* "Sprays."

Water

Winter grass—Keep moist to aid germination.

Azaleas—Moderately water; do not let dry out.

Camellias—Water foliage frequently as in September; do not let soil dry out.

Miscellaneous

Chrysanthemum and *dahlia*—Label all varieties for next year's propagation.

Make notes in garden guide for new varieties for next year's order.

Lily—Prepare bed; *see* "Lilies."

Dahlia—Continue to disbud for specimen bloom.

Add leaves to compost pile.

October Bloom

Ageratum, perennial aster, camellia, celosia, colchicum, chrysanthemum, dahlia, marigold, petunia, rose, salvia, torenia, zinnia.

NOVEMBER

November is the big clean-up month. Pull up all spent annuals, cut off all spent perennials, being careful to mark the spot where some of the dormant or late-sprouting varieties are located. Dig out all unhealthy looking evergreens or flowering shrubs and prepare ground for replacements.

In the garden, the big thrill of the month comes from the *camellias.* Watch the habit of growth of different varieties. Some grow tall, some medium, some quite dwarf. Buy plants in bloom in the nurseries.

Plant

Planting schedule same as for October with these additions:

Lilies—Bulbs from catalogues arrive at this time. Bulbs also available at local seed stores. *Plant immediately.*

Azaleas—Plant early enough for them to get established before severe cold or wait for early spring. Best time is before blooming.

Rose Cuttings—Thanksgiving week is a favored time for this. Select well-drained location. Cover cuttings with glass jars or bank sides of row with wheat straw which lets in light, air, and water but protects from cold. Caution: do not move established roses before December 1st. Early spring planting preferred.

Daffodils—As soon as possible.

Tulips—Do not plant before November 15th.

Trees—*See* "Trees."

Shrubs—*See* "Shrubs."

Dig and Store

Dahlia—*See* "Dahlias."

Caladium, canna, gladiolus, Peruvian daffodil, and *tuberose*—These should be hung indoors in mesh bags to protect from frost.

Fertilize

Top-dress whole garden with 0–20–20 to winterize. Water thoroughly.

Prune

Roses—Look for stem borer; *see* "Roses."

Dogwood—Cut out borers.

Mulch

Azaleas and *camellias*—Mulch if necessary. Do not smother plants.

Cold Frame

Many cuttings may be put in at this time.

Caution in Buying Plants

In selecting plants at the nursery check the ball of dirt on each plant. The size of the ball is more important than the size of the plant. A big plant dug with a small ball suffers a great shock, whereas the small plant dug with a generous ball hardly knows it has been moved and will quickly outstrip the other in growth. Patronize nurserymen who dig plants carefully and who make every effort to handle plants correctly after they have been dug. This kind of handling is more expensive, but it pays off. This includes hilling up around balls with sawdust as protection against drying winds. It also means that in lifting, the left hand is used to support the ball underneath as insurance against the ball's being broken by its own weight. Never pick a plant up by its trunk. Check balls and cans for Bermuda and Johnson grass roots, which will invade entire bed.

Leaves

Do not dispose of leaves. Save them for the garden. They may be utilized in two ways:

1. Half-rotted hardwood leaves make a perfect mulch for azaleas and camellias.
2. Added to the compost pile, leaves are a valuable source of humus for the garden. Chop with lawn mower for speedier decomposition.

November Bloom

Camellias, chrysanthemums, roses, witch-hazel.

DECEMBER

December is a good month for taking inventory, for reviewing the year's successes and failures, and for deciding what to do about the latter. If a plant has failed, there is always a reason for it. The cause usually comes to light with digging. Often it is *too deep planting*, or overaccumulation of mulch and fallen leaves. Sometimes the cause is a diseased root system and the plant is not worth saving. Old plants are seldom worth trying to save. Younger plants can often be restored by the simple process of moving them to a new location or by severe pruning. Since most plants are relatively dormant at this time and since other garden work is less pressing, December is an ideal time for this weeding out.

Roses

See "Roses."

Plant

Because winters can be wet, make use of any period of clear

weather this month when the ground is friable to plant or transplant. Fall and winter planting give a better root start.

Tulips
Shrubs and *Trees*
Spring flowering bulbs

Fertilize

Lawns—Apply agricultural lime; *see* "Lawns." Do not use quick lime.

Miscellaneous

See that evergreen plants go into freezing weather well watered.

Place in jars of water *sweet potato, carrot, beet*. The sprouts will add interesting forms of green to the window garden.

December Bloom

Camellias, osmanthus.

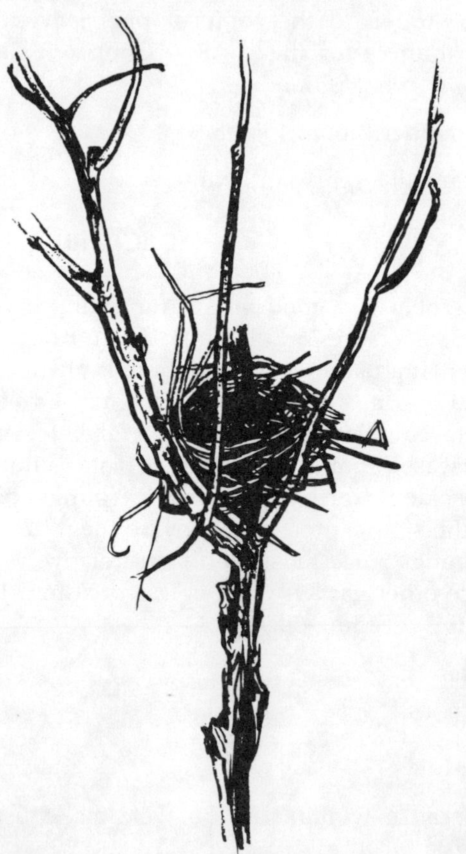

Garden Care

SOIL PREPARATION

Soil Analysis

The soil in this section of the country is mostly neutral clay, which can easily be built up with humus and fertilizers to be highly productive. In some areas there is a white subsoil which is cold and soggy. For this type of soil, drainage and the generous addition of humus are absolutely necessary.

Soil test kits may be purchased at most seed and garden stores, or information regarding soil testing may be obtained from agricultural extension services. Knowing the pH factor in soil is important for it can determine the amount of success achieved in the growing of most plants. *See* "pH Factor in Soil."

Drainage

No single operation is as important to permanent success in gardening as good drainage. It is wise to get expert advice to find out what type of drainage is necessary for each individual garden, for there is no way for the average gardener to know whether or not all or any part of the land needs drainage. Many gardeners think that a sloping land is a guarantee of effective drainage and thus enjoy a false sense of security.

Deep, wide spreading roots are both drouth and health insurance, but root growth will not enter saturated areas. Therefore, if the fundamental drainage is not properly handled, excess water will remain in the soil and all the fertilizers in the world will not make the garden grow. If a severe drainage problem makes it necessary put down agricultural tile (drainage pipes) in the subsoil, be sure the tile has some place to empty, so that surplus water will drain off, not stand. Do not plant anything with a large root system (*i.e.*, willows) near the tiling, as roots will clog drains.

Deep Digging

If the subsoil is tight clay, deep digging is important for drainage and aeration. The practical way of doing this is the same, whether digging a hole for a single shrub or preparing a bed. Dig out the topsoil and lay it to one side, keeping it separate. Then dig out the subsoil (total depth should be at least 2 feet, deeper for trees and large shrubs).

Since the subsoil is poor, it will need more doctoring than the layer of topsoil. Work into the subsoil 2″–3″ of compost or well-rotted or dehydrated manure and a generous sprinkling of cottonseed meal and bone meal. Add one-third clean, sharp builder's sand, and one-third existing soil. The topsoil will not need as much compost and sand, but will need the same amount of cottonseed meal and bone meal. Mix thoroughly. In replacing soil, put the topsoil layer in the bottom of the hole or bed, and the doctored subsoil on top. This mixture will settle several inches and the area should not be planted until after a hard rain. If planting must be made immediately, set plant high enough to allow for settling.

Cultivation

Even after proper preparation, soil in time packs again and needs some cultivation for aeration and proper penetration of water. A narrow spade (sharp shooter) is excellent for this, for it can be driven into the ground in the area between plants without damaging the roots. Doing this assures not only better aeration but a deeper penetration of humus and plant food. Use a small hoe for surface cultivation; weed shallow rooted plants by hand.

Humus

Humus is decomposed organic matter, such as compost, leaf mold, rotted or dehydrated manure, peat moss, etc. Be sure leaves in compost are well decomposed, as whole leaves will cause problems.

Humus is used to lighten and aerate the soil, as well as to provide a good working place for healthy bacteria which is necessary for the successful growth of plant life.

Nothing is more useful than the basic substance of Mid-South soil, which is clay, but it is dense and needs the addition of humus, which allows both water and air to be present together in the soil. Humus decomposes and becomes available as plant food. Because of this, it must be replaced every year or two. If the soil is in particular need, humus can be spaded in between the plants with a sharpshooter, or spread on the surface of an established bed and worked in with a hoe. Rain and snow will help humus penetrate.

Although cinders, gravel or sand will lighten heavy clay, they have no water-holding capacity or food value.

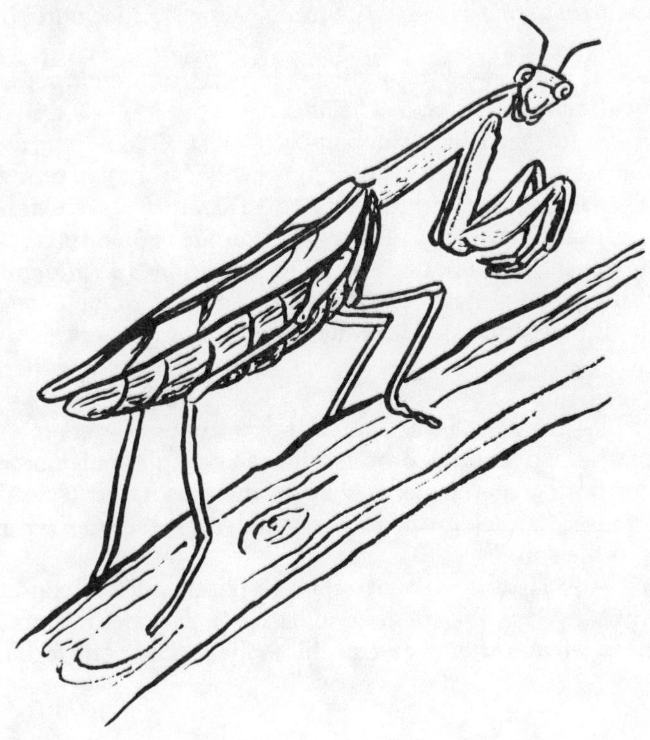

FERTILIZERS AND THEIR USE

Soil fertility can be maintained only in conjunction with proper drainage and watering. Even so, good loamy soil in the garden is temporary and must be augmented from time to time. Beginners are inclined to apply plant food in astonishing proportions, and sometimes with disastrous results. This is true of both organic and inorganic materials. It is best to apply fertilizers sparingly once a month during the entire growing season. Never fertilize when soil is dry or plant is in bad shape. Some experts advise light fertilization every two weeks from spring until fall. This maintains a constant rate. Too much fertilizer will burn leaf tips. If time or temperature prevent such careful attention to detail, then March, July and November are good times to fertilize. *See* "Month-by-Month and Schedule for Fertilizing the Garden." Note exceptions.

Basic Elements

The three basic elements in fertilizer necessary for plant life are nitrogen, phosphorus and potash.

Nitrogen for plants is comparable to protein for people. It is a plant stimulant for luxurious foliage, strong stems, and chlorophyll for color.

Phosphorus is the element producing bloom, fruit, and root growth. It is difficult to maintain in soil balance.

Potash provides what is comparable to vitamins. It improves the general health, strengthens the stem or stalk, promotes root growth (hence very important for bulbs and tubers), and makes plants more disease-resistant. There are also small quantities of a number of trace elements which, while not necessary to sustain life, do add greatly to the health of plants. Both the basic and the trace elements are to be found in both organic and inorganic (chemical) fertilizers.

Organic Fertilizers

Blood meal—contains a large amount of nitrogen. Deters rabbits.

Bone meal—Use steamed product. It is an organic source of calcium and phosphorus, the elements that produce fruit and bloom. Bone meal can be safely used since if not needed by the plant, it merely remains in the soil.

Compost—By far the most attractive fertilizer and soil conditioner. *See* "Compost." Use one spadeful to each square yard of surface.

Cottonseed Meal—After compost, this is the number one fertilizer. In addition to testing high in food value, it is safe to use on any plant. Buy cottonseed meal that has been processed mechanically, not chemically.

Dehydrated Manure—Manure in which weed seeds have been killed. Can be bought in bags at seed and garden stores under various trade names. Can be used as is.

Epsom Salts—A good source of magnesium. Acid-loving plants can become deficient in magnesium or iron. Symptoms of both deficiencies are similar (yellowing leaves).

Fish Emulsion—(5–1–1) An alternate with chemical fertilizers on house plants.

Leaf Mold—Surface soil of the forest; rich, crumbly, desirable, but expensive and scarce. Acid in reaction.

Manure—Chicken, Cow, Horse, Sheep—Even more than for its importance as food and humus, manure is valued as the greatest possible source of beneficial soil bacteria. CAUTION: Fresh manure will burn plants. Because manure contains weed and grass seed, keep separate until well rotted and then add to the compost pile. Do not use with bulbs except as top dressing as it causes fungus and rot. Keep well away from plant stems.

Michigan Peat—A domestic soil conditioner, dark brown and rich looking made from sedge grass and reeds. Acid.

Milorganite—A superb, nonburning product. It is sterilized sediment made from a disposal plant. Do not use on vegetables.

Peat Moss—Best acid reacting soil conditioner. Should be crumbled and moistened before using or it will act as a blotter, taking moisture from the plant.

Chemical Fertilizers—ALWAYS READ DIRECTIONS ON PACKAGE

Chemical fertilizers are sold under trade names such as Vigoro, Fertilome, Ortho, and many others. The proportions of the three major elements are usually written on the package, for instance, 6–10–4 means 6 units of nitrogen, 10 of phosphorus, and 4 of potash. Since all of them except 0–20–20 contain nitrogen, which will burn, they should never be put directly on the stalk or foliage and should be watered in after applying. Some manufacturers change their fertilizer formulas to meet the needs of different areas.

Chemical fertilizers in liquid form ready for use, or as a powder to be dissolved in water, are sold under trade names, such as Miracle-Gro, Rapid-Gro, Ortho-Gro, and many others. Some contain the trace elements. The nitrogen in these preparations is from a source which makes them nonburning and therefore safe to either pour or spray directly on the plant. Foliage feeding, as this is called, reaches both the leaf and root.

In using any chemical fertilizer, be sure to use as directed. One portion may cure but two may kill. All types of fertilizers should be applied frequently but lightly. If too much is applied at one time, some of it will be washed away before it can be used by the plant.

Methods of Using Fertilizers

There are three distinct approaches to the proper choice of fertilizers:

1. *"Organic Gardening."* Only natural materials are used. It is a sure, safe, and long-lasting system.

2. *"Combined Organic and Chemical."* This method always includes the abundant use of humus, which is combined either with measured quantities of chemical fertilizers or with chemical and organic fertilizers. For instance, bone meal may be used to supply phosphorus, muriate of potash for quick acting potash, and nitrate of soda may be added to compost for a shot-in-the-arm growth.

"Organic Gardening" and "Combined Organic and Chemical" are the generally accepted methods.

3. "The Dead End." This is the use of chemical fertilizers only. Although it will seemingly work for a number of years, it is constantly burning up every plant conditioner in the soil until no natural elements or healthy bacteria are left. *Never use chemical fertilizers over a period of time without the addition of humus.*

The pH Factor in Soil (Acid or Alkaline)

The term pH is used to determine the acidity or alkalinity of the soil. All the nutrients in the soil are available to the plant when the pH is correct. pH7 is neutral. Below 7 is acid—above 7 is alkaline. *Vegetables* and *flowers* need fairly neutral soil (pH 6.5). pH5.5 is desirable for such plants as *azaleas* and *hollies*. Moss does not prove that soil is acid—it is more likely low in plant food. *See* "Soil Analysis" for directions on how to test the soil or how to have it tested. The pH factor can easily be changed.

Materials for Increasing Acidity of Soil

1. *Aluminum sulphate*—Works quickly, but overuse can cause soil toxicity.

2. *Chelated Iron*—Has proved very valuable in improving color and

vigor in plants showing iron deficiency (yellowing leaves with dark green veins). Follow directions—too much will burn.

3. *Iron Sulphate*—Adds color to the green of the leaves.

4. *Soil Sulphate*—Has the added advantage of being a fungicide. Available in either powdered or granular form.

Popular plants preferring *acid* soil are azaleas, camellias, gardenias, hollies, and pyracantha. Broad-leaved evergreens, most ground covers, some ferns, and small perennials of the wild garden prefer a soil somewhat on the acid side.

Materials for Making Soil Alkaline

1. *Agricultural Lime*—Longer lasting than hydrated lime. More desirable for lawns.

2. *Hydrated (Liquid) Lime*—Easy to apply, safe to use, economical.

Plants preferring an *alkaline* soil are bluegrass, all members of the bean and pea family (this includes sweet peas), iris, peonies, clematis, fruit trees, and some ferns.

Trace Elements

There are a number of mineral elements in the soil essential for plant growth that are present in such minute quantities that they are known as "trace elements"—such as copper, magnesium, etc. These elements are soon exhausted and need to be replaced frequently. Since many fertilizer products on today's market contain trace elements, experts differ as to the necessity of adding to the soil a commercial trace element mixture. Such mixtures may be hard to obtain, but are worthwhile and should be mentioned. Follow directions.

Summary On Soil And Fertilizers

The above information has been given in order to broaden the gardener's knowledge of the soil, its ingredients and requirements, the types of fertilizers available, the parts these fertilizers play in enriching the soil to ensure successful results, and the different ways in which fertilizers are best used. One fact must always be recognized and remembered: *There is no substitute for "good gardening practices."* The basic foundation for success in horticulture lies in the soil; therefore, it automatically follows that the gardener must understand and respect the soil's needs.

Many successful gardeners prefer using organic fertilizers, plus chemical ones occasionally for quick pick-up treatments. Both types are available at seed and garden stores.

Suggested Schedule for Fertilizing the Garden

Azaleas—At least two fertilizings a year are recommended, applied immediately after blooming in the spring and four to six weeks later. Use prepared azalea-camellia fertilizer available at seed and garden stores. If a dry form is used, water in well after applying. Scatter it on the surface of the ground, but do not scratch it in or the shallow roots may be damaged. Azaleas may also be fed monthly after blooming through August.

Camellias—Fertilize twice a year, once in March and again early in June. Use prepared azalea-camellia fertilizer. Follow directions. The June feeding stimulates the setting of buds.

All the Garden (except acid-loving plants and iris)—Fertilize first in late winter, preferably March. Use a top-dressing of compost, or well-rotted or dehydrated manure, or use a commercial organic fertilizer, such as cottonseed meal or Milorganite. Follow directions.

Fertilize again very lightly about July 1st with a commercial organic product and water in well after applying.

It is highly recommended that the *entire garden* be given a top-dressing of 0-20-20 in November to put it to bed in good condition.

Ambitious gardeners may supplement these main feedings with:

1. Small amounts of balanced commercial fertilizer in granular form at monthly intervals in between feedings; or

2. Small amount of balanced commercial fertilizer in liquid form (foliage feeding) at intervals of two weeks.

These supplementary applications are optional, not necessary. Further information may be found under headings of special plants.

SPRAYS

With constant research for improvement and effectiveness in insect and disease control of the garden, there are many good products sold under various trade names now on the market. In some, different ingredients have been combined so that one product will serve more than one purpose.

Many products for insect control contain systemic poison and are called "systemics." This means that after being used on a plant the poison is absorbed by the plant, travels through the entire system of the plant, and makes it deadly to any attacking insects. Systemics therefore are said to have a longer lasting effect than regular insecticides. Some are for use on the ground and some are made for liquid spraying. Some, such as Cygon or Isotox, can be mixed with a miscible oil for spring and fall spraying. Systemics can be VERY DANGEROUS to people, children, pets, and birds and MUST be used and handled exactly according to directions. For the user a breathing mask (available at drug stores and some garden centers) is strongly recommended, as well as thorough washing of the skin after use, since the poison can be absorbed through the pores.

When spraying any kind of insecticide, put plastic bags over hands and arms, anchored with rubber bands below the elbow. Discard inside out in garbage later.

Insects can build up a resistance to a particular chemical, so a change or rotation occasionally to insecticides other than the one being used is advisable. CAUTION: Insecticides may lose their effectiveness if carried over from the year before. If in doubt, buy and use new products.

For spraying the average garden, there are jars with nozzle attachment sprayers that can be connected to the hose. Be sure to clean equipment thoroughly after using. Any residue may neutralize the effect of the next spray used.

In the following condensed spray guide certain trade name products recommended are similar to others under different labels. As it would be impossible to list here all such products it is suggested that the gardener confer with a reputable seed or garden store for advice.

ALWAYS read first and then follow directions listed on the containers of all products.

Dormant Spray

The most important item for late winter and early spring is to cover the garden with a *dormant spray.* Such a spray at this time will greatly cut down later trouble by killing the eggs and spores of many pests and diseases. Pick a calm day when the temperature is above 40° and under 80°. Spray plants before the leaf buds open to avoid burning them. Practically everything in the garden will be benefitted if included in this spraying, trees, shrubs, evergreens, roses, and perennial border.

The best materials for dormant sprays are *lime-sulfur* (liquid form), and *miscible oil.* In using lime-sulfur care must be taken not to let it come in contact with any kind of painted surface, such as on house, furniture, or car, as it will splotch paint. In the use of either of the two materials listed for dormant sprays, follow directions on containers and be exact in measuring. Some products now on the market combine lime-sulfur and miscible oil. Because this combination is so very strong it should be used only on deciduous plants, not evergreens. Do not use during freezing conditions. *Note:* Do not use oil spray on *sugar or Japanese maple, walnut, beech, or magnolia trees.*

Ants, Beetles, Army Worms, and Diseases in Lawn

Use a *soil insecticide,* such as Diazinon, or a similar insecticide labeled for soil insects. For mildew or rust that appears on lawn grasses, spray with a *fungicide,* such as Captan, Zineb, or Manzate, or consult a professional.

Aphids on tender new shoots of chrysanthemum, roses, etc.

Spray with an insecticide such as Malathion or Diazinon.

Bagworm on Arborvitae and Junipers

Watch for bagworms in May. Picking off "bags" may be sufficient control. If infestation is very bad, spray with an *insecticide* such as Malathion, Diazinon, or Cygon (follow directions—handle with care).

Black Spot, Mildew and Chewing Insects on Roses

Dormant spray in winter. Spray plants and ground. After leaves appear: Spray twice weekly for the first two or three weeks, then once weekly throughout the growing season. Use a weaker mixture at first when the foliage is young, then increase the proportions to the recommended dosage. Use a *fungicide* such as Funginex, Manzate, Benlate, or Phaltan for black spot and mildew, and for insect control an *insecticide* such as Malathion, Isotox, or Cygon (follow directions—handle with care).

Some gardeners combine products which are compatible into one spray. There are many good ones available at seed and garden stores. Always follow directions on containers as to correct proportions and check into which products combine well with others.

The important thing is not to let black spot get started. Start spraying in the early spring, and always remove and dispose of any affected leaves on rose plants.

Blight on Perennials, Peonies, Lilies, Clematis

Healthy plants need no spray. If they had disease last season spray with a *fungicide* such as Manzate (Maneb) as soon as plants come up in spring. Repeat twice at intervals of two weeks.

Holly Leaf Miner

Apply *dormant spray* in February then use a *systemic* such as Cygon or Orthene (follow directions—handle with care). Apply three times: in spring just as new leaves emerge, in early summer, and in early fall. If the problem persists use two or three times at each treatment period. Always dispose of all fallen holly leaves—they harbor pests.

Lace Bug on Azaleas and Pyracantha

Spray three times: after blooming, in summer as a preventative measure, and in early fall (worst period of infestation). If problem arises, use two or three applications spaced a week or ten days apart. Use an *insecticide* such as Orthene, Isotox, Malathion, or Cygon (follow directions—handle with care).

Leaf Spot on Lilacs, Ivy, Chrysanthemums, Vinca Minor, and Ajuga

Use a *fungicide,* such as Zineb, Maneb, or Captan for brownish splotched or spotted leaves. Apply first spray at first sign of leaf spot. Repeat twice at ten-day intervals.

Leaf Roller on Photinia

Use an *insecticide* such as Isotox or Orthene. Apply first spray about June 1st. Follow with two more applications at ten-day intervals.

Mealybugs on house plants, etc.

Remove with cotton swabs dipped in alcohol and rinse with water, or spray with an *insecticide* such as Diazinon or Malathion.

Mildew on Plants

Use a *fungicide* such as Benomyl or Acti-dione.

Nematode on Chrysanthemums, Peonies, Boxwood, Azaleas

When plants look wilted or sick with no trouble visible above ground, dig into roots. If there are small pealike knots along roots, the trouble is nematode. Consult local County Agent. Much research is still needed on nematode control.

Red Spider and Chewing Insects on Dahlias, etc.

Use an *insecticide* such as Malathion, Isotox, or Cygon (follow directions—handle with care).

Scale on Evergreens and Euonymus

In February use a *dormant oil spray*. During the growing season, if needed, use an *insecticide* such as Malathion or Cygon, or a summer oil spray (follow directions—handle with care).

Snails and Slugs

Use product containing the chemical metaldehyde such as Bug-geta, or containing mesurol such as Slug-geta. Follow directions. Wood ashes put on ground around plants, especially funkia, kill snails and slugs by dissolving them as they crawl over ashes. Saucers of beer also are effective.

Spider Mite on Boxwood, Camellias, Junipers

Use a *miticide* such as Kelthane. One application may be enough, but check to be sure.

Thrip on Gladiolus

Before planting, soak corms for 3 hours in a disinfectant such as a solution of 1 to 1½ tablespoons Lysol to 1 gal. water. Spray weekly after plants come up and until buds show color with Isotox or use systemic granules.

Whitefly on azaleas, gardenia, lantana, and house plants

Spray with an insecticide such as Malathion or Diazinon.

Worms on Mimosa

Use an *insecticide* such as Sevin or Malathion. Apply first spray the end of May. Watch for later crops of worms which hatch at three week intervals.

Poison Ivy and Poison Oak

Use Amitrol, Glyphosate (best trade name products are Round-Up or Kleenup), or 2–4–D + MCPP. Follow package directions so as not to kill desirable plants.

The use of chemical sprays needs to be tempered with moderation. Spraying is not recommended as a substitute for good gardening practices, but as a helping hand when problem conditions make it necessary. The excessive use of chemicals can have a toxic effect. Take the diseased branch, leaf, or plant to a garden center for diagnosis before spraying.

WATERING

Watering should be done thoroughly once a week during the summer months. It is amazing how long the hose has to stay in one place for the water to permeate the soil. Make this test just once: water one area for thirty minutes, then dig down next to the bottom of the root of a plant and see whether or not the soil is moist at that level.

Light watering brings roots to the surface of the ground. Flooding washes away plant food and mulch. Proper watering dissolves the elements in the soil and makes them available to the plants. Plants absorb their food in liquid form only. Let hose run slowly for a long time.

Contrary to belief, most plants do not suffer from being watered with the sun on them. There are some exceptions. In very hot weather, water must not touch the leaves of dogwood, boxwood, or ferns while the sun is on them or they will curl and dry up.

Cautions in Watering

Except when washing off foliage, do not stand and hold the hose to water. This does the plant more harm than good, as shallow watering merely brings the roots to the surface and cakes the ground on top, which cuts off air from the roots. Many plants are lost during warm, dry falls because of watering neglect. They need to go into and through cold weather well watered.

Caution in use of soil soakers—some plants in the bed may get skipped entirely because water finds little paths along which to run off.

To soak ground, place nozzle of hose in empty flower pot on its side. Water will flow in and out and not make a hole in the ground.

HYGIENE

Prompt disposal of faded blooms, old stems, and foliage is an important disease preventative.

Diseased branches and foliage should be removed and disposed of in a sealed plastic garbage bag so that the disease will not spread. Never put anything diseased in a mulch pile.

COMPOST

Compost is an odorless vegetable manure made by the decomposition of organic matter. It is an essential element in good gardening for it returns to the soil the same material used to feed the growing plants the previous year.

Leaves make up the main body of the compost, but grass clippings and faded blossoms are also good. Any organic material is a candidate for the compost heap. Table scraps, eggshells, coffee grounds, anything, in fact, that goes in the disposal goes into compost. Fireplace ashes, along with dog and human hair, are a welcome addition. Twigs and branches should not be used since it takes hard woody material too long to break down.

The simplest way to go about composting is to pile leaves in an out-of-the-way spot, give them an occasional turn to aerate them, and wait for them to decompose and turn into a rich, brown organic fertilizer known as compost. This method is no trouble and will require one or more years to complete the breakdown.

But it is possible to speed up the process by the addition of other organic or chemical materials, such as cottonseed meal, blood meal, milorganite, fertilome, and the most treasured of all, manure. The ideal way to do this is to sprinkle it alternately between layers of leaves and compost materials. For example, make a layer of compost material about 6″ deep, sprinkle with lime, another layer, and continue with the rest. Commercial fertilizer containing nitrogen such as 6–10–10 helps the decomposition. Lime reduces acidity, but do not use slaked lime. Commercial additives can be bought at garden centers.

Turning the pile from time to time also speeds up the breakdown. Keep the pile damp. By layering as suggested above and turning a few times, the compost will be ready in three to four months. The use of a grinding machine still further advances the decaying time because the material is reduced to smaller particles.

To build a compost bin, set 4 posts firmly in the ground in a 5′ square. The posts should stand 5′ above ground. Stretch strong chicken wire or hardware cloth around three sides. The wire on the fourth side should be movable to allow leaves and other material to be put in, and compost to be shoveled out. In the center of the square sink an iron pipe which has holes drilled in it. The pipe allows one to water the center of the pile and allows oxygen to penetrate the heart of the compost, partially eliminating the need for turning.

If building a bin is not feasible, there are many ready-made compost bins on the market that are satisfactory. For large gardens, a pair of bins made of loose concrete blocks is suggested. More compost can be made at a faster rate. See diagram on next page.

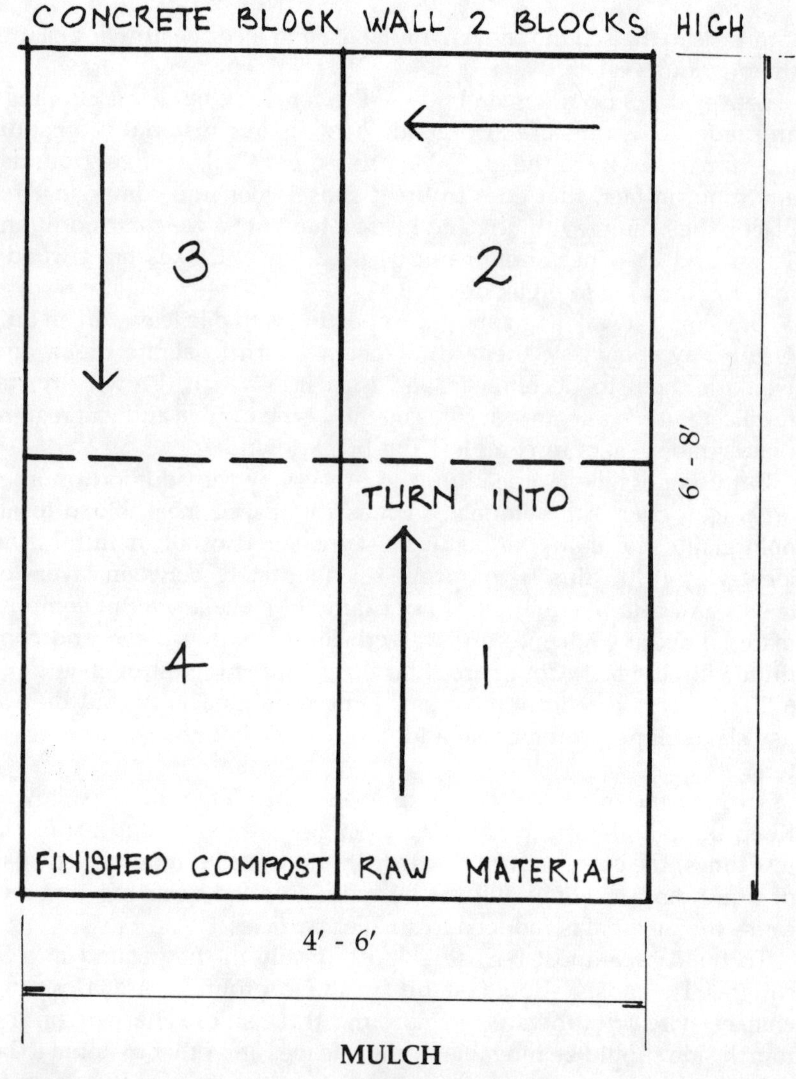

MULCH

Mulch insulates and keeps soil moisture uniform and should remain on all beds at all times. Apply mulch around December 1st and June 1st. Mulch is even more necessary in the summer to protect plants from the scorching heat than it is in the winter months. If only one is used, the June mulch is the more important one.

If the garden has adequate trees, let the leaves stay on the beds, or rake them onto the beds, and they will be a splendid winter mulch.

The beds will not look as neat, but the June mulch can be put directly over the leaves in shrub borders, not flower borders. Mulching soil without first providing the proper drainage and humus is not wise as the roots tend to crowd to the surface. A good mulch holds water, and saves weeding and cultivating.

Organic mulches worked into the soil in the fall will contribute generously to its texture and food value.

Avoid cotton boll hulls. They carry nut grass and weed seeds.

Materials to use for Mulch

Black Plastic—Place on top of worked soil. Especially good if used for beds of annuals and vegetables. Cover with light top-dressing for more attractive appearance.

Brick Bats—Large pieces of broken bricks prevent lawn mower scars on trees, keep weeds down, keep wind from uprooting the ball of newly planted trees, and preserve moisture. Can be removed after well established. Check for slugs.

Compost—excellent. *See* "Compost."

Cotton Seed Hulls—Never work into the soil until well rotted.

Leaves—Oak leaves best for *azaleas* and *camellias*. A small amount of leaves can be pulverized by running a lawn mower back and forth over them. This makes an excellent base for the June mulch.

Michigan Peat—Makes bed look attractive but is expensive. Washes away easily and is acid.

Oak Bark—Acid

Peanut Hulls

Peat Moss—Acid. Shred and moisten thoroughly before using.

Pine Bark Mulch—Nuggets or shredded. Acid, dark brown color.

Pine Needles—Especially good for *daffodils* to keep mud from splashing on blooms.

Straw—Clean

Weedless Dried Grass Clippings

PRUNING

Most amateur gardeners and many who call themselves professionals wield the pruning knife with more enthusiasm than judgment.

Prune for size and shape control and for the forcing of new growth. One safe rule to follow is "When in doubt, don't." Pending the acquisition of adequate knowledge, it is always safe to cut out all dead and diseased wood.

What not to do

1. Do not prune flowering shrubs in the fall.
2. Avoid the "mound habit," the pruning of shrubs, either evergreen or deciduous, into formal shapes. Instead, cut branches back to their point of origin. It is much more beautiful and interesting to preserve the natural shape. Plants used for special architectural effects are an exception.

When to Prune

Broad-leaved evergreens, deciduous shrubs, and trees should be pruned between the first of February and the middle of March. Spring-flowering shrubs and trees should be pruned during or immediately after flowering. Pruning methods for each are different, and will be covered separately. Do not prune after the middle of September as pruning forces new growth which will be killed by cold weather.

General Rules For All Pruning

Always use clean, sharp tools, and prune on a slant. Never leave a stub when cutting off a large branch. If the branch is cut back to the trunk on a slant parallel with the trunk, the cut will heal and bark will grow over it.

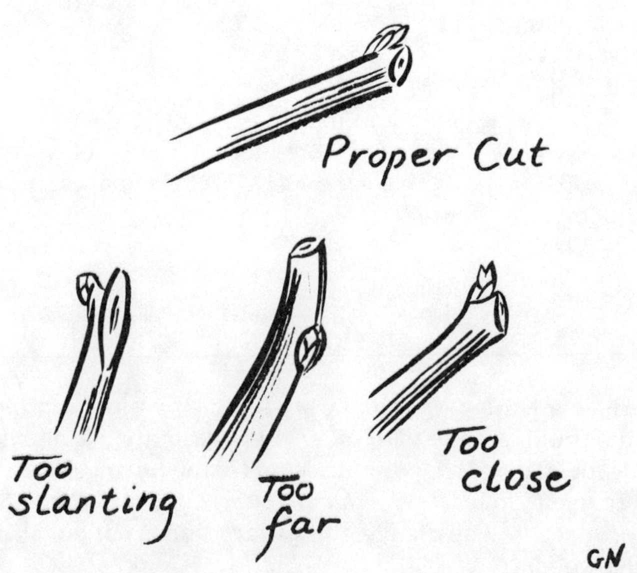

Remove dead and diseased wood at any time of year.

Remove crossed branches.

Remove all sucker growth which weakens the plant.

Limbs larger than a thumb should have the wound painted with tree paint to prevent disease and insect invasion.

Woody shrubs should be pruned, not above a leaf bud, but above a twig turning outward. The flow of sap past the cut into the twig will cause the wound to heal and prevent die back.

If plants, such as Chinese holly, get too tall, they can be pruned into trees. Cut off lower branches and let the top go. Shrubs which are attractive pruned this way are: *Burford Holly, Camellia Sasanqua, Cleyera, Pittosporum,* and *Sweet Olive.*

Specific Suggestions

All plants cannot be pruned alike. Following are some suggestions for the pruning of the more common plants:

Azaleas—if necessary after blooming, clip off faded flowers and cut back to the desired size and shape. Judicious pruning thickens them up, but here too, avoid the mound habit.

Boxwood—The important thing in pruning boxwood is to open up the center to light and air to encourage new growth.

Broad-leaved Evergreens—Begin size and shape control when plants are young. Do not wait until they are old and woody. Branches in center get shaded out. First cut out all the dead wood and the branches that turn in and overlap in the center. This opens up the plant to light. The plant will thicken where it is cut. This is the reason for cutting thin, scraggly growth. Always prune just above a twig growing outward, as for "woody shrubs." In general most evergreens look best if permitted to grow somewhat along the shape nature gave them, so shearing is best confined to straggly shoots that are spoiling the shape of the plant.

Holly should be pruned before new growth starts to encourage branching. A good time to do this is for Christmas decorations.

Dogwood—If cutting for flowers, cutting out borers, or cutting for shape control, cut just above an outgrowing twig—not leaf bud (same as for woody evergreens). In pruning for borers where trunk is badly damaged, often the only way to save the tree is to cut it down almost to the ground. If there is life in the root, it will send up strong new shoots.

Hydrangea—Pruning depends on the species. Prune Hills of Snow and Pee Gee hydrangea in early spring before new growth starts. For large flower heads, cut back 4″–6″ from the ground. These may have to be staked. For smaller, more numerous flowers on strong stems cut back to 2′. Prune big leaved and oak leaf hydrangea immediately after flowering, if necessary.

Hedges—Begin size and shape control when plants are young. Shear hedges slightly narrower and rounded at top to permit sunlight to reach the lower branches.

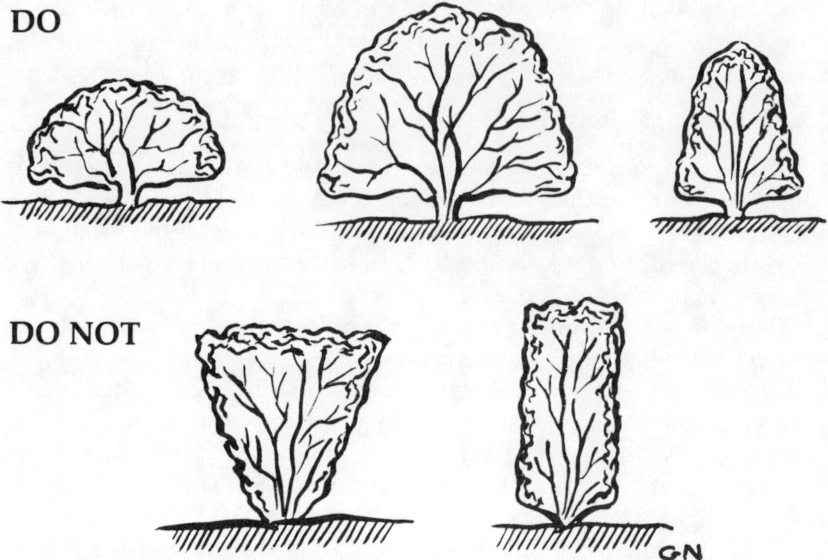

Mahonia and *Nandina*—Need special pruning. Prune in early spring; cut out some of the old wood each year down to the ground. Shorten remaining canes to desired length, being careful always to cut above a bud turning outward. In spring peel off old leaf sheaths on the lower part of leggy nandina canes to promote fullness at the bottom.

Roses — Prune about first week in March. Remove twiggy growth and shorten strong canes to desired length. Do not prune strong roses as hard as weak ones. Paint larger cut ends with tree paint or white glue to prevent invasion of stem borer. Light pruning in July. Climbers require no pruning except cutting horizontally and low on trellis for maximum bloom. See Roses.

Spring Flowering Shrubs—Immediately after blooming in spring, since new growth for next year's bloom is forming. To cut in fall means cutting off next year's bloom. Do not "lop." Until plant reaches a mature size, little pruning is needed beyond light shearing of faded blooms. Then, to keep shrubs vigorous looking, begin to thin. Each spring after blooming, cut out, down to the ground, some of the oldest wood. Repeat this each year or at least every other year. Do not wait until plants get ragged before beginning to prune. It is too late then.

Summer Flowering Shrubs—Prune plants like crape myrtle and althaea in early March. These bloom on the new wood and pruning at this time forces new growth. Prune according to form desired, whether a tall accent plant or a bushy one.

Trees—Do not prune during period when sap is rising. This will cause them to "bleed" too much.

Espalier plants and other trained plants are handled differently. An espaliered plant is grown flat in one plane and only one branch thick so all other growth must be pruned off. This is done after new growth has matured in the spring and again in late August.

Japanese or cloud pruning is an art in itself, and should be done with an artistic eye to accomplish the effect. This pruning can be started in the spring, and continued throughout the growing season.

New plants and trees—The top growth should be pruned back slightly to compensate for roots lost in digging. This pruning balances the top growth with the root structure.

Root Pruning—Trees and shrubs, such as boxwood, which are difficult to transplant, should be root pruned two to six months before planting in order to encourage new feeding roots to develop. With a sharpshooter, cut a circle around the plant two-thirds of the distance from the trunk or at drip line (outer tip of the branches) and as deep as the sharpshooter. The plant can be moved two to six months later.

Conifers—To thicken young pines and other coniferous trees, one-half of the new growth or candles should be pinched out. This will develop two or three new leaders.

Espalier

Espalier (pronounced espal*yer*) is the training and pruning of a plant into two dimensional forms against walls, fences, trellises, or wire frames. Skillful shaping of shrubs, vines, and trees can make them conform to any number of formal or informal designs.

Choose a northern or eastern location where the plant does not receive full, hot summer sun. If possible, a wooden or metal trellis, lattice work, or wires should stand about 6" away from the house or wall so air can circulate. This allows plants to be conveniently sprayed and easier painting of wood structures. However, plants may be espaliered directly on a brick surface using masonry nails.

Start with a young one- or two-year-old plant with lateral branches which will conform to the planned design. Plant the bush or tree just like any other. Do not overfeed because rampant growth is undesirable. A nursery plant which is already growing on a trellis may be quicker.

Gently bend the lateral branches into position, and attach them to the support with a soft material (leather or rubber strips, raffia) which will not cut the bark as wire does. As with any pruning, speed vertical growth by removing side shoots or turn one stem into many by cut-

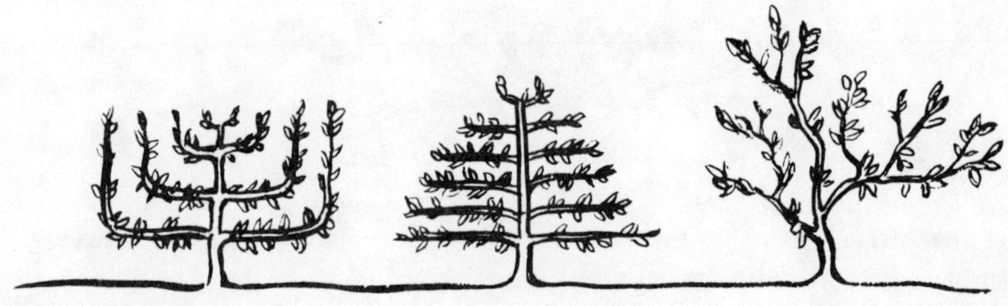

ting back to force branching. Slow growth by turning shoots down or stimulate growth by turning shoots up.

The plants best adapted to espalier produce many side branches and tolerate constant pruning. They are ivy, camellia sasanqua, eleagnus, fig, dwarf fruit trees, forsythia, holly, juniper, lantana, mock orange, photinia, pyracantha, flowering quince, yew (dwarf).

Do not try to espalier large trees or large leaved trees such as magnolia.

Topiary

Topiary is the art of sculpting a plant into a three dimensional shape, usually geometric, but also whimsical figures of animals, etc. Topiary must be continually clipped and pruned so use a very hardy plant species. Two or three plants are needed for some large designs. Elaborate figures usually require a metal frame. It takes four to five years to produce a conventional topiary.

It is much quicker to shape a frame from aluminum wire tied at the joints. Mount the frame securely in a pot. Small-leafed ivy, creeping fig, or other healthy, small-leaved vines will grow up and over it. Keep clipped and use hair pins to tie any loose vine in place.

Another method is to fill a frame with sphagnum moss. Wrap the sphagnum moss with nylon fishing line to hold it in place. Plant the vine in the moss. It will quickly cover the surface.

Keep the potted topiary moist by misting and occasionally add fertilizer to the water. Never allow the moss to dry out.

CONSIDERATIONS FOR LANDSCAPING

Use a professional landscape architect when planning a new garden or renovating an old one to prevent costly mistakes. Before making the master plan, which may require a five- to ten-year budget, a topographical survey is extremely helpful. It is a way of determining the drainage of the entire property, which will affect any and all garden plans.

Before planning a garden, take photographs, consult libraries, and go on house and garden tours. This will determine the most important uses of the property.

Once the style of the house is established, the garden can be the outgrowth of the owners' taste. A well-designed garden brings together plants and trees in a pleasing way.

The following considerations should be incorporated into the plans.

1. Inviting entrance, driveway with proper offstreet parking, and privacy from neighbors.

2. Fencing will determine the bounds of the property and will protect children and dogs. It will also define the background for the ultimate garden.

3. Plans should include a compost bin, garage and utility area, storage for equipment, play area for children, an out-of-the-way area for potting and resting plants, vegetable patch, and terrace, deck or outdoor living area.

4. An underground watering system is desirable, and water and electrical outlets are essential for ease of maintenance. Have an open lawn for a look of spaciousness.

5. Provide access to the terrace, deck, and back yard entrance which does not go through the garage or kitchen.

6. Future plans should be incorporated for eventual family and entertaining needs (i.e., swimming pool and bath house, tennis court, and greenhouse or lath house).

7. Provide night lighting for entertaining, well-lit paths, and wide walks with comfortable steps and risers. White, light colored, and fragrant flowers, and variegated plants are most effective.

8. Laying out beds: To make a bed with straight edges, stretch a string between stakes and dig along the string. Lay a hose on the ground to outline curved beds. Evergreens provide the background for all deciduous plants, perennials, and annuals (*see* "Shrubs"). Plant bulbs, etc. in drifts rather than in rows for a pleasing effect. There should be shade trees for outdoor living area or terrace as well as protection from the western sun. Put plants along the property line for privacy. Plants act as a windbreak and also diminish street noise.

9. Foundation planting: Plant no more than 3 varieties of shrubs, evergreens preferred. Plant at least 3′ away from the house to allow for dripline, pruning, and painting. Plant low shrubs at the doorway to make it inviting and large ones at the far corners of the house. Do not use plants which grow too large and need constant pruning. Do not blot out windows, and make sure there is a pleasing view from each. Put a bird feeding area near a window that is used frequently.

10. Remember that in 10–15 years everything will have changed. All plants will be larger and there will be more shade. Most of all, the garden itself should be geared to low maintenance.

11. Formula for garden steps and risers:

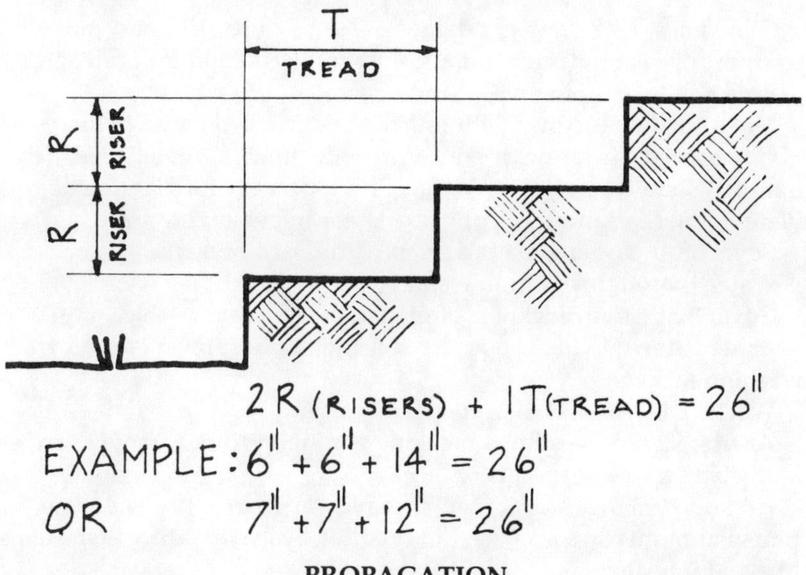

PROPAGATION

Increasing the number of plants from existing ones is known as plant propagation. Plants are propagated from seeds or by vegetative methods (cuttings, etc.). Nearly all annuals, some perennials, and most vegetables are easily grown from seeds. It is usually best to purchase new seeds rather than to plant saved seeds because few seeds remain viable long enough and most seedlings do not "breed true" or duplicate their parents. Because the seeds of some flowers and vegetables are difficult to germinate, it is best to start those from bedding plants purchased from a garden store or catalogue.

Seed Planting

Most garden plants can be grown at home from seeds. A few can be planted directly into the flower bed, but for best results, many fine plants are those that require a long growing season and those not available locally. In general they should be started indoors or in a cold frame about six weeks before outdoor planting time.

In a cold frame, seeds can be planted either in flats or boxes or directly in the soil in the frame. Here they can be protected by glass from frost and beating rains. A miniature cold frame can be improvised with a box and a piece of window glass. When the weather gets warm the glass can be removed and the box or frame shaded with slats or burlap.

Cold Frame—Take any good garden loam, pulverize, and mix with compost or peat moss for humus, and builder's sand for drainage.

Firm soil by tamping with hand or tool.

Make shallow furrows with finger or pencil, drop seed in furrows.

Cover seed lightly with soil, firm with fingers. Small seeds, like petunia, should be barely covered. Check package for planting depth. Plant deeper in sandy soil, and shallower in heavy clay soil.

Level off by firming overall again with board or brick.

Water thoroughly with fine spray.

Cover with two thicknesses of damp newspaper which must be weighted down. This keeps the soil moist and prevents seed from washing away.

Water daily through newspaper.

At first sign of seedlings breaking through ground, remove paper and shade frame with slats or burlap.

As soon as the second set of leaves appears, thin seedlings or transplant into rows 2″ apart. Lift seedling by leaves rather than stems to avoid injuring stem.

Remove to the garden when root system has developed and after the danger of frost is past.

Open Ground—Use the same system with sturdy seeds like zinnias and marigolds. Too much stress cannot be put upon the importance of firming the seed in the ground. If the soil is loose on top, the seed will wash or float away with the first watering.

Starting Seed Indoors—Seeds may be started in a sunny southern window in large flower pots or shallow pans. Put broken flower pot shards in the bottom for drainage and fill to 1″ from the top of the pot with a commercial seed starter mix or a sifted mixture of ½ garden loam and ½ sand. Sow seed as above, water gently, and shade with newspaper. Keep moist and warm (60°–70°). A miniature greenhouse can be made by enclosing the container with a plastic bag or covering it with glass or plastic. Uncover as soon as sprouts appear. When the second set of leaves appears, in two to three weeks, transplant into flats containing a sifted mixture of ⅓ soil, ⅓ sand, and ⅓ humus. Do not crowd. Give the seedlings warmth, full sun, and daily watering until ready to move into the garden. Garden centers have a variety of seed starting materials (sterile soil, peat pots, flats, etc.)

Bedding Plants

Though some perennials and most annuals can be grown from

seed, many are best grown from bedding plants from the nursery. Mark the location of all perennials to avoid disturbing them while working the bed. The following factors are essential to good planting:

1) *Space for the roots*—If the bed is properly prepared the soil will be friable, making it easy to scoop out holes large enough to accommodate the roots without crowding. Spread roots out and downward. For a large crown, build a little mound of firmed soil, set the crown over it and drape the roots over the edges. If bedding plants have remained in the nursery flats too long and have become root bound, make slits in the root ball with a knife and gently loosen the roots by hand before planting.

2) *Proper planting depth*—Set container-grown plants at the same depth at which they were growing. To determine the depth at which dormant plants grew last season, find the soil marks on the old stems. For plants which have no old soil marks at planting time ask nursery for proper depth.

3) *Firmness of soil*—There must be no pockets of air in which roots can dry out. Always firm soil around plants.

4) *Thorough watering immediately after planting.*

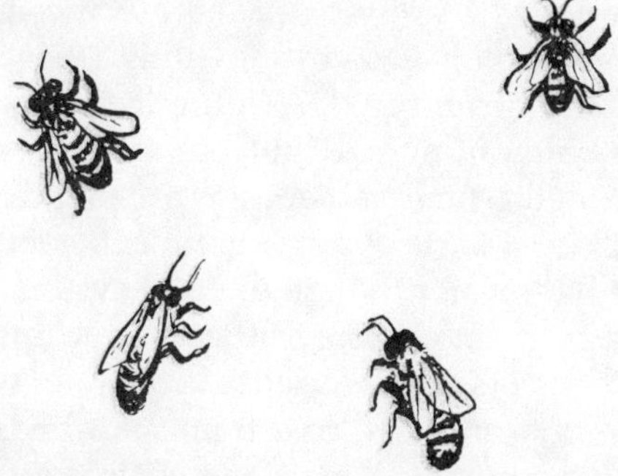

Vegetative Propagation

Many shrubs and perennials and most house plants are easy to reproduce vegetatively. Small pieces of a plant can be rooted and grown into exact duplicates of the parent plant. This offspring is known as a clone. This type of propagation makes it possible to increase one's stock of plants very inexpensively. Only the simplest methods will be described here: divisions, softwood cuttings, leaf cuttings, runners, layering, air layering.

Divisions—Many house plants and perennials can be increased by the division of old plants. Divide plants with multiple crowns or roots and grow the divisions as separate plants. Carefully cut or pull apart the crown or root mass, plant each one individually, and water thoroughly. Keep shaded for a week or so and water sparingly until new plants have begun to grow. The best time to separate house plants such as African violet or Boston fern is when new growth starts. Spring and summer flowering perennials (iris, phlox, columbine, shasta daisy, etc.) should be lifted with a spading fork and divided in September. Divide fall flowering perennials in the spring. Some perennials, such as baby's breath, bleeding heart, and peony, can be left undisturbed for years.

Cuttings—A cutting is a piece of a plant which, when severed from the parent plant, will form new roots and grow into an exact replica of the parent plant.

Softwood Cuttings. Softwood or stem tip cuttings are used to propagate almost all houseplants (begonia, fuchsia, geranium, and philodendron), many perennials (phlox and pinks), and shrubs (azalea, boxwood, euonymus, and quince).

Cuttings from house plants may be taken at any time of the year so long as the plant is in active growth and *not* dormant. Cuttings taken from dormant plants root very slowly. Cut perennials in early summer when the second growth is well advanced. Take cuttings of shrubs from the current season's growth in late spring or early summer as soon as the current season's growth begins to become firm.

The rooting medium should hold moisture, but drain well, and remain well aerated. The best mediums are perlite; clean, sharp sand; or a mixture of equal parts of sand, vermiculite and peat moss. Some plants root easily in water though the root system will be a bit fragile and the cuttings a little more difficult to plant. Put the rooting medium in flower pots, any household container with drainage holes punched in the bottom, flats, cold frames, or beds in shady outdoor spots. Have the medium well moistened before inserting the cuttings. To make the cuttings, choose the tips of short healthy stems, trying to avoid a flowering stem. With a clean, sharp knife or razor blade make a diagonal cut just below a node or place where the stem and leaf come together. The cuttings should be from 2″ to 6″ long, depending upon the size of the plant from which they are taken. Remove all flower buds and the leaves on the lower one-third of the cutting. Large-leaved plants such as hydrangea or fig must have one-half of each leaf snipped off. This allows all energy to be funnelled to root growth.

Dip the bottom of the cutting in a commercial root hormone powder and shake off excess. With a pencil or sharp stick make a hole for the cutting in the rooting medium. Insert the cutting and firm the medium around it to hold it upright. Space the cuttings about 3″ apart. Keep shaded. Keep moist but not wet. This is easier if the container is enclosed in a plastic bag or covered with glass or plastic for a greenhouse effect. The humidity stays high and the soil moist with little watering. It may be necessary to raise the cover daily and wipe off excess moisture to prevent fungus, mildew, or decay. Rooting time varies from a few weeks to months, depending on the type of plant.

As roots begin to grow well, gradually remove the covering to harden the new plants. House plants should be planted in small pots just large enough to hold them. When the roots are ½″ to 1″ long move to progressively larger pots as needed. Increase only one size at a time. Plant perennials and shrubs in the garden as soon as the root systems are well established. Water new plantings well and shade for 7–10 days. Pinch out the tiny growing tips to make bushy plants. Do not fertilize until plants are well established. If new growth has not appeared on cuttings of slow growing shrubs by fall, leave them in the rooting medium and keep protected in a cold frame until spring.

Leaf Cuttings. Leaf cuttings are used to propagate house plants with thick fleshy leaves, such as African violets, gloxinias and other gesneriads, begonias, peperomias, and many succulents. Cut a healthy mature leaf with about 2″ of leaf stalk. Set into moist rooting medium so that the leaf just touches the medium. Cover with plastic or glass to create a greenhouse effect. Give plenty of light. Roots will form and eventually small shoots will appear at the base of the parent leaf. When the plantlets are one-third the size of the parent, gently pull the new shoots away from the parent and pot separately.

Many plants, such as Rex begonias and African violets, are propagated by *vein leaf cuttings.* Slit the large veins on the underside of the leaf with a razor blade. Lay the leaf, right side up, on wet sand or other rooting medium. Push the leaf stem down into the rooting medium. Secure the cuts by hair pins or weight the leaf with sand or a pebble. Cover and treat as above. New plants will grow at each incision.

Runners: It is a simple matter to propagate plants which produce runners (Boston fern, pick-a-back, spider plant). Runners are prostrate shoots which appear at the base of the plant and root at the joints, forming plantlets. Simply fasten down a runner into a pot filled with potting soil and keep moist. When a good root system is established and new leaves appear, sever the new plant from its parent.

Layering: Layering is a good method of increasing plants like azalea, boxwood, and forsythia. Bend a flexible branch to the ground, a foot from the tip. Dig a shallow trench and mix in sharp sand and peat. Scrape away about 2″ of the bark on the underside of the branch. Dust with hormone powder and bury the branch 3″ deep. Secure it with wire or a brick. The buried stem will have roots by spring. At this time cut the plant from its parent and transplant.

Air Layering: Air layering is recommended for woody plants such as camellia, hibiscus, and magnolia which are difficult to root. Use this method with house plants which have grown too tall or leggy or those which are hard to root (croton, corn plant, dieffenbachia, rubber plant, schefflera). Any time of the year is satisfactory, but spring is most successful. Make a slanting cut one-half way through a stem or branch 8″–14″ below the growing tip. Do not detach from the parent plant. Treat the cut with hormone powder and place wet sphagnum moss over it and wedge it into the cut. Wrap the moss with plastic and tie it with string at each end. Do not allow the moss to dry out. When new roots are plentiful, sever the stem below the ball of moss, remove plastic, and plant without disturbing the roots. Cover with a plastic bag until the new plant is well established. Be sure to allow air circulation on hot days.

Propagation is fun, economical, and rewarding.

SHELTERED GARDENING

Cold Frame

A cold frame is a bottomless box with a transparent cover which is used to extend the growing season. Cold frames can be bought or built. They may be made of wood, brick, or concrete. If wood is used, it should be painted or treated to prevent rot. Dimensions of 6′ long by 3′ wide fit a standard glass sash which may be used for the covering or use clear plastic. While not as transparent as glass, plastic has the advantages of being lighter and nonbreakable. The top should be hinged either at the back of the frame or from a central bar in the middle to allow ventilation. A cold frame gets hot even on cold days and ventilation is a must. In this area there are very few days cold enough to keep the glass down tight. For most of the time, glass should be kept open a crack at the low end by inserting a notched stick or other device. On warm days, when the temperature gets to 70° or above, ventilation should be provided on the high side as well.

Ideally the frame should face south so that it gets full benefits of the winter sun. The rear of the frame should be 18″ high, sloping to 12″ in the front. This sloping toward the front allows more sunlight in the frame.

The frame can be placed directly on the ground or can be secured to a foundation of brick or concrete. The soil must be well drained. This may be achieved by digging down 12″, adding a 4″ layer of sand or pea gravel, and replacing the dirt. The soil inside a cold frame should be a rich mixture of equal parts soil, humus, and sand. The soil needs to be revitalized each year with the addition of humus.

Cold frames have many uses. They can be used to start seedlings in advance of the outdoor season. In the cold frame seeds may be sown directly in the ground or started in peat pots or flats. Cold frames are also useful in hardening off seedlings and other small plants that have been grown in the greenhouse and are not ready for full exposure to outdoors. They can be used to carry less hardy patio plants over the winter and to propagate plants from cuttings in late summer. *See* "Propagation" in "Garden Care."

Bulbs for the house may be forced in cold frames. Put the pots in the frame, fill the frame with wet leaves, cover with the glass top and two months later the pots should be filled with vigorous roots. After moving the bulb pots into a lighter area, there is still plenty of time to start seedlings for spring planting.

Cold frames can be converted to hot frames by the addition of electric heating cables placed 6″ under the soil. These cables with directions are readily purchased from garden supply stores or catalogues.

Bay Window Greenhouse

Some of the successful indoor gardeners in this section have accomplished amazing results by the use of a "bay window greenhouse." Southern exposure is by far the best, with an eastern one next in choice. Build or place a copper lined plant box (copper prevents rust) across the entire window space. Length and breadth depend on individual requirements, but the depth should be 6 to 12 inches. Fill the bottom of the box with sand or pebbles to retain moisture. Set the flower pots on this base and water them when the surface of the soil begins to dry out. The constant evaporation from the wet sand or pebbles will furnish the necessary humidity for the plants. In this manner the three indoor gardening essentials—good drainage, moisture, and sunlight—are provided. It is also desirable to keep the room temperature as cool as possible.

Using this method, one can successfully grow a number of beautiful plants other than the hardy ones included in the article "House Plants."

The Camellia House

Camellia japonicas and other species and hybrids of the camellia family offer a long blooming season from October to April. They must be protected however from extremes of temperatures, as too much sun in summer and below freezing temperature in winter are both detrimental to specimen blooms. The proper protection may be provided by a "camellia house," thus assuring blooms even more brilliant than those pictured in catalogues.

Two types of camellia houses are described here, a glass one and a slat one. In either one camellias may be planted in pots and tubs, or directly into the ground which has been made into a camellia bed. Plants in tubs require less space, their size is readily controlled and they may be removed for decorative purposes. Camellias in the ground are more easily fertilized and watered, do not require transplanting, and can be grown to larger size.

It is imperative to have a close-by hose connection for watering and syringing, as plant foliage and the floor of the house should be sprinkled every day to provide the proper humidity. An *accurate* thermometer is a very important piece of equipment in either type of house.

Both types of camellia houses are highly successful and should include the following requirements:

40°–50° winter temperature.
Adequate ventilation.
Semishade.
Plentiful water.
Good drainage.
Good soil. See special article on "Camellias."

GLASS HOUSE. An ornamental glass house should be near your home or even built against a side of the house or garage to provide easy care and added enjoyment of flowers. This proximity is a great advantage; almost any type of heating equipment can be chosen since electricity, gas, and water are available. Never allow a glass house to become too warm, for this causes camellias to lose their buds.

Heating—Standard greenhouse heaters are available which may be purchased for either glass house or slat house use. Manufacturers give advice as to the ratio of heaters to space. If electric wires are conveniently near, these may be used, or a portable radiator with a thermostat will work. Companies which sell greenhouses offer small gas burners with controlled heat.

Ventilation—Camellias do not flourish in a hot greenhouse. Their home must have adequate ventilation; either use a large number of removable glass sections or many windows and automatic ventilators.

Shade—Shade is provided by frames of slats, which are removable, made to fit over the glass allowing for 50% shade.

Evaporator Air-conditioning—Not essential but very beneficial for summer. Not much extra expense involved.

SLAT HOUSE. A slat house may be constructed at minimum expense. If it is not pretty, screen it with shrubs.

Construction—Use posts supporting a slanting (for drainage) roof. Make the roof of slats, roughly 2 inches wide and 2 inches apart. The slats run approximately north and south. This makes moving shadows on plants. The roof should be approximately 8 feet high, depending on the desired height of your camellias.

Ventilation—The side walls are made of slats somewhat farther apart. Build large openings on the south wall. The entire south wall can be made of hinged sections which open at the top and fasten there with hooks. When open, their weight rests on the ground outside. These are easily handled with cords through pulleys. During average winter weather this side of the house remains open during the day and the heat is turned off.

Shade—Usually the slats make enough shade (50% shade imperative) and syringing cools the plants.

Heat—The same types of heating equipment listed for the glass house are suitable for the slat house. In the fall, before the first frost, staple 6 mil. polyethylene on the house. It comes in rolls of 100 ft. and is 10 ft. wide. The wind may cause a few small tears during the winter but they are easy to patch. Camellias usually require some heat during winter nights, and in coldest weather heat is sometimes needed during the day. Remember that 40°–50° winter temperature is required. After danger of frost is over, remove the polyethylene and store it for use the following winter. In the summer, if gas heaters are used, cover them with polyethylene to prevent their rusting from water and humidity.

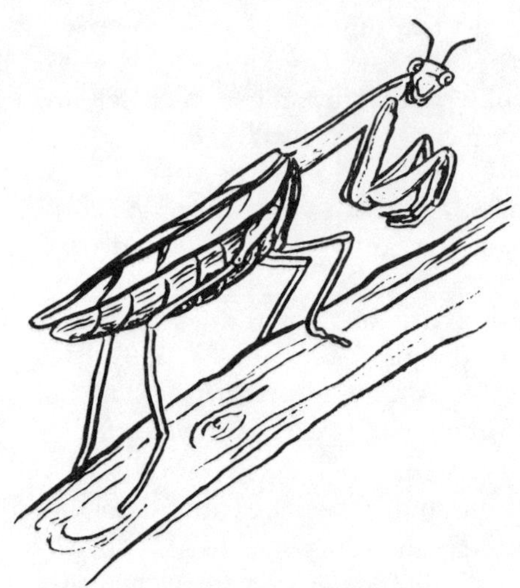

COMPANION GARDENING

Companion gardening is based on the theory of planting for protection against harmful insects and diseases. Many plants function effectively as insect attractants or repellants, and also help to improve the growth of certain companion plants. Companion gardening offers an alternate approach to today's overreliance on chemicals.

Basil—Companion to tomatoes; improves growth and flavor; repels flies and mosquitoes.

Beebalm—Companion to tomatoes; improves growth and flavor.

Borage—Companion to tomatoes, squash, and strawberries; deters tomato worm; improves flavor and growth.

Castor Oil Plant—Repels moles and chipmunks.

Chives—Companion to carrots; improves growth and flavor; repels aphids.

Coriander—Contains an oil which will repel spider mites and aphids.

Garlic—Plant near roses and raspberries; improves growth and health; deters Japanese beetles and aphids.

Horseradish—Plant at corners of potato patch to deter potato bug.

Marigolds—The workhorse of the pest deterrants. Plant throughout the garden. It discourages Mexican bean beetles and nematodes. Companion to tomatoes. Deters asparagus beetle, tomato worm, and general garden pests.

Mint—Repels ants.

Nasturtium—Companion to radishes, cabbage, and cucumber; plant under fruit trees. Deters aphids, squash bugs, striped pumpkin beetles.

Petunia—Protects beans.

Peppermint—Planted among cabbages, it repels the white cabbage butterfly.

Rosemary—Companion to cabbage, bean, carrots, and sage; deters cabbage moth, bean beetles.

Sage—Discourages troublesome insects.

Lawns

RENOVATING AN EXISTING LAWN

To renovate an old lawn, first test the soil to determine its acidity and/or alkalinity (pH), and, if needed, apply lime to lower acidity and iron sulphate to reduce alkalinity. Consult local garden center or local agricultural extension service for soil testing information. Fertilize the grass with a good commercial fertilizer and water deeply once a week (*see* fertilizing). Raise the height of the mower blade to 2½″ or 3″. If thatch (mulch from clippings, etc.) is too thick and is smothering the grass, a rake or dethatcher should be used. Holes should be made in heavily compacted soil with an aerator or spiker.

For any small, dry places spread a 2″–3″ layer of moistened compost over the spot, and work it into the ground to a depth of 5″. Tamp firmly and sow grass seed. Sprigs, plugs, or strips of sod may also be used, but be sure to level the latter with a roller.

ESTABLISHING A NEW LAWN AND COMPLETELY REBUILDING AN OLD LAWN

Completely rebuilding an old lawn can be more expensive than starting a new one on bare ground. Spring is the optimum time to plant. Lay sod in March. Plant seeds after May 15. Run a rotary tiller back and forth across the lawn until turf is reduced to finely cut organic matter. Then turn the soil with a tiller to a depth of 4″–6″, adding top soil, moistened and crumbled peat moss (1 bale to 300 square feet), organic humus, sand, fertilizer, and lime or sulphur. Any hard clods must be removed. Also, check the contours of the land for proper drainage.

A new lawn should be graded so that it slopes away from the house. In leveling do not alter the existing grade around large trees as burying the roots or scraping away existing soil will kill them. Where natural drainage will not take away excess water, an underground drainage system of pipes may be needed.

Next, level the soil by going over it with a light roller. Remove any small pieces of concrete or debris by working a rake back and forth, at the same time smoothing the tilled soil. Relevel at this time by dragging a light soil leveler, such as a board, across the lawn.

Sod, plugs, sprigs, or seeds can now be planted. Use a spreader to sow seeds evenly, and cover them lightly with a little dirt or humus. Water the seeds with a fine mist and keep moist until established.

The cost of grass seed should be judged not by bulk but by the quality of the seeds. Read the label carefully.

When planting sprigs, lay them on prepared ground about 6″ apart. Cover all but the leafy part of each sprig, and keep the soil moist.

When planting plugs (small 3″–5″ pieces of sod) place the plug in a hole (2″ apart for Bermuda, 3″ apart for Zoysia) and press firmly into the ground with a roller. Keep the soil moist until established. Plugs and sprigging are superior to, but more expensive than seeding. Bermuda plugs will cover the lawn the first summer, Zoysia not until the second summer.

Sodding, though still more costly, is the easiest and quickest way to create a lawn. The sod is laid on prepared ground in a bricklike pattern so that the joints butt together. Fill in any gaps with a mixture of peat and soil. Be careful with Zoysia which does not tolerate dirt fill on top of it. Press the roots into the soil with a roller and water twice a week until the sod is established. Do not mow until the grass is 3″ tall. All new lawns need frequent watering.

POPULAR GRASSES AND THEIR CARE

There are many strains and mixtures of lawn grasses. The new hybrids are expensive, but in many cases are hardier and more beautiful. The choice depends upon soil, climate, and amount of money one is willing to invest.

In the South a lawn is generally one variety of grass such as Bermuda or Zoysia rather than a mixture. Bermuda and Zoysia become dormant in the winter and are often given an overplanting of annual rye for winter color.

Bermuda

Bermuda, with its deep, drouth-resistant roots, is the most widely used Southern grass. All Bermuda turns straw-colored in cool weather. It requires full sun; however, only five hours of sun are sufficient for survival. Bermuda is fast growing and relatively hardy. It needs more frequent feeding, edging, and mowing than Zoysia, and, in addition, becomes a pest in flower beds. There are many new hybrids which are hardier, finer in texture, and stay green longer, but are expensive as they cannot be seeded. Do not seed Bermuda before May 15.

Water Bermuda deeply once a week in dry weather. Do not allow a thick thatch to build up.

The soil for a Bermuda lawn should have a pH of between 6.5–7.5. To maintain Bermuda, fertilize three or four times a year, starting in early spring (*see* Fertilizer).

In addition to the common Bermuda species there are several hybrids which are finer bladed and more attractive, but less winter hardy and cannot be propagated by seeds. Recommended varieties are Tiffway 419, Tiffgreen 328, and Tiff Dwarf.

Zoysia

Zoysia, while initially more expensive than Bermuda, needs less frequent mowing and edging. It must be planted by plugging or sodding. Zoysia remains green until the first heavy frost. Avoid heavy traffic on winter dormant Zoysia. It does well in light shade, but prefers full sun with frequent, deep watering. It will live but not spread in total shade. Some of the new hybrids are much hardier. Zoysia is slow growing, but when established forms a thick turf which smothers out weeds. It does not tolerate weed killers as well as Bermuda does. Zoysia needs a pH of 5.5. to 7.0 (6.5 is the best). Rust disease (a fungus) is sometimes a problem in cool, wet springs or falls (*See* Weeds, Fungus, and Insects).

The most popular varities of Zoysia are:

Meyer's Z-52, which is coarse but tolerant of traffic and general abuse; more shade tolerant. Do not spot sod, use solid coverage. Emerald is more attractive but less hardy and slower growing.

Shade Tolerant or Cool Weather Grasses

These grasses are used for a green winter lawn (Winter Grass) or for problem areas which are too shady to grow anything else. All must be started from seed in the early fall. The seed germinates faster in warm weather. The last week in September is the best time to plant, but these grasses may be sown all through October. In bare places, loosen the soil before planting. Lightly rake in the seed and keep moist until germination, then water frequently. The seedlings can easily be smothered by fallen leaves. Rake lightly to prevent injury to the shallow rooted blades. Use any well balanced slow-release fertilizer after seeding and water in immediately to prevent burning. All of these grasses will look best in spring, early summer, and fall. The perennial shade grasses will suffer from heat and must be watered frequently in the summer.

Winter Grass—Annual rye grass. For a green winter lawn broadcast seed over lawn, 1 pound per 100 square feet. The planting of rye grass over a Bermuda lawn may slightly harm the Bermuda, but if the winter grass is cut frequently, it is not apt to choke out the Bermuda.

Perennial Rye—Shade grass. Attractive and hardy, but requires more sun than Blue Grass and Fescues. The best varieties are Regal and Derby.

Blue Grass—Blue grass is a perennial shade grass. The new hybrids (Touchdown, Bristol, Glade) are very hardy. It dries out in hot, dry weather, but can survive with frequent watering as far south as Tennessee, Georgia, and Alabama. It grows best with a pH of 5.5–7.0 and should be fertilized in early spring, early summer, or early fall.

Fescue—A perennial shade grass frequently mixed with blue grass for a more sturdy lawn. Creeping Red Fescue is attractive but clumpy. Kentucky 31 is used extensively in problem shade areas and best heavily seeded. New varieties (Falcon, Rebel & Olympic) are finer bladed and quite heat resistant.

LAWN CARE

Mowing—A well-cared-for lawn will keep insects and weeds to a minimum. Rake leaves from the lawn and mow grass often enough to prevent weeds from reseeding. Be sure that the lawn mower blades are sharp. When first mowing the lawn (in March) set mower blades very low to cut the grass closely and kill emerging weeds. Be sure to rake after the first mowing to prevent heavy thatch buildup. Raise mower blades (2″–3″) as summer progresses. By September 1 have the blades high enough to allow Bermuda to grow to a height of 1½″–3″ before growth stops in October. Taller grass is more cold resistant. Cut Zoysia higher than Bermuda. Too thick a thatch will kill all grass and will have to be removed by dethatching.

Aerating—Heavily compacted soil should be opened up with an aerator, an inexpensive tool which may be purchased or rented at a garden center.

Watering—Lawns should be soaked thoroughly once a week during drouth. An automatic sprinkler system makes lawn care easier. Consider installing one before planting a new lawn.

WEEDS, FUNGUS, AND INSECTS

New grasses should be 6 weeks old before a contact weed killer is applied. In early spring remove any heavy thatch from Bermuda and Zoysia with a rake or a dethatcher. Use a preemergence weed killer every spring to prevent the germination of broad-bladed weeds. It can be applied with a balanced fertilizer. If a preemergence weed killer is not used, a postemergence weed killer containing MSMA such as ANSAR may be applied when the temperature is above 85° to kill weeds. Several applications at weekly intervals are necessary. It will turn Bermuda brown but will not kill it. Zoysia is less tolerant of MSMA so use less and make an additional application or two. Caution: Always use care in the application of weed control chemicals to avoid burning desirable grasses.

In spring, preemergence herbicides need to be watered into the soil to be effective for a period of several months. When applying selective **broad-leaf** (dandelion, chick weed, henbit, plantain, etc.) weed killers (2-4D based) and **broad-bladed** (crab, dallis, goose, foxtail) grass killers (ANSAR-MSMA) select a time when there is no rain for 48 hours. Use 2-4D based weed killers when temperature is between 55° and 80°. FOLLOW DIRECTIONS.

Hand weeding with a weeding tool is still a good way to get rid of weeds in a small area. Most weeds can be eliminated from Bermuda by covering with black plastic for about a week or so, and then watering deeply.

Removal of thatch tends to prevent and clear up fungus (mildew, rust). If the fungus persists, use a fungicide such as Zineb, Maneb, or Fore.

Beetles, grubs, and army worms are controlled by an insecticide such as Malathion. Follow directions carefully. Check local extension service.

FERTILIZING LAWNS

In spring (April or May) and early fall (September or October) apply a top-dressing of commercial lawn fertilizer at the rate of 4 or 5 pounds to every 100 square feet of lawn. In the spring use a fertilizer high in nitrogen (urea or ammonium nitrate) to stimulate top growth. Use little or no nitrogen after August 1. Instead use one high in potassium (muriate of potash). Two or three applications of a balanced fertilizer will benefit the lawn during the growing season. During hot spells however, either halve the dosage or eliminate it entirely. So that the grass will not be injured by burning, water the lawn thoroughly, immediately after application.

The soil should be neutral or slightly alkaline. As the roots tend to create acidity in the soil, some lime is often needed. The best time to apply lime is around December, January or February, at about the rate of 50 to 100 pounds of ground limestone (agricultural lime) to 1000 square feet, depending on the soil pH factor.

Do's and Don'ts

Do not allow children or pets to come in contact with sprays. Do not apply more than the directions call for, as an overdose may burn the grass. Never use broadleaf herbicides (2-4D based) near trees or shrubs as it can kill both, especially dogwood, boxwood, and azaleas. Read all labels carefully. Remember to water deeply after applying inorganic fertilizers to prevent grass burn. Water all new lawns frequently. Reapply fertilizer when the grass loses its rich green color.

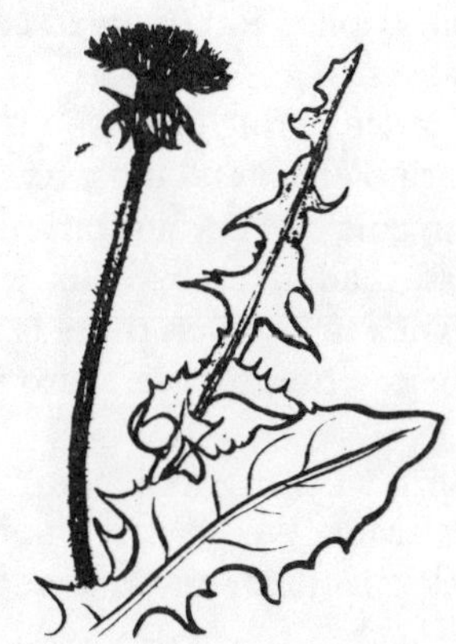

Trees

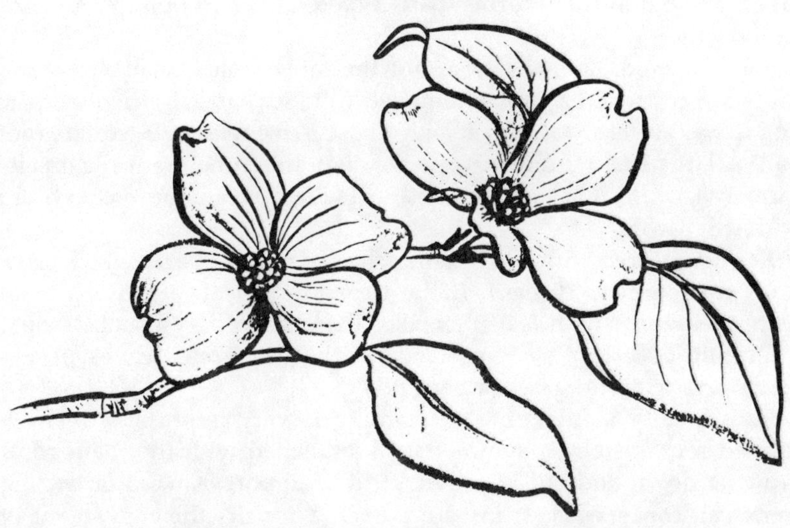

In choosing a tree to plant its primary purpose must first be determined. Plant for hardiness, shade, beauty, and good landscaping effect, fall color, screening, and spring bloom.

Limit the selection to trees that are available and hardy in local area and can adapt to the particular spot where they will be planted. A tree planted north of its adapted range may grow satisfactorily through a series of milder-than-normal winters, but may be killed by a severe one.

In buying trees always take into consideration the potential size of a tree with regard to the actual size of the property. Select the tree that is best for the intended use. A broadly spreading tree will be ideal for the lawn; a slim upright tree would be perfect beside a driveway but be of little use for shading a patio. Be sure the eventual size and shape will be suitable for the area in which it is used. Also consider how long it will live, and how fast it will grow. Never use a tree as foundation planting.

In the city trees must tolerate pollution, soil compaction, and fairly dry situations near the street. Choose tolerant varieties or create favorable conditions. Ginkgo and London plane trees do well in the city; sugar maples do not.

PURCHASING A TREE

Trees are sold in three forms: bare-rooted, balled in burlap and container-grown.

Select a medium-sized tree, not the largest one available. Many roots are cut when a tree is removed from its natural growing spot, and it may suffer from the shock. Choose a tree with an adequate root ball. A large tree requires two years of attention before it regains its former vigor. In this length of time a smaller tree will have caught up with its growth.

Reject any tree with broken branches or injured bark, which is an open invitation to disease. If the trees are in leaf, avoid any with wilted leaves or with leaves smaller than the variety usually bears, indicating poor root systems. Look for healthy green leaves. Avoid containers with nut grass or bermuda grass.

Root quality at the time of planting is very important. A well-formed root system is symmetrically branched with the main roots growing down and out to provide trunk support. Kinked or circling roots can cause weak trunk support and restrict the movement of water and nutrients. Check for a well-formed root system.

PLANTING

Trees which are bare rooted and balled in burlap should be purchased and planted when they are dormant, from about October 15 to March 15. Planted at any other time, extra care must be provided. Container-grown trees can be kept for a long time and planted at any time of the year.

Never pick up trees by the trunk only; always support the ball. Between purchasing and planting a tree it is very important to keep it moist and cool.

All trees should be planted in a large hole as cramped roots stunt growth. Dig a hole at least twice as wide and deep as the root system. Mix the soil that has been removed with an equal amount of leaf mold, peat moss, compost, or other organic matter, and for heavy clay soil, use sand. This mixture is called backfill soil. In some areas there may be strata of gray, puttylike earth which is usually sour with an unpleasant odor. Replace this dirt with good soil or find a different location.

Never plant a tree too deep. In gauging the depth be sure to allow for settling of loose dirt. Set the tree a little high in the beginning. If the tree is a graft, be sure the graft union is at least 2″ above soil level. For bare-rooted trees, mound backfill soil into a cone within the hole, and adjust the tree to the correct height. Carefully spread the roots around the cone and fill with backfill soil and water. Firm soil with foot, being careful not to injure the roots. Do not mix fertilizer with backfill in the planting hole as this can injure the roots. Most trees will grow well the first season without additional fertilizer.

For balled and burlap trees shovel enough soil mixture into the hole to raise the top of the ball at least 2″ above the level of surrounding ground. Place the tree in the hole and pull burlap away from trunk, rolling it down below the soil level. Remove all grass roots, especially bermuda. It is not necessary to remove the burlap since it will rot within a year. Make a few slices in the sides and bottom to allow for easy root penetration. Add the backfill soil and pack it firmly; water the plant thoroughly.

Container-grown trees: Be sure to have the nurseryman slit the sides of a metal container, as it will be difficult to remove the plant without damaging it. Remove the plant from the container and inspect the roots. Slice firmly through the ball in 3 places vertically with a sharp knife to loosen any roots that may be matted around the ball. Fill in with backfill soil, pack firmly, and water thoroughly.

After the tree is planted, make a 4″ high rim or saucer with extra dirt at the perimeter of the hole. Fill with 1″ or 2″ of mulch to retain moisture and discourage weeds. Covering the entire surface with bricks, brick bats or stones will hold the ball firmly in the wind, retain moisture, prevent lawn mower nicks on the trunk and keep down weeds. Check occasionally for slugs under bricks. Remove bricks after a couple of years. Trees planted in woodland gardens need no levee or bricks as the leaves, mulch, and ground cover hold the moisture. A small barrier of wood or wire is also a protection from lawn mowers.

Trunks of newly planted trees should be wrapped with tree wrapping tape to prevent sun scald and to protect them from rodents, rabbits, and insects. Remove wrapping in about 2 years.

Do not stake the tree unless it will not stand up without it. A young tree standing alone with its top free to move usually becomes a stronger tree and better able to withstand the elements. Remove one-third to one-half of the top growth, retaining only those branches that will become the main structure branches.

Water the tree frequently and thoroughly the first year, and spray the leaves each time. The second year it should be watered during hot, dry spells, and after that it should be on its own except during periods of extended drouth.

WATERING AND FERTILIZING

Trees are never too old to respond to water and fertilizer. A newly planted tree must have water every ten days during the first two summers. Let the hose trickle slowly for two or three hours.

Trees should be fed regularly. Fertilize during January, February, or March. There are many ways to fertilize. Spread the fertilizer directly on the ground or use a crowbar to form holes 8″ deep, making a circle below the tips of the branches and fill with fertilizer.

Cottonseed meal or milorganite are excellent because they release nutrients slowly and will not burn the roots. A good chemical fertilizer is 10–8–6. Slow release lawn fertilizers are also effective. There are special fertilizer sticks which can be hammered into the ground. Nutrients can also be squirted into the soil with an injector, called a needle probe or root feeder, which is attached to a garden hose. Foliar feeding (spraying nutrients on the leaves) works quickly and often produces dramatic results. This method is highly recommended in combination with punch-hole or injector feeding for trees that are seriously undernourished and for trees whose roots spread under paving and cannot be reached otherwise.

PEST CONTROL

Well-tended trees are less susceptible to pests and diseases than neglected ones and, if attacked, recover faster. Borers are attracted by the odor of a wounded tree. Place mothballs or yellow laundry soap around the base of the tree or use a spray such as Ortho Lindane Leaf Miner Spray for borers. If a pest problem should arise, first identify the cause so the proper controls can be applied.

Because of the height of most trees and the difficulty in reaching top limbs and foliage, it is recommended that gardeners consult experienced professional help should serious diseases or pests occur, and when damage to trees has been severe from snow, wind, or ice storms.

HELPFUL HINTS

Watch any grading done around trees. Fine trees have been killed by dirt being dumped on top of their roots or having the dirt cut away. Do not plant large-leafed trees near a house because it is disproportionate to the house. Do not espalier magnolias against the house because they tend to crack foundations as well as overgrow the location.

If a limb has been removed from a tree or if a tree has been cut by a lawn mower, trim the bark smoothly to form an oval wound and apply tree paint (available at seed and garden stores). This prevents insects from attacking unprotected wood.

Large leathery leaves (magnolia, sycamore, etc.) should not be left on the ground in large quantities. They decay slowly and do not allow enough moisture and nutrients to reach plant roots.

FLOWERING TREES

American Basswood
Buckeye
Catalpa
Chaste Tree
Crape Myrtle
Devil's Walking Stick
Devil-wood
Dogwood
Dove Tree
Epaulette-tree
Fringe tree
Franklin tree
Golden-Chain
Golden Rain
Hawthorn
Horsechestnut
Paulownia
Red Bud
Service Berry
Silver Bell
Snow Bell
Sourwood
Sweet Olive
Tulip
Yellowwood

Flowering Fruit

Apple
Apricot
Cherry
Crab Apple
Peach
Pear
Plum

TREES FOR FALL COLOR

Ash	Ginkgo	Sourwood
Beech	Golden Rain	Sugar Maple
Black Gum	Hickory	Sweet Gum
Chinese Tallow	Japanese Maple	Sumac
Dogwood	Scarlet Oak	

TREES

KEY

B—Broadleaf evergreen	E—Evergreen
bf—Bird Food	F—Showy Flower
C—Coniferous	*—Very desirable
D—Deciduous	

COMMON NAME SCIENTIFIC NAME	KEY	HEIGHT	COMMENTS
American Basswood (American Linden) *Tilia americana*	D, bf	70′–90′	Fragrant white flowers in summer; yellow fall foliage; heart-shaped leaf. Fast grower; broad shade tree. Bee forage tree.
American Elm *See* Elm			
American Hornbeam (Blue Beech, Ironwood) *Carpinus caroliniana*	D	40′	Leaves pest-free and resemble elm. Yellow in fall. Slow grower. Grown from Maine to Texas.
American Holly *Ilex opaca*	B, bf	40′–50′	Not for foundation planting. Subject to leaf miner (See sprays). Heavily fertilize for masses of berries.
Angelica Tree *See* Devil's-walking-stick			
Apple *Malus*	D, F	to 30′	Many varieties. Check local nursery.
Apricot *Prunus armeniaca*	D, F	to 20′	Many varieties. Check local nursery.
Arborvitae *Thuja occidentalis*	C	2½′–20′	Good loamy, well-drained soil. Sunny. Easily grown; dwarf and giant varieties.
Ash *Fraxinus*	D, F bf	30′–90′	Many varieties. Hardy. Rapid growth. Yellow leaves in fall.

TREES

COMMON NAME SCIENTIFIC NAME	KEY	HEIGHT	COMMENTS
Bald Cypress *Taxodium distichum*	C, D*	150′	Handsome. Forest size. Good in large garden. Forms knees only under water. Grows very old. Excellent for shutters, coffins, and shingles.
Beech, American *Fagus grandifolia*	D, bf*	50′–90′	Light gray bark. Young trees retain leaves all winter. Leaf similar to elm.
Beech, Copper *F. sylvatica*	D*	80′	Bronze-colored leaf. Handsome accent.
Birch, European White *Betula alba* or *pendula*	D	30′–60′	Short-lived. Sun. Single or multiple trunk. Prefers northern climate. White peeling bark.
Birch, River *Betula nigra*	D, bf	60′–80′	Stream and river banks. Fast growing. Bark orange and scaly. Tolerates poor drainage. Do not plant near terrace as roots tend to surface. Yellow fall foliage. Messy.
Black Cherry *See* Cherry			
Black Gum (Sour Gum, Tupelo) *Nyssa sylvatica*	D bf*	60′–90′	Handsome tree. Slow growing. Scarlet in fall.
Black Locust *See* False Acacia			
Black Walnut *Juglans nigra*	D	50′–150′	Valuable for nuts. Do not plant ornamentals or vegetables underneath.
Buckeye *Aesculus pavia*	D, F	to 20′	Native. Bright red spiky flower. Late spring. Nut is good luck charm.
Catalpa *Catalpa bignonioides*	D, F	40′	Forest size. Attracts worms. Showy white flower in early summer. Long slender seed pods. Very large leaves.
Cedar, Red *See* Juniper			
Cedar Atlantic Cedar *Cedrus atlantica*	C	40′–100′	Feathery, bluish green needles. Also pendulous form.

TREES

COMMON NAME SCIENTIFIC NAME	KEY	HEIGHT	COMMENTS
Deodar Cedar *C. deodara*	C	to 100′	Dark blue green needles. Handsome, graceful, drooping branches. Large accent or background tree.
Cedar-of-Lebanon *C. Libani*	C*	to 130′	Closely resembles *C. deodara* but darker green and larger. Very handsome long-lived tree.
Chaste-Tree (Vitex) *Vitex agnus-castus*	D, F*	to 25′	Biblical tree. Purple blue spiky flower in June-July. Pungent odor. Gray green palmate foliage. White variety available.
Cherry *Prunus*			
Black Cherry *P. serotina*	D, F, bf	50′–75′	Birds love berries. Fast grower. White flower in spring.
Flowering Cherry *P. cerasus*	D, F*	to 25′	Early spring bloom. White or pink flowers. Also double flower variety. Check local nursery.
Japanese Cherry *P. serrulata*	D, F*	to 30′	Unsurpassable. Blooms with daffodils. Upright or weeping. Tufts of pink flowers.
Chestnut *Castanea*			
American Chestnut *C. dentata*	D, F	100′	White spike flower. Subject to blight. Sweet-meated nuts. Other varieties, including pink.
Chestnut Oak *See* Oak			
Chinaberry *Melia azedarach*	D, bf	to 50′	Fast grower, short-lived. Good for quick shade. Lacy foliage, yellow fruit.
China Fir *Cunninghamia lanceolata*	C, E	100′	Handsome. Hardy in Zones 7 & 8. Spiny foliage.
Chinese Parasol Tree (Phoenix Tree) *Firmiana simplex*	D	50′	Palmate leaf 12″ across. Resembling sycamore. Grown in South for shade. Lemon yellow flower in Zones 8 & 9.
Chinese Quince *Cydonia sinensis*	D	20′	Insignificant pink bloom. Spring

TREES

COMMON NAME SCIENTIFIC NAME	KEY	HEIGHT	COMMENTS
Chinese Scholar *See* Pagoda Tree			
Chinese Tallow Tree *Sapium sebiferum*	D	40′	Fast grower. Weedy, poisonous juice. Yellow, purple, crimson in fall. White berry. Not very hardy.
Chinese Wingnut Tree *Pterocarya stenoptera*	D*	to 30′	Ornamental fast grower, pinnate leaf. Attractive pale green-winged nut chains in May. Moist soil. Tolerates hot summers.
Cornelian Cherry *Cornus mas*	D, F	20′	See Dogwood. Yellow bract flowers. Valuable in shady place. Can stand dry soil. Also variegated. Check local nursery.
Crabapple *Malus*	D, F	10′–25′	Sun, many varieties. Showy spring flower, easy to grow. "Calloway" outstanding. Do not cut off lower branches until well established.
Crape Myrtle *Lagerstroemia indica*	F*	to 20′	Beautiful bark. Blooms mid-June through September; pink, white or magenta. "Near East," pale pink. Do not treat as shrub. Dwarf varieties available. Blooms 100 days.
Cryptomeria *Cryptomeria japonica*	C*, E	to 125′	Pyramidal growth. Background tree. Distinctive greenery. Angular foliage.
Cucumber Tree *See* Magnolia			
Cypress *Cupressus* Bald Cypress—*See* Bald Cypress			
False Cypress *Chamaecyparis*	C, E		Many varieties, sizes, and colors. Check local nursery.
Italian Cypress *Cupressus sempervirens*	C	to 80′	Narrow, columnar. Dark green foliage. Used in formal European gardens.
Dahoon *Ilex cassine* See special article on Holly			

TREES

COMMON NAME SCIENTIFIC NAME	KEY	HEIGHT	COMMENTS
Dawn Redwood *Metasequoia glyptos-troboides*	D*	50′–100′	Extremely handsome. Resembles Cypress. Fast growing.
Devil's walking-stick (Angelica Tree) *Aralia spinosa*	D, F	to 30′	Very thorny. Graceful tree with huge clusters of tiny white flowers in summer, turning to rust in fall. Shady wild area.
Devilwood *Osmanthus americanus*	B	20′–30′	Leaves 7″ long. Fragrant, greenish flowers in early spring. Hard wood.
Dogwood			
Flowering Dogwood *Cornus florida*	D, F bf*	to 30′	Many cultivars. White and pink bracts in spring before leaves. World's favorite, native to U.S. Scarlet leaves in fall.
Asian *C. Kousa*	D, F	to 20 ′	June bloom. Pointed white bracts. Scarlet fruit. Flowers appear with leaves.
Cornelian *C. mas*	D, F	20′	Yellow flowers; *see* Cornelian Cherry
Dwarf *C. nana*	D, F	5′ to 6′	Dwarf form of *florida*.
Weeping *C. pendula*	D, F	20′	Weeping form of *florida*.
Double *C. plena*	D, F	20′	Double form of *florida*.
Red-Osier *C. sericea*	D, F	10′	Red branches. Shrub. Does not like hot climate.
Dove Tree *Davidia involucrata*	D, F,*	to 30′	Great beauty in bloom. Dense head with large creamy, drooping bracts like a white dove.
Elder *Sambucus nigra*	D, bf	30′	Large umble flower 12″ across, resembling Queen Anne's Lace. Shrublike and coarse genus. Also a variegated variety.
Elm			
American Elm *Ulmus americana*	D	to 120′	Graceful wine-glass shape. Forest size. Subject to Dutch Elm disease. If it dies, dispose of it immediately. Yellow fall foliage.

TREES

COMMON NAME SCIENTIFIC NAME	KEY	HEIGHT	COMMENTS
Elm, winged *U. alata*	D	10′–20′	Winged bark. Twigs are corky. Dry soil. More of a shrub than a tree.
Epaulette Tree *Pterostyrax hispidus*	D	45′	Large elmlike leaf. Abundant creamy, pendulous, fragrant flowers. Moist, sandy loam. Flowers in spring.
False Acacia (Black or Yellow Locust) *Robinia pseudoacacia*	D, F	40′–80′	Spiny branches. Fragrant white flowers. Suckers. Avoid poisonous thorns.
False Cypress *See* Cypress			
Fig (common) *Ficus carica*	D, bf	30′	Many varieties. Grown for fruit. Consult local nursery.
Franklinia (Gordonia) *Franklinia alatamaha*	D, F*	6′–20′	White waxy flower in late summer and fall. Shade and protection needed. Damp, peaty soil.
Fringe Tree (Old-man's beard) *Chionanthus virginicus*	D, F*	30′	Good ornamental. Fragrant white feathery flower in spring.
Ginkgo (Maidenhair Tree) *Ginkgo biloba*	D*	120′	Hardy. Prehistoric. Very handsome ornamental. Yellow in fall. Good on city streets or parks. Only one species. Female has foul smelling fruit.
Golden-chain Tree *Laburnum anagyroides*	D, F*	30′	Large pendulous racemes of yellow flowers in spring. Needs protection.
Golden Rain Tree *Koelreuteria paniculata*	D, F*,	30′	Large clusters of tiny yellow flowers in late spring. Golden rain is the falling of yellow flowerlets. Very ornamental. Large brown seed pods in fall.
Gordonia *See* Franklinia			
Hackberry *Celtis laevigata*	D, bf	100′	Wide-spreading, airy branches. Thrives in poor soil. Native. Disease and insect free. Yellow fall foliage.

TREES

COMMON NAME SCIENTIFIC NAME	KEY	HEIGHT	COMMENTS
Hawthorn *Crataegus laevigata*	D, bf	25′	Hawthorn of English literature. White flowers in May. Red fruit. Thorny. Subject to caterpillars.
Hemlock *Tsuga canadensis*	C, E*	25′–50′	Feathery conifer. Cool damp location. Many species. Consult local nurseries.
T. canadensis pendula	C, E	15′	Drooping.
T. diversifolia	C, E	20′	Very compact.
Hickory *Carya*	D	to 100′	Many species. Hardy. Food for wildlife. Wood used for smoking meat and fish. Yellow fall foliage. Native.
Holly *Ilex* See special article on Holly			
Honey Locust *Gleditsia triacanthos*	D	35′–70′	Thornless varieties. Yellow in fall. Tolerates pollution. Fast grower.
Hop Hornbeam *Ostrya virginiana*	D	20′–50′	Very hard wood. Hardy, pest free. Slow grower. Yellow in fall. Native.
Horse Chestnut *Aesculus hippocastanum*	D, F*	50′–100′	Pink or white flower spike in spring. Sun or light shade. Any soil. Also dwarf varieties.
Ilex *See* Special article on Holly			
Ironwood *See* American Hornbeam			
Japanese Pagoda Tree *See* Pagoda Tree			
Japanese Persimmon *Diospyros kaki*	D	40′	Large orange edible fruit. Very attractive tree. Hardy Zones 7, 8, 9.
Japanese Tree Lilac *Syringa reticulata* var. *japonica*	D, F	20′–30′	Large white raceme flowers in midsummer

TREES

COMMON NAME SCIENTIFIC NAME	KEY	HEIGHT	COMMENTS
Judas Tree *See* Redbud			
Juniper *Juniperus*	C, E	to 50′	Many species and varieties. Foliage mostly gray green. Many forms from columnar to ground cover. Subject to rust, fungi, galls, bagworms. Remove rust galls.
Common Red Cedar *J. virginiana*	C, E	to 50′	Many cultivars; fragrant wood used in cedar closets.
Katsura *Cercidiphyllum japonicum*	D	to 50′	Round 4″ leaves. Scarlet and yellow in fall. Rich, moist soil. Female, spreading; male, columnar.
Linden (American) *See* American Basswood			
Loblolly Bay *Gordonia lasianthus*	B, E*	60′	Not hardy above Zone 7. White flowers, glossy dark green leaves.
Locust *See* False Acacia and Honey Locust			
Loquat *Eriobotrya japonica*	E, F	to 20′	Not hardy above Zone 7. Handsome large-leaf foliage. Edible fruit. Fragrant white flowers in panicles in fall.
Magnolia Cucumber Magnolia *Magnolia acuminata*	D, F*	to 100′	Early very large foliage, greenish flower and leaves. Seed pod resembles cucumber. Pyramidal shape.
M. grandiflora	E, F	100′	Large leathery leaf. Huge white fragrant flower, 8″–12″ diameter. Roots surface. Red fruit.
M. heptapeta (denudata)	D	to 30′	Large coffee-cup-sized flower before leaves. Early bloomer. Bloom often caught in late freeze.
Large-Leaved Cucumber Tree *M. macrophylla*	D, F	20′–50′	Leaves 2½′ long. Very large fragrant, rumpled white flower. Very dramatic.
M. quinquepeta nigra	D	to 12′	Red purple flowers appear before foliage.

TREES

COMMON NAME SCIENTIFIC NAME	KEY	HEIGHT	COMMENTS
Chinese Magnolia *M. soulangiana*	D	to 12′	Prolific bloomer. Fragrant white flower, streaked with orchid. Some subspecies dark reddish purple. Flowers appear before foliage.
Star Magnolia *M. stellata*	D*	to 15′	Sweet smelling, narrow-petaled flowers, 3″ diameter. Often shrub form, blooms early. White flowers appear before foliage.
Sweet Bay *M. virginiana*	D or E, F*	to 60′	Grayish leaves. Small fragrant white flowers. Red fruit.
Maidenhair Tree *See* Ginkgo			
Maple Japanese *Acer palmatum*	D*	20′	Slow growing. Brilliant coloring early spring and fall. Desirable.
A. palmatum dissectum	D*	4′–5′	Finely cut leaves divided into segments. Scarlet in fall. Extremely slow growing.
Norway *A. platanoides*	D	to 90′	Rounded head, desirable tree for wooded lots. Yellow fall foliage. Street tree.
Red *A. rubrum*	D	to 120′	Scarlet, orange in fall. Good street or park tree
Silver *A. saccharinum*	D	60′–100′	Softwood. Native to eastern U.S. Good roadside ornamental. Fast grower. Has shallow spreading root system so not good for small garden. Yellow red autumn foliage.
Sugar *A. saccharum*	D*	100′	Hardy all over Eastern U.S. Source of maple sugar. Does not tolerate pollution. Autumn foliage gold, orange, scarlet.
Mimosa *Mimosa*	D	40′	Pink flowers mid-June to August. Spreading crown, short-lived. Trees drip. Subject to worms.
Mountain Ash *Sorbus americana*	D	30′	Prefers cool climates. Showy in fall with clusters of red berries.
Mulberry *morus*	D, bf	50′	Edible fruit that stains. Undesirable. Roots surface. Several varieties.

TREES

COMMON NAME SCIENTIFIC NAME	KEY	HEIGHT	COMMENTS
Oak			Some varieties subject to leaf gall. No known cure.
Black *Quercus velutina*	D	80′ up	Fast grower. Dull orange in fall.
Burl *Q. macrocarpa*	D	to 80′	Has very large acorns. Insect and disease resistant. Dull yellow fall foliage. Drops leaves in winter.
Chestnut *Q. prinus*	D	70′	Likes dryness. Shapely leaf. Dull orange in fall.
English *Q. robur fastigiata*	D	to 80′	Very upright, columnar. Subject to mildew.
Live *Q. virginiana*	E*	to 60′	Wide spreading. Not hardy north of Zone 5. Handsome tree, slow grower, glossy dark green leaves.
Pin *Q. palustris*	D*	60′–70′	Pyramidal head. Long pendulous branches. Red in fall. Fast grower. Good for avenues and as a specimen shade tree. Subject to leaf gall.
Post *Q. stellata*	D	50′–60′	Retains brown leaves all winter. Hardy from Zone 3 southward.
Red *Q. rubra*	D	60′–75′	Red fall foliage. Rapid grower. Subject to leaf gall.
Scarlet *Q. coccinea*	D	60′–80′	Scarlet in fall. Likes dry location. Erect and symmetrical. Holds leaves in winter.
Shingle *Q. imbricaria*	D	to 60′	Round topped in age. Russet in fall. Holds leaves in winter.
Water *Q. nigra*	D*	60′–70′	Holds leaves in winter. Fast grower. Inconspicuous fall foliage.
White *Q. alba*	D*	to 100′	Handsome. One of the most noble of hardwood trees. Should be planted in large open space. Russet fall foliage. Holds leaves in winter.
Willow *Q. phellos*	D*	40′–60′	Narrow leaves. Pendulous branches. Fast grower. Pale yellow fall foliage. Any soil. Subject to leaf gall.

TREES

COMMON NAME SCIENTIFIC NAME	KEY	HEIGHT	COMMENTS
Osage Orange *Maclura pomifera*	D	50′–60′	Large, fast-growing, pest-free. Large round green fruit not edible. Invasive roots.
Pagoda Tree *Sophora japonica*	D	50′–75′	Late summer cluster of tiny flowers followed by yellow pods. Shade tree. Fast grower. Withstands pollution.
Paulownia (Royal Empress Tree) *Paulonia tomentosa*	D, F* bf	to 50′	Large sturdy tree with showy fragrant violet flowers in spring. Creates dense shade, fast grower. Not hardy above Zone 7.
Pawpaw *Asimina triloba*	D, bf	20′–30′	Native. Fast grower. Bananalike fruit. Yellow fall foliage.
Peach *Prunus*	D, F	to 15′	Many varieties; see local nursery. White to pink flowers in spring. Also dwarf varieties.
Pear *Pyrus*	D, F	to 15′	Many varieties; see local nursery. White flowers.
Pecan *Carya*	D	to 100′	Dull yellow fall foliage. Many varieties; consult local nursery. Troubled by caterpillars. Not hardy north of Zone 7.
Persimmon *Diospyros virginiana*	D	to 40′	Fall fruit edible, good for birds and wildlife. Very hard wood, used for golf clubs. Yellow to red fall foliage.
Phoenix Tree *See* Chinese Parasol Tree			
Pine	C, E	to 100′	80 species. Needlelike leaves in cluster. Hard, woody cones. Tolerates poor soil, prefers well-drained sandy loam. Plant nursery grown trees rather than digging from woods. Fast growing.
Austrian *Pinus nigra*	C, E	to 100′	Pyramidal growth. Stiff dark green needles.
Japanese Red *P. densiflora*	C, E	to 100′	Fast grower. Widespread. Hardy. Blue green needles.
Japanese White *P. parviflora*	C, E	50′	Dense bluish needles forming tufts at tips of branches.

TREES

COMMON NAME SCIENTIFIC NAME	KEY	HEIGHT	COMMENTS
Loblolly *P. taeda*	C, E	90′	Fast grower. Tolerates poor soil.
Red *P. resinosa*	C, E	to 80′	Upright and domelike. Hardy. Dark green, glossy needles.
Scotch *P. sylvestris*	C, E*	to 70′	Spreading, drooping branches. 2½″ cones. Stiff bluish green needles. Very hardy.
Swiss mountain *P. mugo*	C, E	1′–3′	Shrubby, dense. Good for bonsai.
White *P. strobus*	C, E*	100′	Graceful. Picturesque in age. Symmetrical, pyramidal. Soft bluish green needles. Needs water in dry weather.
P. strobus fastigiata	C, E	20′	Narrow, upright growth.
P. strobus nana	C, E	1′–2′	Bush form.
P. strobus prostrata	C, E	3′	Low, trailing branches.
P. strobus umbraculifera	C, E	2′–3′	Umbrella-shaped
Plum *Prunus*	D, F	to 20′	Many varieties. Early bloom. Pale pink flower. Susceptible to insects. Green or purple leaves.
Plum-yew *Cephalotaxus drupacea*	E	30′	Hardy in sheltered areas. Slow growing.
C. fortunei	E	30′	Slender branches. Graceful. Under cultivation it remains shrubby.
Poplar *Populus*	D	to 50′	Many varieties; check nursery. Fast grower, soft wood. Roots can damage drains and walks.
Pussy Willow *Salix discolor*	D	10′–20′	Good for flower arrangments. Easily propagated in water. Catkins appear before leaves.
Redbud *Cercis canadensis*	D, F	25′	Native, showy purplish pink flowers. Blooms before dogwood. Volunteers from seed. Fast grower. White variety, double variety.
Sassafras *Sassafras albidum*	D*	30′–60′	Fragrant, greenish blossom. All parts aromatic. Tea from roots is a medicinal tonic. Orange and red fall foliage.

TREES

COMMON NAME SCIENTIFIC NAME	KEY	HEIGHT	COMMENTS
Serviceberry *Amelanchier*	D, F bf	20′–30′	Many varieties. Early bloomer. White spring blossom. Native. Yellow, orange, or red fall foliage.
Silver-Bell Tree (Lily of the Valley Tree, Snowdrop Tree) *Halesia carolina*	D*, F	35′	Branches in spring become lined with snowdroplike flowers. Azaleas and rhododendron grow well below them. Well-drained acid soil. Yellow fall color.
H. monticola	D, F	to 50′	Larger leaves and white flowers than *carolina*. Also pink variety.
Smoketree *Cotinus coggygria*	D*	to 15′	Coppery purple leaf, feathery plumes in May and June. Hardy.
C. obovatus	D	to 30′	Brilliant orange scarlet fall foliage.
Snowbell *Styrax japonicus*	D*	30′	Sprays of bell-like fragrant white flowers in early summer. Very curvaceous branches. Native. Needs protection. Slow grower.
Sourwood *Oxydendrum arboreum*	D*	to 30′	Second only to flowering dogwood. Hanging clusters of fragrant white bell-shaped flowers in May and June. Scarlet in fall. Native. Sourwood honey is famous. Slow grower.
Spruce Colorado Blue *Picea pungens*	E*	80′–100′	Bluish green or silvery blue foliage.
Norway *P. abies*	E	to 150′	Dark green, shiny needles, drooping branches.
Sumac *Rhus*	D	30′	Beautiful red foliage in fall. Red, fuzzy fruit clusters. Also bushes. Many varieties. Some poisonous, rank.
Sweet Gum *Liquidambar styraciflua*	D, bf	80′	Quick growth. Crimson, purple, and scarlet fall foliage. Winged bark. Trashy fruit balls. Maplelike leaf. Pest free.
Sweet Olive *Osmanthus fragrans*	E*	20′–30′	Dark green shiny foliage. Fragrant white flowers. Blooms fall and winter. Needs protected location.

TREES

COMMON NAME SCIENTIFIC NAME	KEY	HEIGHT	COMMENTS
Sycamore (Buttonwood, Plane Tree) *Platanus occidentalis*	D	70′	Large, fast growing; will outgrow small spaces. Dull yellow fall foliage; attractive peeling bark. Wood good for butcher blocks. Leaves not good for compost.
Trifoliate Orange *Poncirus trifoliata*	D, F	to 20′	Hardy to New Jersey. Fragrant white flowers. Small, orange, very acid fruit.
Tulip tree (Poplar) *Liriodendron tulipifera*	D	to 100′	Green and apricot flower in late spring. Fine forest tree. Not easily transplanted.
Tupelo *See* Black Gum			
Vitex *See* Chaste Tree			
Yellowwood *Cladrastis lutea*	D*	30′–50′	White panicles, like wisteria. Fragrant. Deep rooted. Drought resistant. Blooms profusely every other year. Prune only in summer as it bleeds severely if pruned in winter or spring.

Shrubs

Both trees and shrubs are woody plants. Trees generally have a single trunk while shrubs have multiple trunks and rarely reach a height of more than 20 feet. Some shrubs can be pruned into trees; refer to the shrub chart for eventual size. In planting, select young plants because older plants suffer shock when moved. The choice of shrubs is infinite. Shrubs can be chosen for size, shape, leaf color, evergreen or deciduous, flowers, berries, fruit, attractive bark, tolerance to sun, shade, dampness, or drought. Shrubs can be allowed to grow naturally and informally, or they can be sheared into formal shapes, but this is an unending chore. Shrubs massed in a staggered pattern, forward and back, and low and high, create a soft natural background or border. The most interesting borders are not planted in straight rows, but are designed with curves and bays that are lovely when underplanted with low-growing annuals, perennials, and bulbs. Hedges can also be planted low to outline an area or high to block out an undesirable view. Shrubs are planted for accent, background, sound barrier, privacy, and screening. In selecting foundation plants do not use large-leaved plants or shrubs which will grow too large for the space. Do not choose brittle, messy, or short-lived shrubs.

Planting

Same as Trees. *See* "Trees, Planting." Be sure to plant shrubs far enough apart to allow for future growth. Water deeply once a week until established and during dry spells.

BROAD-LEAVED EVERGREENS

Broad-leaved evergreens are the South's most prized group of garden plants. They create a pleasant setting even in winter. They thrive in the climate, like the soil, and add interest to borders with the texture, size, and color contrast in their leaves. To further enhance the garden picture, quite a few add the beautiful colors of their blooms, while many produce clusters of vivid berries. They make beautiful specimen, foundation, border, and accent plants and are very good as hedges and espaliers.

Culture

Broad-leaved evergreens may be planted any time from October through March. Earlier planting lets the plant take root before the growing season starts and so gives it quite an advantage over later planting.

Almost all the broad-leaved evergreens will stand sun or shade. Those that should be planted in shade only will be so noted. They should be planted in a well-drained location with the top of the root ball slightly above the surrounding soil. Mix planting soil with sand, humus, and wet peat moss for acidity. Pack soil well around the root ball and build a soil saucer to hold water. Water well until plant is established.

The only serious pests are scale insects which can be controlled. *See* "Scale on Evergreens." Do not spray right after the new growth comes out, or if the temperature is below 40° or over 80°.

Scale on Evergreen and Euonymus

In February use a *dormant oil based spray.* During the growing season, if needed, use an *insecticide,* such as Malathion or Cygon. Be sure to spray undersides of leaves. *Follow directions—handle with care.*

Fertilizer

With properly prepared soil the only fertilizer necessary will be an annual light dusting of cottonseed meal, 5–10–5, or an azalea-camellia fertilizer.

Shrubs with shallow root systems need to be mulched. Oak leaves, pine needles, shredded pine bark mulch or pecan shells are all excellent. Do not use finely milled peat moss because it forms a hard crust and water runs off without soaking into the ground. Shade-tolerant ground covers, such as ajuga, pachysandra, or vinca minor, provide a living mulch.

BOXWOOD

Boxwood is truly an aristocrat among shrubs and at home with the finest architecture. On the other hand, it will add elegance and beauty to the most modest landscape, and it is no snob as to soil requirements.

The secret of successful boxwood in this area is simple and inflexible. The two musts are *perfect drainage and partial shade.*

Healthy, rich green boxwood is usually found on the north side of a house, or on shaded, well-drained or sloping grounds. Location plays a large role in the success of boxwood. They need protection from western sun.

Planting

Boxwood does not like to be crowded. For maximum health it needs plenty of room with free circulation of air around it. It does best grown as a specimen plant. Take care in planting not to set ball too low.

Boxwood is easily transplanted with a good ball of dirt around the roots. Plant any time between October 1st and May 1st. It will flourish in any good garden loam. In preparing the hole, incorporate plenty of humus, such as leaf mold or compost, also some sand, and moistened peat moss.

Cultivation

Boxwood roots are near the surface. Very shallow cultivation is advised, just enough to keep down weeds or to supply a light mulch in summer. *Boxwood does not like heavy mulching.*

Watering

Boxwood likes plenty of moisture, not only until the plant is well established, but also during drought and summer heat. Do not wet foliage or apply any spray in hot sun as the foliage will burn.

Pruning

Boxwood can be trimmed in any desired form, preferably in early spring. *B. sempervirens* may be cut to resemble Japanese cloud pruning. This lets in light and air and encourages leaf growth far back on branches, making it easier to maintain sanitary conditions. Remove all dead or diseased branches.

Feeding

Do not overfeed boxwood. One feeding in spring should suffice. Well-rotted or dehydrated manure is excellent but cannot be repeated yearly without building soil too high on roots. A recommended fertilizer is 6 parts Milorganite, 2 parts bone meal, 2 parts cottonseed meal. Spread evenly over root area and a little beyond the edge of the branches. Do not scratch in as shallow roots may be damaged. Apply lime occasionally.

Pests

The principal enemy of boxwood in this area is red spider mite. The worst period of infestation is late summer. It may also appear in the spring. The mite is too small to see on foliage, and it attacks the underside of the leaf. If the foliage begins to look speckled and whitish, the chances are this is the trouble. For a further test, hold a sheet of white paper below a branch and tap sharply. If present, the very tiny insects will fall to the paper and begin to move about, where they can be seen. Spray with a mixture of a miticide, such as Kelthane, and a fungicide, such as Manzate. Follow directions on containers. Repeat this for three successive weeks. This spray will also help control any fungus that may be present on plants. At the time of first spraying make a light application of nitrate of soda around the roots. This helps the foliage to recover.

In late spring watch for wooly or cotton aphids (white) that turn into winged insects. Look closely inside the plant to discover them as they attack the stalks and woody branches, not the leaves. Spray with an insecticide, such as Malathion.

Propagation

Boxwood is easily rooted from cuttings. For this a cold frame is not needed. Choose a spot in partial shade where the soil is loamy. The addition of 1 part sand to 2 parts soil makes a good rooting mixture. Clippings may be taken in spring before the new growth appears or late summer (August) as boxwood is pruned. Pull clippings apart at the joints, leaving a "heel," or cut, just below a leaf bud. Select cuttings 4"–6" long. Dip ends in rooting medium. After trimming out some of bushy growth at top (to reduce evaporation) insert half the length of each cutting in the ground. From this time on, keep moist. With minimum care about 75% of the cuttings will root, sometimes more. They may be left in the cutting bed the first year. Cuttings may be transplanted bare-rooted to their permanent location.

Principal Varieties

Buxus arborescens—tree box, large green leaf, typical large form

B. harlandii—easily recognized by its longer leaf. Recommended by southern nurseries as the variety that best stands heat

B. microphylla var. *arborescens*—tree box

B. microphylla—"Curly Locks," curvaceous medium leaves

B. microphylla var. *japonica*—wide oval leaf, medium green

B. microphylla—*"Kingsville"*—dwarf, compact, 8"–10"

B. microphylla koreana—small, medium green leaf

B. sempervirens—standard American boxwood

B. sempervirens var. *argentea marginata*—variegated, light green-edged wavy leaves

B. sempervirens var. *arborescens aurea pendula*—mottled leaves, variable in color, white, dark green, rose tint with no definite pattern

B. sempervirens var. *aurea maculata*—part of leaf variegated with irregular patches of white

B. sempervirens var. *"Elegantissima"*—dark green leaves with white margins

B. sempervirens var. *"Fastigiata"*—dark green, tall, and upright

B. sempervirens "Handsworthiensis"—large, oval, smooth, dark green leaf

B. sempervirens var. *"Koreana"*—small, light green leaf

B. sempervirens L.—avocado green leaf

B. sempervirens var. *"Rotundifolia"*—big, rounded, dark green leaf

B. sempervirens var. *"Suffruticosa"*—edging box, bush, dark green leaf

Helpful Hints

Variegated plants do better in the shade as they have less chlorophyll and burn easily. They also brighten shady areas.

HOLLY (ILEX)

The Mid-South area is a favored one for the growing of a great variety of hollies. There is a holly for every purpose, whether it is a ten-inch-high hedge or a tall screen. There is great variation in leaf form, size, and color, also in growth habit, such as open, natural or thick, lateral or conical. There is even variation in individual plants of the same species. Nursery rows offer the best opportunity for making individual choices. Each year additional varieties are put on the market. Hollies are the evergreens to which one looks for permanence. Most of them are singularly free from pests and diseases and are good in any soil, so long as it is slightly acid. They do not seem to mind heat provided they do not get too dry, and they take either sun or shade. They also tolerate pollution.

Holly Tips

Planting—*See* "Trees, Planting."

Hollies must be *planted high* to insure drainage.

In moving large hollies—defoliate or spray with an antitranspirent.

For berries—apply superphosphate at time of blooming.

If holly plants look anemic—Check planting depth. Also see "pH Factor in Soil."

Dispose of leaves as they shed in spring to keep down disease.

For leaf miner—See "Sprays."

Holly hedge does not require as frequent pruning as other hedges because it makes its main growth only once a year, in spring.

One cupful Epsom Salts sprinkled around each plant as berries first begin to turn color makes the berries distasteful to birds. The effect, however, will have worn off by January when birds most need help in obtaining food. Hollies will tolerate severe pruning or, if they become too tall to prune, cut off lower branches and shape into trees.

HOLLIES

All bloom in spring. Most are evergreens.

COMMON NAME SCIENTIFIC NAME	HEIGHT	COMMENTS
American varieties *Ilex aquipernyi*	6′	Lacy foliage, red berries. Cross between English *aquifolium* and American *pernyi*, very hardy.
East Palatka *I. East Palatka*	30′–40′	Smooth light green leaf, scattered red berries. Vigorous grower. Tree.
Howardi *I. Howardii*	20′	Smooth dark green leaf, red berries in clusters. Tall background or specimen tree.
I. Humes' Hybrid	20′	Similar to *I. Howardii*, one of the many of Dr. Humes' hybrids. Very desirable.
Old Heavyberry *I. opaca*	30′	Dull green leaf. Good variety for red berries. Loses most of its leaves in March.
Savannah	30′	Outstanding light green leaf. Less spiny; heavily berried.
Xanthocarpa *I. Xanthocarpa*	50′	Yellow berries.
Dahoon *I. cassine*	18′	Narrow grey-backed leaf, small red berries. Loose growth; tolerates wet feet.
Myrtle Dahoon *I. cassine myrtifolia*	3′–4′	Very small narrow dark green leaf, black berries.
Foster Holly *I. fosteri*	5′–6′	Hybrid of Dahoon and American hollies. More hardy than Dahoon. Rapid grower, dark green foliage, heavy fruit production.
Inkberry *I. glabra*	4′–6′	Smooth glossy leaves. Black berries. Good for naturalizing or clipping. Cold resistant.
Possum Haw *I. decidua*	18′–20′	Not evergreen. Distinctive for its masses of orange red berries that remain all winter. Similar to *I. verticillata*.
Winterberry *I. verticillata*	16′	Not evergreen. Profuse bright red berries. Loose open growth.

HOLLIES

All bloom in spring. Most are evergreens.

COMMON NAME SCIENTIFIC NAME	HEIGHT	COMMENTS
Yaupon *I. vomitoria*	to 15′	Oval leaf, red berries, spreading branches, clip for density. Grows anywhere. Good for hedges.
Columnar Yaupon *I. vomitoria fastigiata*	12′	Columnar form.
Weeping Yaupon *I. vomitoria pendula*	9′	Weeping form.
Chinese varieties *I. cornuta*	to 20′	Shiny, very spiny, dark green, thick leathery leaf, large red berries. Upright growth. Strong grower, makes excellent hedge. Keeps out children and dogs. Grows too large for foundation planting.
Burford *I. cornuta burfordii*	30′	Leaf more rounded and not as spiny as *I. cornuta,* lush red berries, rapid grower. Can become a tree. Berries must be pruned off by March for flowers to make new berries.
I. cornuta compacta	5′	Dark green oval leaf, red berries.
I. cornuta latifolia	20′	Large leaf similar to rhododendron, red berries in clusters. Slow grower. Bold dense accent. Subject to scale.
I. cornuta "Willow Leaf"	5′	Small, dark green, narrow leaf, red berries.
I. pernyi	4′	Small toothed leaf, large red berries. Good foundation plant. Medium pyramidal size.
English variety *I. aquifolium*	to 50′	Very dark, spiny, curled green leaf, red berries. Most beautiful of all hollies, but not as dependable as others. Shade from west, needs acid soil plus good air circulation.
Japanese variety *I. crenata*		All varieties have very small, smooth leaves, black berries. Grow compactly even when unpruned. This family produces many dwarf forms. Needs water when dry.

HOLLIES

All bloom in spring. Most are evergreens.

COMMON NAME SCIENTIFIC NAME	HEIGHT	COMMENTS
I. crenata convexa	2′	Small, shiny, dark green convex leaf. Can be used in place of American box, part shade.
I. crenata helleri	2′	Dark green leaf, twiggy red stems, low spreading growth. Japanese in feeling.
I. crenata hetzii	3′–5′	Dark shiny green leaf, leaf larger than *I. convexa*. Vigorous grower, semispreader, can be espaliered.
I. crenata macrophylla	2′	Foliage lighter green than *I. convexa*, makes good low hedge.
I. crenata rotundifolia	4′	Rapid grower, excellent for hedge.
Nellie Stevens Holly *I. "Nellie R. Stevens"*	18′–20′	Hybrid of English and Chinese hollies. Fast grower to 20′ in 15–20 years. Conical when young, spreads with maturity. Dark green foliage, heavily berried. Cold resistant.
	DWARF HOLLIES	
Chinese *I. cornuta cornuta*	2′	Hybrid, no berries.
I. cornuta rotunda	12″–14″	Dark green spiny leaf, hybrid, no berries. Spreading growth.
Japanese *I. crenata helleri*	2′	Foliage lighter green than *I. convexa*, makes good low hedge.
I. crenata nummularia	14″	Small leaves, cloud form.
Yaupon *I. vomitoria nana*	12″	Very hardy.

HEDGES

Hedges are living walls. They are beautiful architectural features and make interesting divisions between various parts of the garden. Extremely tall hedges are a protection from displeasing views and noisy highways, and act as a wind break. The privacy of a secluded garden is one of a hedge's greatest assets.

Choice of Plants

Evergreens with small leaves are widely used, and preference is usually given to plants which will respond to clipping and thicken into smooth unbroken shapes. Flowering shrubs are also excellent hedge material and provide welcome beauty at bloom time. Prune or shear after blooming.

Planting

Plant in continuous trench so all plants receive equal water. The distance at which shrubs should be planted varies according to the nature of the plant. Small shrubs and quick growing shrubs, like small privets, should be planted 9″ apart, the average evergreens 18″ apart, and tall shrubs 24″ apart.

Deciduous plants should be pruned severely when they are first put in the ground. Cut them back to a height of 8″–10″. Large evergreens need only shaping and topping.

Shape

The form of the hedge is of first importance; the top must not obstruct the sunlight from lower branches. Make the hedge narrower at the top than at the bottom. The top should be gently rounded, the sides should slope to the somewhat broader base.

Maintenance

When the hedge is new, shape and prune it carefully; during this period its future beauty is determined. Clip along the sides but not between the plants. Allow the hedge to make new growth in the spring. Then prune when growth slows down in May. The subsequent frequency of shearing depends on the rate of growth of the plants since neatness and precision are essential to the beauty of a clipped hedge.

Evergreen Hedges—Tall (over 5 feet)

Eleagnus
Camellia sasanqua
Holly—*Ilex cornuta*
I. cornuta burfordi
I. opaca
Yaupon Holly
Red Cedar
Cherry Laurel
Photinia glabra
Photinia fraseri
Hemlock

Evergreen Hedges—Medium (2–5 feet)

Abelia grandiflora
Azalea
Barberry
Boxwood
Holly—*Ilex crenata rotundifolia*
Ligustrum
Weeping Privet

Evergreen Hedges—Low (up to 2 feet)

Boxwood
Euonymus japonica microphylla
Holly—*Ilex crenata bullata*
I. crenata helleri
I. crenata macrophylla
I. vomitoria nana (Dwarf Yaupon)

Flowering Hedges

Plants used for flowering hedges should not be pruned into formal shapes, but allowed to grow in their natural form. Prune only for thickening and uniformity.

Tall—Camellia sasanqua, Forsythia, Spirea prunifolia, and Spirea vanhouttei, Azalea.

Low—Deutzia gracilis, Floribunda roses, and Spirea Anthony Waterer, Azalea.

FLOWERING SHRUBS

The Mid-South is rich in flowering shrubs which supply blooms the year round. The exact time of blooming for the different varieties depends to a large extent on soil as well as the weather, therefore the blooming dates will vary from year to year and in different localities.

Flowering shrubs can be used as backgrounds, color accents, and specimen plants. They are easy to grow, and if given reasonable care and pruned as needed, will add greatly to the beauty of the garden.

They may be planted anytime from the first frost in the fall through the middle of April.

They must have at least 8 hours of sun a day to set their bloom, and the deciduous shrubs prefer full sun to develop their best display.

The following information is for *deciduous flowering shrubs.* The culture for evergreen flowering shrubs, such as azaleas, camellias, and others, is covered under special articles.

Culture

Flowering shrubs will set more buds if adequately watered once a week during dry weather.

Fertilize in the spring.

Aphids (tiny green insects which suck the sap) are about the only pests that bother these shrubs. Spray with *insecticide* such as Isotox or Malathion. Wash off pests with hard spray of water.

Prune *spring flowering shrubs* immediately after blooming by thinning. Prune *summer flowering shrubs,* like crape myrtle and althaea, in February or March because they bloom on new wood. *See* "Pruning."

Check Month by Month for flowering time.

Helpful Hint

Most spring flowering shrubs, especially quince and forsythia, can be cut as soon as buds show a little color, brought into the house, and put in warm water to force blooms.

FLOWERING SHRUBS

January

Camellia	Winter Sweet
Winter Honeysuckle	

February

Almond	Pussy Willow

Camellia
Forsythia
Loropetalum
Quince
Spiraea thunbergi
Witch Hazel

March

Camellia
Pearl Bush
Photinia
Spirea prunifolia
Star Magnolia
Viburnum burkwoodi

April

Azalea
Barberry
Beauty-bush
Deutzia gracilis
Kerria
Lilac
Scotch Broom
Spiraea cantoniensis
Spiraea vanhouttei
Storax japonicus
Sweet Shrub
Tamarisk
Viburnum

May

Abelia
Azalea
Deutzia "Pride of Rochester"
Hardy Orange
Honeysuckle
Mock Orange
Pomegranate
Weigela

June

Butterfly Bush
Elderberry
Hydrangea macrophylla
Hypericum
Oak leaf Hydrangea
Spiraea "Anthony Waterer"
Yucca

July

Althaea
Bottlebrush Buckeye
Butterfly Bush
Candlestick Tree
Crape Myrtle
Hypericum
Lavender Cotton
Gardenia
Hydrangea
Tamarisk

August

Althaea
Bluebeard
Butterfly Bush
Crape Myrtle
Hydrangea
Hypericum
Summer Sweet
Tamarisk

September

Althaea
Butterfly Bush
Crape Myrtle

October

Camellia
Fatsia
Tea Plant

November

Camellia
Sweet Olive

December

Camellia

SHRUBS FOR FALL COLOR

Abelia
Azalea
Barberry
Burning Bush
Nandina
Sumac

SHRUBS AND TREES FOR BIRD FOOD

Ash
Barberry
Beauty Berry
Beech
Birch
Black Cherry
Black Gum
Chinaberry
Cotoneaster
Devil's-walking-stick
Dogwood
Fig
Elderberry
Euonymus
Hackberry
Hawthorn
Holly
Ligustrum
Linden
Mahonia
Mulberry
Nandina
Paulownia
Paw-paw
Photinia
Serviceberry
Sumac
Sweet Gum

Helpful Hints

Birds—

Plant berried plants for bird food.

Pine cones: tuck shortening into crevices for birds in winter.

It is said that each bird eats its own weight in insects and seeds every day. Their beauty and entertainment and their great help in insect control make them worth encouraging. Provide feeding boxes and bird baths and keep filled daily. Birds like wild bird seed mixture, crumbs, suet, apples, and sunflower seed. Don't forget water in icy weather. Mix one tablespoon peanut butter with one-half cup cornmeal and one-half cup bacon grease for a special treat.

In heavy snowfall, put a piece of black plastic out, throw seeds on top.

Place suet in a pocket of chicken wire attached to a tree for super bird watching.

SHRUBS

KEY
E—Evergreen
D—Deciduous
A—Annual

COMMON NAME SCIENTIFIC NAME	KEY	HEIGHT	COMMENTS
Abelia *Abelia grandiflora*	E	to 10′	Pinkish white flowers on arching branches, leaves green in summer, bronze in winter. *Bloom Time:* June to Nov.
Alexandrian Laurel *Danae racemosa*	E	3′–4′	Inconspicuous white flower, red berries in fall, shiny spiny leaves. Likes shade. Not hardy north of Zone 6. Not a true laurel. *Bloom Time:* March–April.
Almond (Flowering) *Prunus glandulosa*	D	4′	Pink "pom-pom" blooms, very hardy. *Bloom Time:* March–April
Althaea (Rose-of-Sharon) *Hibiscus syriacus*	D	6′–12′	White to rose to lavender, single day flower. Rank. Check local nursery and catalogues. *Bloom Time:* July–August
Andromeda *See* Pieris			
Anise Tree *Illicum anisatum*	E	6′–19′	Rarely produces flowers. Desirable for light olive green elliptical leaves; aromatic. Partial shade, pest free. Lasts well in water for arrangements; roots easily in glass container.
Aucuba *Aucuba japonica*	E	to 6′	Inconspicuous white flower, large glossy leaves, solid or variegated. Prefers shade. Bright red berries in fall. Roots in water in glass. *Bloom Time:* June
Azaleas *See* special article			
Barberry *Berberis*	E&D	4′–8′	Leaf colors vary from red, pink, yellow, bronze, green or variegated. Many varieties, including dwarf, check local nurseries. Small yellow flowers, spiny stems, foliage handsome in fall. Good for spiny hedge. Full sun, tolerates shade. *Bloom Time:* April

SHRUBS

COMMON NAME SCIENTIFIC NAME	KEY	HEIGHT	COMMENTS
Beautyberry French mulberry *Callicarpa americana*	D	4′	Insignificant flowers; large bright orchid, lavender whorls of berries; leaves golden in fall. *Bloom Time:* May
Beautybush *Kolkwitzia amabilis*	D	6′–10′	Gracefull bell-shaped flowers, pink with yellow throat, on well-established plants. Leaves dull red in fall. Sun. *Bloom Time:* May–June
Bluebeard *Caryopteris*	*D*	*2′-3′*	Violet blue flowers, gray green foliage. Mulch in winter. *Bloom Time:* Sept.
Bottlebrush Buckeye *Aesculus parviflora*	D	10′–12′	White spike flower; foliage forms dense mound. Any good soil; partial shade; difficult to transplant. Slow grower. *Bloom Time:* July
Boxwood *See* special chart			
Bridal Wreath *See* Spirea			
Burning Bush *See Euonymus atropurpurea*			
Butterfly-Bush *Buddleia alternifolia*	D	8′–12′	Clustered spikes of fragrant lavender purple flowers; wide-spreading, arching branches. Attracts butterflies. Good for cutting. Cut back to 1′–2′ in spring. *Bloom Time:* July
B. davidii	D	8′–12′	Similar to above, many varieties. *Bloom Time:* Mid-July to frost
Camellia *See* special article			
Candlestick Tree *Cassia alata*	A	6′–8′	Bold yellow clusters of flowers, 6″–8″ long locustlike leaf. Treat as an annual. Best grown from seed. *Bloom Time:* July–Sept.
Cape Jasmine *See* Gardenia			
Carolina Allspice *See* Sweet Shrub			

SHRUBS

COMMON NAME SCIENTIFIC NAME	KEY	HEIGHT	COMMENTS
Cherry Laurel English Laurel *Prunus laurocerasus*	E	12′	Short clusters of fragrant, white flowers, glossy leaf. Can be used as a hedge. Subject to borers. *Bloom Time:* April
Zabelle Laurel *P. laurocerasus zabeliana*	E	9′	Inconspicuous flower, blue black berries, horizontal branches. Sun or shade. Not suited for foundation planting. *Bloom Time:* April
Chinese Red Bud Judas Tree *Cercis chinensis*	D	to 15′	Bright magenta flowers blooming on stem and trunk. *Bloom Time:* March
Cleyera *Cleyera japonica*	E	3′ to 5′	New foliage reddish turning glossy green, leathery texture. Handsome in arrangements. Pest free, acid soil, sun or partial shade. Low and spreading. *Bloom Time:* May
Cotoneaster Cranberry *Cotoneaster apiculatus*	D	18″–24″	Pink flowers, crimson fruit in fall. Dense growth, needs no pruning. Suitable for low hedges. *Bloom Time:* April
C. dammeri	E	18″	White flowers, red berries in fall, prostrate form. *Bloom Time:* April
C. divaricatus	D	3′–5′	Pink flowers, crimson berries in fall. Small, round, highly polished, dark green leaves. Desirable for specimen plant or hedge. *Bloom Time:* April
C. franchetii	E	6′	Pink flowers, orange red berries. Tolerates any soil. Deciduous in North. *Bloom Time:* April
C. horizontalis	Semi-E	3′	Pink flowers followed by red berries. Low spreading habit. Many other varieties, check local nurseries or catalogues. *Bloom Time:* April
Crape Myrtle *See* "Trees."			
Daphne *Daphne cneorum*	E	1′	Fragrant pink clusters of flowers. Often has second bloom in fall. Suitable for rock garden. *Bloom Time:* March–April

SHRUBS

COMMON NAME SCIENTIFIC NAME	KEY	HEIGHT	COMMENTS
D. odora	E	to 4′	Dense heads of very fragrant, white or purplish flowers. Not hardy above Zone 7. Slow grower, partial shade. Can be difficult to grow. Pest free. *Bloom Time:* March–April
Deutzia *Deutzia gracilis*	D	2′–4′	Clusters of pure white flowers on slender delicate arching stems. Pest resistant. *Bloom Time:* April
D. scabra var. *"Pride of Rochester"*	D	6′–8′	Double white flowers brushed with pink. *Bloom Time:* May
Elderberry *Sambucus canadensis*	D	12′–15′	Large white flower cluster, followed by black berries. Favorite of birds. Rank, suckers freely. Berries used for wine, jam, and pies. *Bloom Time:* June
Elaeagnus *Elaeagnus pungens*	E	to 8′	Insignificant flower, silvery green foliage on underside of leaf. Many varieties; requires frequent shaping. Good screening material. *Bloom Time:* April
E. pungens variegata	E	to 5′	Leaves light green, margined yellowish white. Semishade, any soil. Pest free. Easily transplanted. Slow grower. *Bloom Time:* April
Euonymus *Euonymus alata*	D	to 8′	Insignificant flower, scarlet leaves in fall, winged bark. *Bloom Time:* April
Hearts-a-busting with love *E. americana*	D	4′	Hot pink fruit with orange seed, dark red fall foliage. *Bloom Time:* April
Burning Bush or Wahoo *e. atropurpurea*	D	to 25′	Insignificant flower, yellow fall foliage, scarlet fruit. *Bloom Time:* April
E. japonica aureo-variegata var. "Gold Spot"	E	8′–10′	Insignificant flower, variegated yellow leaves. *Bloom Time:* April
var. "Silver King"	E	8′–10′	Insignificant flower, variegated white leaves. *Bloom Time:* April

SHRUBS

COMMON NAME SCIENTIFIC NAME	KEY	HEIGHT	COMMENTS
E. japonica microphylla	E	6″–24″	Insignificant flower; dwarf, compact evergreen foliage. Similar to boxwood. Also variegated form. *Bloom Time:* April
E. fortunei	E	3′–6′	Evergreen; trailing or climbing; 2″ leaves. Orange yellow berries in fall. Good, quick cover for cyclone fence. *Bloom Time:* April
Fatsia *Fatsia japonica*	E	4′–8′	Ball-like heads of white flowers; large glossy leaf. Shade. Not hardy above Zone 7. *Bloom Time:* October
Firethorn *See* Pyracantha			
Forsythia *Forsythia*	D	1′–8′	Yellow flowers; "Lynwood Gold" very fluorescent variety. Many varieties. Sun. Do not prune into ball. Can be forced in winter. Remove old canes to ground level after blooming. *See* White Forsythia. *Bloom Time:* February
Border Forsythia *F. intermedia*	D	6′	Yellow bell-like flower; handsome fall foliage. *Bloom Time:* February
F. intermedia spectabalis	D	6′–10′	Showiest yellow flowers; handsome fall foliage. Strong grower. *Bloom Time:* February
F. suspensa	D	6′–10′	Blooms later than above. *Bloom Time:* March
Cape Jasmine Gardenia *Gardenia* *Gardenia jasminoides*	E	to 6′	Large white waxy, very fragrant, flowers, some bloom into fall. Not hardy in severe winter, needs protection. All gardenias subject to white fly. *Bloom Time:* Spring & Summer
G. jasminoides radicans	E	1′–2′	Dwarf. Culture similar to camellias: acid soil, humus, use iron chelate for yellowing leaves. Requires sun for setting of buds. *Bloom Time:* May–June

SHRUBS

COMMON NAME SCIENTIFIC NAME	KEY	HEIGHT	COMMENTS
G. stricta-nana	E	1′	Fragrant white flower; dark green leaves. Subject to nematodes and white fly; needs spraying. More hardy than radicans. All gardenias eminently suitable for containers. *Bloom Time:* Summer
Hardy Orange *Poncirus trifoliata*	D	15′	White flowers, sour orange fruit, thorny. Very good to espalier on south or west wall. *Bloom Time:* May
Hazel *Corylus avellana contorta*	D	to 7′	Twisted, corkscrew-like branches, desirable for flower arrangements, slow growing. Also called Harry Lauder's Walking Stick.
Hearts-a-busting with love *See* Euonymus			
Holly *See* Special Chart on Holly			
Honeysuckle Winter Honeysuckle *Lonicera fragrantissima*	Semi-E	6′–8′	Spicy fragrant creamy white flowers. Inexpensive screen or hedge material. Many varieties. Branches easy to force in midwinter. Any soil; pest-free. *Bloom Time:* Early Spring
Hydrangea Hills of snow *Hydrangea arborescens grandiflora*	D	3′–4′	White flowers, turning greenish, remain for months. Can be dried. *Bloom Time:* July–August
Big-Leaved or French Hydrangea *H. macrophylla*	D	to 10′	Blue, pink or white flowers. Many named varieties. Use aluminum sulfate for blue, lime for pink, and neutral soil for white. Needs water. Prune 3′–5′ for best results. *Bloom Time:* June–July
PeeGee hydrangea *H. paniculata grandiflora*	D	3′–15′	Large, creamy white flowers turning to pink; coarse leaf. Interesting grown as standard. Can be dried. *Bloom Time:* June—Sept.
Oak-leaved hydrangea *H. quercifolia*	D	to 12′	Creamy white large panicles turn to rosy color in late summer. Leaves like red oak. Interesting bark, can be dried. Very desirable, native. *Bloom Time:* June

SHRUBS

COMMON NAME SCIENTIFIC NAME	KEY	HEIGHT	COMMENTS
Hypericum *Hypericum frondosum*	E	3′	Yellow wild roselike 2″ bloom, dull green leaf. Sun. *Bloom Time:* June–Oct.
H. calycinum	E	12″–18″	Blooms like single yellow rose on low spreading plant. Good ground cover. Tolerates shade. *Bloom Time:* June–Oct.
Jasmine *Jasminum floridum*	E	4′–5′	Yellow flowers, trilobed leaf. Good clipped to a low hedge overhanging a wall. *Bloom Time:* May
Winter Jasmine *J. nudiflorum*	D	3′–4′	Yellow blossoms before leaves appear. Young branches green in winter. Low spreading form. Can be forced indoors. Sun. *Bloom Time:* February
Juniper Creeping Juniper varieties *Juniperus horizontalis*	E	6″–11″	Spreading form. Also used as ground cover.
Pfitzer Juniper *Juniperus chinensis pfitzerana*		6′–8′	Steel blue foliage; massive shaggy form. Spreading habit to 10′. Sun; poor soil.
Kerria *Kerria japonica*	D	4′	Single strong yellow flower; neat slender growth; dark green foliage. *Bloom Time:* April
K. japonica pleniflora	D	5′–7′	Double orange pom-pom-like flowers. Growth too insubstantial and color too strong for foundation or border planting. Naturalizes well. Semishade. *Bloom Time:* April
Laurel. *See* Alexandrian Laurel Cherry Laurel Mountain Laurel			
Lavender Cotton *Santolina chamaecyparissus*	E	18″	Undesirable yellow flower which should be pinched off. Desirable for aromatic, fine-textured silvery gray foliage. Sun, any soil, tolerates dry areas. *Bloom Time:* July
S. virens	E	18″	Green foliage. Form of above. *Bloom Time:* July

SHRUBS

COMMON NAME SCIENTIFIC NAME	KEY	HEIGHT	COMMENTS
Leucothoe *Leucothoe axillaris*	E	5′	Bronze leaf in spring. Not very hardy, needs shade. *Bloom Time:* May
Drooping Leucothoe *L. fontanesiana*	E	6′	Lily-of-the-Valley-like flower. Hardy. Sandy loam. *Bloom Time:* May
Sweet Bells *L. racemosa*	D	10′	Same as above. Upright. Scarlet in fall. Very desirable. *Bloom Time:* May
L. recurva	D	10′	Similar to above but more spreading habit. Can stand drier conditions. *Bloom Time:* April–June
Ligustrum Glossy Privet *Ligustrum japonicum* var. *coriaceum*	E	to 4′	Small curly waxy leaf. Not hardy above Zone 7. *Bloom Time:* June
Black Wax *L. lucidum*	E	to 25′	White, very fragrant flowers in racemes; dark green shiny leaves; dark blue berries that birds like. Sun or shade. Fast grower in any area but wood is weak. May be considered a small tree. Useful for tall screen. *Bloom Time:* June
Chinese Privet *L. sinense,* var. *pendulum*	E	12′ or more	Weeping privet, good for hedge. *Bloom Time:* June
Common Privet *L. vulgare*	D	15′	Rank, takes over, must be pruned. Not desirable. Plant young hollies instead. *Bloom Time:* June
Lilac Persian Lilac *Syringa persica*	D	5′–6′	Very fragrant. Hardiest of all lilacs. Cut out old flower heads. *Bloom Time:* April
Common or French Lilac *S. vulgaris*	D	10′–15′	Lavender to white fragrant flowers; old fashioned garden lilac; many varieties. Not the standbys they are in North. All syringas need alkaline soil, cool nights, wood ashes. Periodically remove old stems after flowering to maintain a process of constant renewal. *Bloom Time:* April

SHRUBS

COMMON NAME SCIENTIFIC NAME	KEY	HEIGHT	COMMENTS
S. vulgaris var. "Charles X"	D	to 10′	Light red buds, free bloomer. *Bloom Time:* April
S. vulgaris var. "President Grévy"	D	to 10′	Double blue flowers, hardy. *Bloom Time:* April
S. vulgaris var. "Vertale"	D	to 10′	Single white flower. Sun. *Bloom Time:* April
Loropetalum *Loropetalum chinense*	E	to 10′	Fringy white flowers which resemble witch-hazel. Small dark leaves of medium texture. Foliage and bloom good for filler in arrangements. Partial shade. *Bloom Time:* April
Magnolia Star Magnolia *Magnolia stellata*	D	10′	Very early white starry flower, also pale pink; shrub, or tree. Often frost-bitten. *Bloom Time:* Feb.–March
Mahonia *Mahonia*	E	5′	Clusters of bright yellow flowers followed by blue green grapelike fruit, stiff holly-shaped spiny leaves. Shade. When pruned, new foliage comes from top only. *Bloom Time:* March
Holly grape *M. aquifolium*	E	5′–6′	Large coarse spiny leaves. Irregular form. Showy yellow blooms in March followed by conspicuous blue black fruit. Cut back older stems in early spring. *Bloom Time:* March
Leather-Leafed Holly Grape *M. bealei*	E	7′	Large coarse, leathery blue green foliage; yellow flowers in early spring followed by bluish berries. Light shade. Moist soil. Keep cut to 4′–6′ to prevent legginess. *Bloom Time:* March
Chinese Mahonia *M. fortunei*	E	4′	Similar leaves, less spiny. Plant in protected area; not hardy above Zone 8. Light shade. *Bloom Time:* Late March
Oregon Grape *M. nervosa*	E	3′	Much smaller than above. Leaves turn bronze spring and fall. *Bloom Time:* March

SHRUBS

COMMON NAME SCIENTIFIC NAME	KEY	HEIGHT	COMMENTS
Mock Orange *Philadelphus*	D	12′	White and yellow fragrant flowers on long graceful branches. Sun or partial shade. Many varieties, check local nurseries or catalogues. *Bloom Time:* May
Mountain Laurel *Kalmia latifolia*	E	10′	Pink and white flowers. Likes cool mountain climates. Sun or partial shade. Very desirable. *Bloom Time:* May
Nandina Heavenly Bamboo *Nandina domestica*	E	5′–6′	Small white raceme flower; beautiful airy foliage; clusters of red berries in fall and winter; bronze in spring. Should be pruned by thinning, not lopping. Very desirable.
N. domestica nana purpurea	E	12″–18″	Dwarf, thick foliage that is vivid bronze purple.
Osmanthus Devilwood *Osmanthus americanus*	E	20′	Spiny oval leaves; fragrant greenish white flowers; light gray bark. Open growth. Fast grower; trouble-free. Dislikes cold winters; plant in protected area. *Bloom Time:* March–April
Fortunes Osmanthus *O. fortunei*	E	6′	Small white fragrant flowers; profuse bloomer; lighter green foliage. A more hardy hybrid. *Bloom Time:* Summer
Sweet Olive or Osmanthus *O. fragrans*	E	10′	Tiny white very fragrant flowers. Upright growth habit. Not hardy below 10 degress. Very desirable in winter gardens. *Bloom Time:* Freely throughout winter
O. heterophyllus	E	15′–20′	White or yellowish fragrant flowers. Small dark leaves resembling miniature holly but leaves are opposite instead of alternate. Peaty soil. Adapts well to clipping. *Bloom Time:* June–July
Pampas Grass *Cortaderia selloana*	E	20′	Ornamental showy grass. 1′–3′ flower plumes. Good for drying. Many other varieties.

SHRUBS

COMMON NAME SCIENTIFIC NAME	KEY	HEIGHT	COMMENTS
Paper Plant *Tetrapanax papyriferus*	D	to 10′	Very large leaf. Dies back in winter. Multiplies rapidly, not for small gardens. Immature leaf good for stylish arrangements. Cut leaf with a piece of the trunk. Burn stem.
Pearl Bush *Exochorda racemosa*	D	6′	Waxy white clusters of flowers. Strong rank grower. Sun or partial shade. *Bloom Time:* March
Photinia *Photinia glabra*	E	6′–10′	Smooth leaf; can be kept in vivid red foliage by clipping every two weeks. Sun. *Bloom Time:* March
P. fraseri	E	15′	White umbel flowers; red berries; New foliage red. Will stand shade. *Bloom Time:* March
Pieris *Pieris floribunda*	E	to 6′	White Lily-of-the-Valley-like flower, dull green leaves. *Bloom Time:* April–May
P. formosa	E	to 20′	Flowers tinged with pink; somewhat more tender than above. *Bloom Time:* April–May
P. japonica	E	to 10′ or more	Drooping panicles of white flowers. Larger and faster grower than *P. floribunda. Bloom Time:* April–May
P. japonica variegata	E	18″	Dwarf form with white-edged leaves. Suitable for bonsai. *Bloom Time:* April–May
Pittosporum *Pittosporum tobira*	E	6′–8′	Old plants have fragrant clusters of creamy flowers. Smooth oval leaves in whorls. Spreading growth. Not extremely hardy in cold areas. *Bloom Time:* April–May
P. tobira variegata	E	4′–6′	Green and white leaf, same as above. Not hardy above Zone 7. Try as house plant. *Bloom Time:* April–May
Podocarpus *Podocarpus alpinus*	E	10′	Handsome dark green needlelike leaves. Sun or shade. Needs protection. Good for arrangements. No flowers or fruits of merit. *Bloom Time:* April–May

SHRUBS

COMMON NAME SCIENTIFIC NAME	KEY	HEIGHT	COMMENTS
P. macrophyllus	E	20′	Tree form of above. Not hardy in severe winter. *Bloom Time:* April–May
Shrubby Yew Podocarpus *P. macrophylla Maki*	E	6′–8′	Shrubby form. *Bloom Time:* April–May
Pomegranate *Punica granatum*	D	to 10′	Flame-color double flowers; delicious red fruit; handsome foliage. Not hardy in severe winter. *Bloom Time:* April–May
Privet *See* Ligustrum			
Pussy Willow *Salix discolor*	D	10′	Gray catkins. Severe pruning after blooming produces longest stems and largest catkins. Fast growing, also a tree. *Bloom Time:* February
Pyracantha Firethorn *Pyracantha*	E	6′–15′	Many varieties. White flowers followed by red or orange berries; poisonous thorn; suitable for espalier. Acid soil. Subject to red spider and scale. *P. lalandei* has orange berries.
Quince *Cydonia oblonga*	D	2′–8′	White through red flowers appear before leaves. Blossoms easily forced in winter. Many varieties, spreading or erect. Sun, any soil. Fruit makes good jelly or cooked with applesauce. *Bloom Time:* February
Raphiolepis *Raphiolepis umbellata*	E	to 8′	Clusters of fragrant pink flowers; small shiny leaf; dark blue berry in fall. Will not tolerate very cold winters. Interesting branch structure. *Bloom Time:* Mid-Spring
Redbud *See* Chinese Redbud			
Rhododendron *Rhododendron*	E	to 15′	Many species and varieties. Huge flowers from white to red, large handsome leaf. Dislikes extreme summer heat and fluctuating winter temperatures. In the South choose coolest spot in light shade. Avoid winter sun, especially after noon. Acid soil.

SHRUBS

COMMON NAME SCIENTIFIC NAME	KEY	HEIGHT	COMMENTS
Rose of Sharon *See* Althea			
Santolina *See* Lavender Cotton			
Sarcococca Sweet Box *Sarcococca*	E	to 6′	Inconspicuous white flower; attractive glossy green leaves; red fruit. Dislikes very cold winters. *Bloom Time:* Spring
St. Johnswort *See* Hypericum			
Scotch Broom *Cytisus scoparius*	E	4′–6′	Yellow or white flowers; bright green supple stems; leafless. Prized by flower arrangers. Good drainage essential; good for dry gravelly areas. *Bloom Time:* April
Snowball *See* Viburnum			
Snowberry Waxberry *Symphoricarpos albus laevigatus*	D	3′–6′	Tiny pink flowers in early spring followed by clusters of white waxy berries that cling until late fall. Sun or light shade. Tolerates dry soil. Informal hedge. *Bloom Time:* Spring
Spirea *Spiraea bumalda* var. "Anthony Waterer"	D	3′	Pink or rose flowers; dwarf. Prune old branches after blooming except "Anthony Waterer." *Bloom Time:* June
Bridal Wreath *S. prunifolia*	D	6′	Double white flowers; erect form. *Bloom Time:* April–May
S. reevesiana (cantoniensis)	D	4′	Clusters of white flowers. Bushy grower, not hardy in North. *Bloom Time:* April
S. thunbergii	D	3′–5′	Dainty white flowers; feathery branches; twiggy; orange to scarlet in fall. *Bloom Time:* March
S. vanhouttei	D	6′	Clusters of single white flowers in profusion on arching branches; most popular. *Bloom Time:* April
Star Magnolia *See* Magnolia			
Storax Japanese Snowbell *Styrax japonicus*	D	15′	Showy fragrant lily-of-the-valley type flower; lacy foliage; curvaceous branches; good for arrangements. *Bloom Time:* April

SHRUBS

COMMON NAME SCIENTIFIC NAME	KEY	HEIGHT	COMMENTS
S. obassia	D	10′–20′	White flower clusters, round leaves which are velvety beneath. *Bloom Time:* April
Strawberry Bush *See Euonymus america*			
Sumac *Rhus*	D	2′–20′	Many varieties, all native. Inconspicuous yellow or green flowers before leaves in early spring; hairy red fruit in late summer; brilliant in fall. Pest free; good for naturalizing. *Bloom Time:* Spring
Staghorn *R. typhina*	D	20′	Large clusters of green flowers; hairy crimson fruit; hollow stem. *Bloom Time:* Spring
R. vernix	D	20′	Poisonous. 7 to 13 leaflets; bright scarlet in fall; flat round gray fruit. Grows in marshland. *Bloom Time:* Spring
Summer-Sweet Sweetpepper Bush *Clethra alnifolia*	D	4′–6′	Fragrant white spikelike flowers lasting 4–6 weeks. Shade; wet, peaty or acid soil. *Bloom Time:* July–August
C. alnifolia rosea	D	4′–6′	Pink flowers. *Bloom Time:* July–August
Sweet Olive *See* Osmanthus			
Sweet Shrub Pale Sweet Shrub *Calycanthus fertilis*	D	2′–6′	Very faint fragrant chocolate-colored flowers. Often mistaken for *C. floridus.* Lacks brownish fuzz on leaf. *Bloom Time:* April
Carolina Allspice, Common Sweet Shrub *C. floridus*	D	6′	Sweet-scented chocolate-colored flowers; brownish fuzz on underside of fragrant leaves. Rich damp soil, will tolerate shade. *Bloom Time:* April
Tamarisk *Tamarix parviflora*	D	to 9′	Pink flowers on slender branches; reddish bark; long feathery branches. Full sun; well-drained soil; tolerates wind and salt air; also good in ordinary gardens; grows well from cuttings. Prune right after blooming. *Bloom Time:* April

SHRUBS

COMMON NAME SCIENTIFIC NAME	KEY	HEIGHT	COMMENTS
T. ramosissima	D	12′–15′	Pink flowers on purple branches. Strong grower; prune back to 3″ stubs of previous season's growth before new growth starts. *Bloom Time:* August
Tea Plant *Camellia sinensis*	E	4′	Fragrant cream-colored flowers; shiny green leaf. Same culture as camellias; subject to scale. *Bloom Time:* October
Viburnum Arrowood *Viburnum burkwoodii*	Semi-E	4′–6′	Round clusters of pink or white star-shaped flowers; fragrant, red to black berries; dark red fall foliage which remains late. Not particular to soil or position; soil should not be too dry. Many varieties and hybrids; check local nurseries. *Bloom Time:* March
V. carlcephalum	D	6′–7′	Fragrant ball-shaped clusters of white star-shaped flowers; red to black berries; red fall foliage. Strong grower; hybrid; fragrant; "Snowball." *Bloom Time:* April
V. carlesii	D	5′	Most fragrant pink and white clusters of flowers; dark green foliage. *Bloom Time:* April
V. macrocephalum	Semi-E	7′–12′	Large snowball clusters of white flowers. *Bloom Time:* April
Old Fashioned Snowball *V. opulus*	D	12′	Large showy clusters of white flowers followed by scarlet juicy fruit. Vigorous grower; subject to aphids. *Bloom Time:* April–May
V. plicatum tomentosum Mariesii	D	6′–7′	Large sterile white flowers, small fertile ones in center; red berries in fall. Insect resistant; very desirable. *Bloom Time:* April–May
V. rhytidophyllum	E	10′	Large flat cluster of yellowish white flowers followed by red to black berries; wrinkled leaves. Not hardy in North unless protected. *Bloom Time:* May
V. trilobum	D	8′–12′	Large sterile white flowers surround small fertile ones in center; bright red berries; red fall foliage. *Bloom Time:* April

SHRUBS

COMMON NAME SCIENTIFIC NAME	KEY	HEIGHT	COMMENTS
Wahoo (Burning Bush) *See* Euonymus			
Winter Honeysuckle *See* Honeysuckle			
Wintersweet *Chimonanthus praecox*	E	to 10′	Straw yellow flowers marked with maroon; spicy perfume; coarse and dense foliage; irregular branch form. Sun or semishade; average garden soil; good for cutting. *Bloom Time:* January
Weigela *Weigela florida*	D	8′–10′	Rose pink clusters of tubular flowers on arching branches of previous year's growth. Many varieties. *Bloom Time:* May
Witch-Hazel *Hamamelis virginiana*	D	3′–6′	Very fragrant pale yellow flowers; yellow fall foliage. *Bloom Time:* February
White Forsythia *Abeliophyllum distichum*	D	2′–3′	White flowers resembling forsythia; not a true forsythia. *Bloom Time:* April
Yaupon *See* Holly			
Yew English Yew *Taxus baccata repandens*	E	4′	Feathery rich green foliage. Low spreading mound; good for informal masses or clipped hedges or border. Acid soil, good drainage; shade; dislikes extreme heat.
Japanese Yew *T. cuspidata*	E	to 20′	Red fleshy berries in fall; vigorous spreading growth. Good for hedges; hardy.
Dwarf Japanese Yew *T. cuspidata nana*	E	to 6″	Dwarf; slow grower.
Hybrid Yew *T. x media*	E	30′	Cross between English and Japanese. Needlelike foliage; red, fleshy, one-seeded berries in fall.

SHRUBS

COMMON NAME SCIENTIFIC NAME	KEY	HEIGHT	COMMENTS
Yucca Spanish Bayonet *Yucca aloifolia*	E	4′	Large spikes of creamy white bell-shaped flowers, rising above sharp-pointed foliage. Makes interesting contrast in garden. Any well-drained soil; sun or light shade; not bothered by heat, drought or pests. *Bloom Time:* Mid-Summer
Spanish Dagger *Y. gloriosa*	E	2½′	Smaller and less sprouting than above; leaves a brighter color. *Bloom Time:* Mid-Summer

Vines and Ground Covers

GROUND COVERS

Among the most practical and beautiful landscaping materials are ground covers, or low growing plants used to blanket the ground. They can prevent erosion on banks and be used in shady areas where grass will not grow. They also help to eliminate weeding and preserve moisture in flower beds. All ground covers may be fertilized in the spring and again about July 1 with Milorganite or cottonseed meal. Sprinkle fertilizer over them and quickly wash off their leaves with a gentle spray of water.

Moss is a good ground cover under trees, but dangerous on walks (brick, slate, etc.). To remove slippery moss from brick walks use a solution of equal parts of a laundry bleach such as Clorox and water. For removal of weeds check with a garden center for a long-lasting spray.

Some ground covers are subject to fungus in periods of damp weather. Use a fungicide such as Captan or Benlate. For scale, use an oil-based spray or an insecticide such as Malathion. See "Garden Care" for instructions on sprays.

GROUND COVERS

KEY
A—Annual
P—Perennial
E—Evergreen

COMMON NAME SCIENTIFIC NAME	KEY	COMMENTS
Ajuga Bugleweed *Ajuga genevensis*	P, E	Hardy creeper. 6″ spike of brilliant blue flowers. Sun or partial shade. *Bloom Time:* April
A. reptans		Many varieties; bronzed to dark purple leaf; white to rose flower. Shade or partial shade; all subject to fungus. *Bloom Time:* April
Asiatic Jasmine *Trachelospermum asiaticum*	P, E	Creeping vine, cream-colored flowers. Keep sheared to 6″ for best ground cover. *Bloom Time:* Early Summer
Begonia *Begonia grandis (B. evansiana)*	P	1′–2′; large pink flowers. Self sows, hardy. Angel wing leaf, red on underside. Dies back in winter. *Bloom Time:* August thru Fall
Bishop's Weed *See* Goutweed	P	
Confederate Jasmine *Trachelospermum jasminoides*	P, E	Fragrant white flower, shiny, waxy leaf. Slow grower. Will tolerate very hot conditions; sun or shade. Not hardy above Zone 8. *Bloom Time:* April–May
English Ivy *Hedera*	P, E	Many varieties. Hardy creeper and climber, strong fast grower, invasive. Sun or shade.
Epimedium *Epimedium*	P, E	Yellow, white, red, pink flowers, irregular heart-shaped leaf. Shade, slow grower. *Bloom Time:* Spring
Euonymus *Euonymus radicans*	P, E	Insignificant flower, orange berries in fall. Hardy climber or creeper up to 20′ or more. Sun or shade; subject to scale. *Bloom Time:* Spring
Ferns *See* "Hardy Ferns"		
Funkia *See* Plantain Lily		

GROUND COVERS

COMMON NAME SCIENTIFIC NAME	KEY	COMMENTS
Goutweed Bishop's Weed *Aegopodium podagraria*	P, E	White parsleylike flower, 14"; variegated foliage. Sun or partial shade. Good for edging, spreads rapidly. *Bloom Time:* Summer
Hosta *See* Plantain Lily		
Lantana *Lantana camara*	A	Creeper. Orange, pink, yellow, red, white. *Bloom Time:* Summer
Lavender Cotton *Santolina chamaecyparissus*	A	Aromatic; silver grey wooly foliage. Small yellow flower which should be cut off for appearance. 12", sun. *Bloom Time:* Summer
S. virens		Green variety. *Bloom Time:* Summer
Lily-of-the-valley *Convallaria majalis*	P	White and pink fragrant flower. Semishade. Native. *Bloom Time:* Spring
Liriope *Lirope muscari*	P, E	Green or variegated leaves, lavender or white spike, broad grasslike foliage. 15"–20". Sun or shade, hardy. Good for large areas or borders. Cut back in February before spring growth. Several varieties. *Bloom Time:* August or September
Mondo Monkey Grass *Ophiopogon japonicus*	P, E	Dwarf variety similar to liriope. Cobalt blue berry in fall. Sun or shade, hardy. Forms sodlike mat. *Bloom Time:* Spring
Oxalis *Oxalis*	P	Pink, white, yellow flowers; delicate, shamrock-shaped leaf. Many varieties. Sun or shade. Small bulb can be a pest. *Bloom Time:* Spring
Pachysandra *Pachysandra procumbens* "Allegheny"	P, E	Flowers greenish or purplish. Mottled leaf larger than *terminalis*. Same as below. *Bloom Time:* Spring
P. terminalis	P, E	Whitish flower, attractive foliage. "Silver edge" is variegated variety. Shade or partial shade; hardy. 8"–12." Easily propagated from cuttings. *Bloom Time:* Spring
Periwinkle *See* Vinca		

GROUND COVERS

COMMON NAME SCIENTIFIC NAME	KEY	COMMENTS
Plantain Lily *Hosta*	P, E	Attractive broad leaf; lavender spike flower to 2′; variegated forms. Dies back in winter; subject to slugs. Many varieties, some fragrant. *See* Flower Border. *Bloom Time:* Summer
Portulaca *Portulaca grandiflora*	A	Mix fine seed with soil. Red, yellow, orange, purple. Needs sun. *Bloom Time:* All Summer
Santolina *See* Lavender Cotton		
Sedum Stonecrop, Live-forever *Sedum*	P	Many varieties; *See* catalogues. Very hardy in any soil, succulent leaf and stem; sun or shade, best in rock gardens. *Bloom Time:* Summer
Strawberry Geranium (Strawberry Begonia) *Saxifraga stolonifera*	P	White, pink or scarlet flowers, dull green-gray foliage, geranium-shaped leaf. Propagates by runners. Shade, good for rock gardens; dies back in winter. *Bloom Time:* May–June
Trailing Juniper *Juniperus horizontalis*	P	Small blue fruit which birds love. Woody, treelike trunk, gray green foliage, coniferous evergreen. 12″ to 24″ high. Sun, good in rock garden, hardy. *Bloom Time:* Spring
Vinca Greater Periwinkle *Vinca major*	P, E	Coarse, dark green leaves on long runners, lavender blue flower. Variegated variety good for window boxes and hanging baskets. Prolific. *Bloom Time:* Spring
Common Periwinkle *v. minor*	P, E	Long, vinelike creeping stems, lavender or white flowers. Shade, hardy, subject to fungus. Var. "Bowles" slower growing, more and larger flowers over a longer period. *Bloom Time:* Spring
Violet *Viola*	P	White, blue, yellow, purple flowers. Sun or shade. Prolific. Use miticide for red spider. Many varieties. *Bloom Time:* Spring

GROUND COVERS

COMMON NAME SCIENTIFIC NAME	KEY	COMMENTS
Wild Ginger *Asarum canadense*	P	Kidney-shaped leaf, small maroon flower close to the ground. Moist, humus soil, deciduous; will not tolerate deep shade. *Bloom Time:* Early Spring

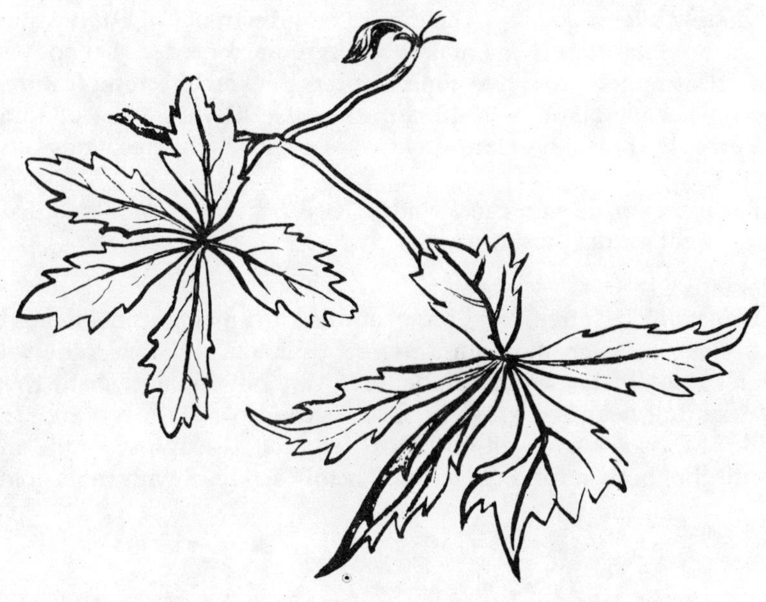

VINES

Vines come in a never-ending variety of leaf shapes, textures, and colors. Many are desirable for their decorative leaf patterns and flowers. Vines can be pruned and trained for a variety of uses. They can be used as screening for privacy, shade above a patio, and as a cover for unsightly fences, such as chain link. Some can be trained into standards in containers. Vines are useful in narrow areas where there is no room for shrubs.

When planting, dig a large hole, adding humus, sand, and slow release fertilizer. Soil adjacent to a building wall may be filled with concrete and debris which will kill acid-loving plants. Remove all debris and add good soil. Water thoroughly and do not let vines dry out. Do not let any vine go into winter with dry soil. A spring feeding before flowering is adequate.

Give vines a suitable support on which to climb; use a trellis or wire framework for heavy nonclinging vines or simply wall nails with flexible ends for small runners. Stretchable plastic tape is very good for tying vines. Remember: climbers need support, and clingers adhere to any surface.

Pruning is important. Vines which flower on new growth must be pruned very early in spring, and all vines may be pruned immediately after blooming. The evergreen growth of English ivy must be sheared in order to maintain a well-groomed garden. Do not permit unrestrained growth to conceal interesting architectural features. Do not let ivy climb any structure because it will loosen building material. Do not let ivy climb any tree as it will kill the tree, and is also unsightly.

For insect or disease check with a local nursery or county agricultural agent for diagnosis and remedy.

Clematis

Unusually pest free, extra hardy and bearing magnificent blooms in many colors, clematis require perfect drainage and rich loose soil. Prefer at least 5 to 6 hours sun daily. In very hot climates, shade roots by planting near low growing shrubs. Dig hole 2½′ deep and 2½′ wide. Mix soil with well-rotted or dehydrated manure, sand, and handful of bone meal. Set crown 2″ below soil level with roots going

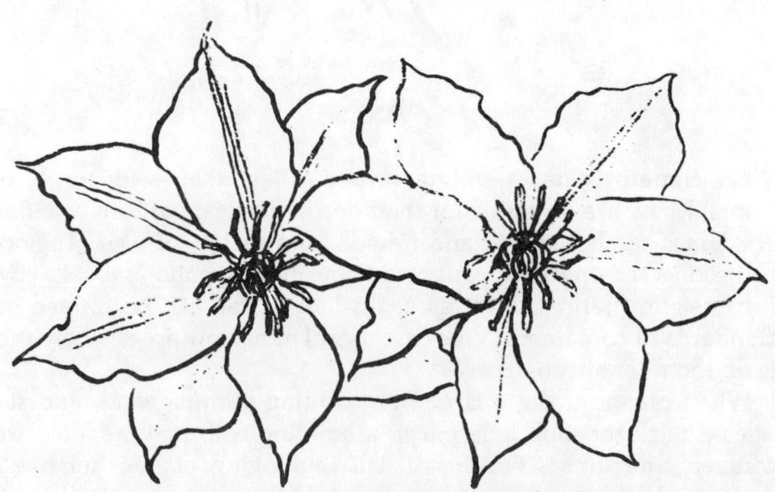

straight down. Be careful that no manure touches roots. Mulch 2" deep. Provide support for climbing and carefully help fragile new growth to attach itself to it. Apply 1 cupful of lime plus small amount of commercial fertilizer to each plant in spring. Water well in hot weather. The woody stems of clematis should be protected at ground level with half circle of chicken wire to prevent their being cut when weeding. In winter, protect stems with covering of leaves, straw, or other loose material.

Cut back *Large Flowered Clematis* to 18 inches above ground in *very* early spring to increase number of stems.

Prune *Small Flowered or Species Clematis* after blooming by removing dead wood only.

A few of the many lovely varieties of clematis are listed below:

(Large Flowered)

1. Comtesse de Bouchard—rose to rich pink; prolific bloomer
2. Crimson Star—large, bright red flowers
3. Duchess of Edinburgh—double white
4. Henryi—large, beautiful white flowers, 8" across
5. Jackmanii—popular, hardy grower, purple blossoms, 5" across
6. Jackmanii rubra—red variety of above
7. Jackmanii superba—dark violet purple and larger
8. Lanuginosa—choice, pure white, waxlike blooms, good for cutting; strong grower
9. Nelly Moser—small red stripe on lavender petals
10. Ramona—lavender blue
11. The President—popular, rich purple flowers

(Small Flowered)

1. Montana alba—white; fine used as screen
2. Montana rosea—rosy pink blooms in spring; lovely over stone wall or fence
3. Mrs. Robert Brydon—small pale blue flowers in late summer
4. Paniculata—old fashioned, fragrant white feathery flowers in late summer; very hardy
5. Tangutica—tiny golden bells; fall seed pods good for arrangements. One of few yellow clematis available.

Ivy

Ivy *(Hedera)* is a hardy, shade-tolerant, evergreen vine. All ivy has two stages of growth. During the juvenile stage, the plants have attractive leaves with 3 to 5 lobes and aerial roots that cling to any surface. Upon maturity, the stems become thick and woody while the leaves change to an oval shape and inconspicuous flowers are followed by small poisonous berries. As ivy is usually clipped and slow to mature, few plants are seen in the adult stage.

Hedera Helix, or English Ivy, is the most common with over sixty named varieties, some variegated. All ivy can be propagated by cutting or layering. It grows best in shade where the morning sun will not burn it. Ivy prefers rich, moist loam, but it will grow in ordinary garden soils. Although it is rather slow to establish, it will tolerate much abuse.

Ivy has many uses in the landscape. It is an excellent ground cover for shady areas, such as under trees where grass cannot survive. However, do not let ivy grow up tree trunks as it will eventually kill the tree. Ivy can be planted on slopes to prevent erosion. It is attractive when lining a drive if one is willing to keep it clipped. Do not plant ivy in flower beds because it will smother annuals and perennials. When planted beneath azaleas, camellias, or other ornamental shrubs, ivy must be constantly thinned or it will rob the plants of nutrients and moisture. Plant shallow rooted ground covers instead.

Ivy transforms a chain link fence into a soft green screen. It is also lovely grown on the wall of a brick house, but this is not recommended because over a period of time it ruins the mortar. It has to be constantly trimmed, not only for neatness, but to keep it from stopping up gutters and rotting wood trim.

Ivy has long trailing stems and is perfect for hanging baskets, garden urns, and window boxes. The small-leaved varieties make excellent house plants (See "Container Plants"), and are desirable for large topiaries.

Prune ivy in early spring. When grown on walls, the heavy woody stems should be cut back to promote lacy new growth. If ivy is used as a ground cover, clip the plants rather close to the ground for a thicker, more attractive foliage. To get new plants in bare spots, cover the middle of a trailing stem with dirt and keep it moist. Alternatively, place the stem in water and transplant it after it has rooted.

Water ivy during drouth. Feed it once a year with 6–10–10. On the rare occasion when insects are a problem, spray with an oil based insecticide in early spring.

VINES

COMMON NAME SCIENTIFIC NAME	KEY	COMMENTS
Akebia *Akebia quinata*	P	Semievergreen climber. Delicate curly foliage, mahogany flowers—fragrant. *Bloom Time:* Early Spring
Banksia Rose *Rosa Banksiae*	P	Only thornless rose climber. Not hardy above Zone 7. Clusters of yellow or white tiny roses. *Bloom Time:* June–August
Bittersweet *Celastrus scandens*	P	Climber. Yellow or orange berry in fall, inconspicuous flower. Deciduous. *Bloom Time:* Spring
Boston Ivy *Parthenocissus tricuspidata*	P	Fast growing; sturdy.
Cardinal Vine *Ipomoea multifida*	A	Climber. Small red and white morning glory-like flower, leathery leaf. Sun, light soil, native vine. *Bloom Time:* Summer
Carolina Jasmine *Gelsemium sempervirens*	P	Woody evergreen, yellow flower, graceful climber. Very fragrant native. Sun. *Bloom Time:* Spring
Carolina Moonseed *Cocculus carolinus*	P	Deciduous, woody climber. Red fruit in clusters, attractive foliage. Keep moist. *Bloom Time:* Summer
Cat's Claw *Macfadyena uniquis-cati*	P	Evergreen clinger. Yellow trumpet flowers, 4"; Sun, dry soil. Very tender, prefers greenhouse. *Bloom Time:* Spring
Cherokee Rose *Rosa laevigata*	P	Climber, 15'. Fragrant white flower, 2"–3" across, evergreen. Not hardy in North *Bloom Time:* Summer
Clematis *Clematis* *See* special article.	P	Many varieties; deciduous woody climber. Handsome red, white or purple flower. Plant in sun with roots in shade or heavy mulch. Cut back to 18" in March. *Bloom Time:* Spring; some again in late summer
Climbing Fern *See* "Hardy Ferns"		

VINES

COMMON NAME SCIENTIFIC NAME	KEY	COMMENTS
Climbing Hydrangea *Hydrangea anomala*	P	Deciduous clinger. Fragrant large white cluster flower. Partial shade, moist. Bare trunk attractive; keep pruned. *Bloom Time:* Early summer
Confederate Jasmine *See* "Ground Covers"		
Coral Vine *Antigonon leptopus*	P	Climber. White or bright pink flowers. Sun, moist; best grown from root; cut back in fall. *Bloom Time:* All summer to fall
Cross Vine *Bignonia capreolata*	P	Evergreen in the South. Yellow trumpet flower. Sun. Prune hard after flowering. *Bloom Time:* Early summer
Cypress Vine *Ipomoea quamoclit*	A	Climber. Feathery leaves, red and white flowers. Sun, light soil. Red attracts hummingbirds; native. *Bloom Time:* Summer
Deadly Nightshade *See* Nightshade		
Euonymus *Euonymus radicans*	P	Trailer or climber. Many varieties. Evergreen; Check nursery for scale resistant varieties. *Bloom Time:* Spring
English Ivy *Hedera helix* *See* special article	P	Many varieties, hardy evergreen creeper and climber. *Bloom Time:* Spring
Fig Vine Creeping Fig *Ficus pumila*		Thin, green, heart-shaped leaves. Clinging stems, desirable for foliage. May die back in winter but recovers. Does well in hanging baskets, topiary, or walls.
Grape Vine Muscadine grape, Scuppernong *Vitis rotundifolia*	P	Heavy green screen in summer. Many varieties, see catalogues. Native vine. *Bloom Time:* Spring
Gourds *Cucurbita*	A	Runners or climbers. Inedible fruits in many colors and shapes; when dried, serve many useful and decorative purposes. Sun, long growing seasons. Mulch. *Bloom Time:* Spring

VINES

COMMON NAME SCIENTIFIC NAME	KEY	COMMENTS
Honeysuckle *Lonicera japonica*	P	Fragrant yellow flowers. Invasive. *Bloom Time:* June
L. sempervirens		Orange, yellow, or scarlet trumpet, fragrant flowers. Sun. Often used on mail boxes. Native vine, keep pruned. *Bloom Time:* Summer
Jackson Vine *Smilax lanceolata*	P	Evergreen, hardy climber, can be invasive. Good for out-of-water decoration. *Bloom Time:* Spring
Jasmine *Jasminum*	P	Many varieties. Evergreen climber. Yellow flower. Sun or shade. *Bloom Time:* Spring
Moonvine Moonflower *Ipomoea alba*	A	Climber up to 20′. Fragrant white flower. Blooms at night. Sun. Soak seed overnight before planting. Native vine. *Bloom Time:* Summer
Morning-glory *Ipomoea*	A	Many varieties. Climber. Red, white, blue; "Heavenly Blue" is good color. Sun. See seed catalogues. *Bloom Time:* Summer
Nasturtium *Tropaeolum majus*	A	Climber; 8′ to 12′. Yellow, orange. Good vine for cool greenhouse. *Bloom Time:* Early summer; winter in greenhouse.
Night Shade *Solanum dulcamara*	A	Climber. Poisonous, red berry, shiny oval leaves, violet flowers. Deciduous. *Bloom Time:* Summer
Passion Flower Maypop *Passiflora incarnata*	P	Climber. Lavender flower; edible fruit. Sun. Invasive native vine. *Bloom Time:* Early summer
Silver Lace Vine *Polygonum aubertii*	P	Chinese fleece-vine. Twining vine, 20′. Greenish white fragrant flowers in long, drooping clusters. Sun. Zone 5, South. Pest-free native vine. *Bloom Time:* Summer
Smilax *Smilax glauca*	P	Climber. Spreads rapidly. Pest, sharp prickles, insignificant bloom. Undesirable. Sun. *Bloom Time:* Summer

VINES

COMMON NAME SCIENTIFIC NAME	KEY	COMMENTS
Trumpet Vine Trumpet Creeper *Campsis radicans*	P	Creeper up to 30′. Orange and scarlet tubelike flowers. Can be trained into standard. Sun. Rank growth pattern. Native vine. *Bloom Time:* Summer
Virgin's Bower *Clematis virginiana*	P	Climber. Festoons of white flowers. Good to ramble over slopes and rocky places. Sun. *Bloom Time:* Late summer
Virginia Creeper Woodbine *Parthenocissus quinquefolia*	P	Clinger. 5-leaved, often confused with poison ivy (3-leaved). Scarlet in fall. Insignificant bloom.
Wisteria (sometimes Wistaria) *Wisteria floribunda*	P	Japanese wisteria. Hardier than Chinese. Flowers white, lavender, pink; woody. Fast grower. Fertilize in fall. *Bloom Time:* Spring
W. sinensis		Chinese wisteria. Vigorous climber. Shorter racemes than *W. floribunda*. Bluish violet, fragrant flowers. Prune roots about 3′ from main trunk for heaviest flowering. Can be trained into standard. Sun. All wisteria, if allowed to run rampant on gates, fences, and gutters, will pull them apart. If not blooming, root prune with a sharp shooter 3′ from trunk.

Bulbs

Bulbs are classified into five categories: true bulbs (tulip, daffodils), corms (crocus, gladiolus), tubers (caladium), tuberous roots (dahlias), and rhizomes (iris). All have one common characteristic: a food storage system for underground living.

Buy Grade A bulbs without soft spots or bruises. When choosing bulbs, consider color, height, and bloom time. By carefully selecting varieties of bulbs, the bloom time may be prolonged from February through October. The season begins with the early spring-flowering crocuses, snowdrops, scillas, hoop petticoats (miniature daffodils), and grape-hyacinths. Then come the daffodils, Dutch hyacinths, and tulips. Next anemones, gladioli, lilies, and tuberoses, followed by hardy amaryllis and colchicums.

Bulbs that bloom in the spring are planted in the fall. Autumn-blooming bulbs are planted in the spring or summer. The proper planting depths are: true bulbs twice the depth of the bulb from the tip; corms about 2–3 inches; tubers, rhizomes, and tuberous roots are planted shallow. For naturalizing, plant deeper as the bulb will not multiply as quickly, thus precluding lifting. Most of the small bulbs and many of the larger ones, like the daffodil, tulip, hyacinth, and lily, are not lifted for three years or more until they have multiplied sufficiently to be separated and replanted.

All require good, well-drained garden soil, preferably dug to a depth of 12″, and prepared with coarse builders sand, bone meal, and peat moss. When planting, put a handful of a low nitrogen bulb food in the bottom of the hole, cover with 2″ of sand, and fill with soil. Feed spring-flowering bulbs after blooming with 0–20–20. In the fall all bulbs should be included in the overall top-dressing of the garden with 0–20–20.

A good mulch, like pine needles, will keep the mud off the flowers. Water in spring and after planting and during dry spells in fall and winter. All bulbs need sun. Bulbs will not bloom in deep shade. Do not cut back foliage until dead, as it provides needed nourishment for the formation of the next year's bloom.

If bulbs are attacked by rodents, try moth balls, red pepper, or tobacco mixed in the soil, or enclose bulbs in wire mesh.

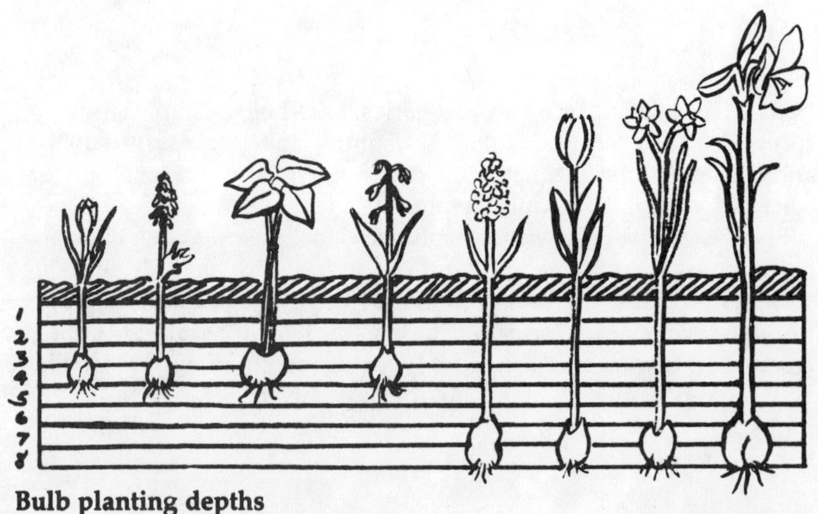

Bulb planting depths

DAFFODILS

Daffodils, indigenous to the northern hemisphere, are members of the Amaryllis family. Although they are called by many names, such as jonquils or buttercups, the proper name is "daffodils" (English) or "*narcissus*" (scientific) which are interchangeable. Jonquils are one of the twelve classifications of daffodils.

There are thousands of exciting and beautiful daffodils, ranging in colors from white, pink, yellow, orange, to red, and combinations of colors. The forms vary greatly—trumpets, large and small cups, doubles, clusters, and miniatures.

The time of bloom varies with different varieties. A long season of bloom can be enjoyed from early to late spring. Selection may be made from studying the many catalogues available, and visiting local daffodil shows.

General Culture

Daffodils are one of the easiest flowers to grow; however, the better the culture, the better the bloom. Plant in the fall when soil is cool to avoid early sprouting. Daffodils require sun, and should not be planted in deep shade.

Soil—Daffodils will grow in almost any type of soil, but proper preparation of the soil will enhance the size and beauty of the bloom. The bed should be dug at least a foot deep (the deeper the preparation, the better). Four ingredients should be well mixed with the existing soil before planting begins: (1) builder's sand for drainage, (2) well-matured humus with good nitrogen content for the tissue building elements, (3) sulphate of potash for bloom and root development, (4) dry peat moss. Put a quarter cup 0–20–20 or bone meal in the bottom of each hole, and then add an inch of sand so that the base of the bulb does not rest directly on the soil or the fertilizer.

Depth—To some extent the type of soil regulates the depth at which the bulb should be planted. In a good friable soil 4″ of dirt over the top of the bulb should be sufficient. A lighter soil or a sandy one will require a deeper covering, and a heavier soil will require less depth. A shallow planting will require more frequent lifting and division as the bulbs tend to split up more quickly. Plant small and miniature bulbs twice the depth of the bulb from its tip.

Daffodils may be planted in a show bed, a flower border, or a natural wooded place, but not in dense shade. In the border try planting them in the back instead of the front because daffodils bloom early and later the drying foliage may be hidden by perennials and annuals. Do not plant in grassy areas as grass cannot be mowed until foliage turns brown.

For the best effect plant only one variety in each clump. Label each bulb for show flowers or each clump when naturalizing. When entering a flower show, the name of the flower is required, so make a chart in case of lost labels.

For a large area a naturalized planting more closely resembles the flower in its wild state. The best effect is created by planting fifty to a hundred bulbs of one variety in each drift, and include bulblets.

Fertilizing—The first year after planting, daffodils need little or no fertilizer provided soil is properly prepared. Top dress with 0–20–20 or bone meal in spring as tips emerge and again in fall. Wood ashes from the fireplace may be used in winter.

Mulching—Mulching is important to survival of plants during the hot summer, and adds protection during winter freezes. Almost any type of cover may be used as long as it does not crust, mat, or blow away. Pine needles and shredded pine bark make a good mulch while providing the proper pH, and are resistant to the wind. They also prevent mud splashing on flowers.

Watering—During growing season, deep soak about once a week unless there has been adequate rainfall. Daffodils have deep roots, and therefore, need plenty of water. Proper drainage is essential to prevent rotting of bulbs.

Lifting—Lifting should be done every two years for show flowers, every three or four years for the flower border, and every five or six years when naturalized. Bulbs should be dug with care as soon as foliage browns, then cleaned and dipped in a fungicide. They should be allowed to dry in a shady place for one or two weeks before storing or replanting. This is the time to look for basal rot or soft spots, and if any appear, all infected bulbs should be destroyed. Now, the healthy bulbs should be replanted or show flowers placed in shallow flats, onion or potato sacks and stored in a cool, dry place. Be sure to label each variety.

Daffodils may also be moved in clumps while in bloom. This is an aid to landscaping as it is easier to place and find bulbs. When transplanted with a ball of dirt bulbs do not know they have been moved. Replant carefully, leaving all foliage and as much root as can be saved.

After blooming, if the flower has not been picked, cut off flower stem below seed pod as it will draw strength away from the forming bulb. Stem, roots, and foliage should be left intact because they furnish food for the new flower.

The six things to remember are:

1. Deep, heavy watering during the active growing season.
2. Let bulbs dry out during summer months.
3. Keep beds free of weeds.
4. Provide good drainage.
5. Examine all new or lifted bulbs, and destroy those that have soft spots.
6. Fill the small hole left in the ground after the foliage has been separated from the bulb to prevent pests attacking the bulb.

Daffodil Classification

1. *Trumpet*—1 flower to a stem; trumpet or crown as long as or longer than perianth segments.
2. *Large Cup*—1 flower to a stem; cup, or crown more than one-third, but less than equal to length of perianth segments.
3. *Short cup*—1 flower to a stem, cup or crown not more than one-third length of perianth segments.
4. *Double*—Crown double, perianth double, or both.
5. *Triandrus*—Usually more than 1 flower to a stem, head drooping, perianth segments often reflexed.
6. *Cyclamineus*—1 flower to a stem, perianth segment reflexed, crown straight and narrow.
7. *Jonquil*—Usually several flowers to a stem, often fragrant. Usually stem is round, dark green rushlike foliage.
8. *Tazetta*—Usually 2 to 6 or more flowers to a stem, generally globular shaped, sweet scented, very short cup. Perianth segments rounded and somewhat crinkled.
9. *Poeticus*—1 flower to a stem, very white perianth segment, small, flat crown, edged with red or green throat.
10. *Species—Wild Forms*—All species and wild forms—double forms of these varieties are included.
11. *Split Crown*—Crown split for one-third of its length.
12. *Any Others*

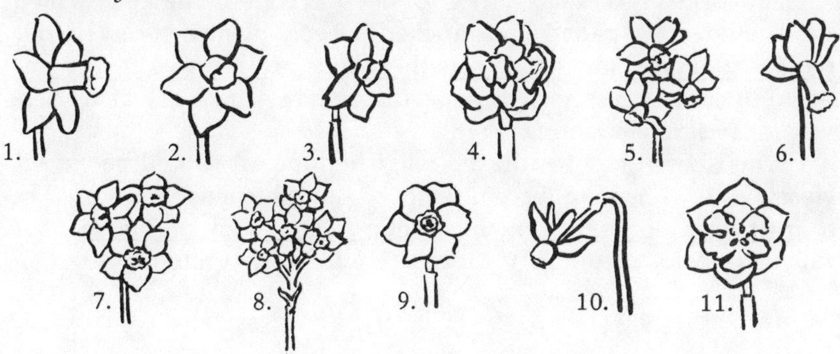

DAHLIA, DAHLIA HYBRIDS

Dahlias come in sizes from 1′ to 12′. Blossoms range from 2″ to dinner plate size. Their colors are white, red, rust, orange, pink, peach, and yellow. There are many forms: Decorative, Cactus, Ball, Pompom or Miniature.

Dahlias need well-drained soil and a sunny location, and require a full season's growth. Plant in May for a blooming season in October. Some miniatures will bloom all summer. Cover with soil 5″ deep for large varieties which must be staked—and this must be done at planting time so as not to impale tubers. Use uniform stakes painted green, which makes them less visible. Large varieties should be planted 3′ or 4′ apart. Fertilize with a balanced fertilizer such as 5–10–5 lightly and often. They require plenty of water during the growing season. Mulch, but do not let mulch touch the stem as it will cause rot.

In fall, after the blooming season, carefully dig tubers, knock off dirt, dry in sun, and cut off all but 1″ of stem. Store in peat moss and/or vermiculite, and keep tubers from touching.

In the spring remove from storage and put into damp peat moss. When buds appear, divide carefully with a sharp knife. Each section must have at least one bud to produce a plant. If storage is a problem, new tubers can be bought in the spring or old ones may be left in the ground and protected with a heavy mulch, such as straw.

Select dahlia tubers or plants from catalogues or garden centers.

GLADIOLI

Gladioli have spectacular floral value. Their tall, handsome, flowering spikes in radiant colors will bloom all summer if given sun, room, and care. By setting the corms out at one- to three-week intervals, after danger of frost is past, there will be an extended succession of bloom. Generally they bloom 90 days after planting.

Plant corms 4″–6″ apart and 4″–6″ deep in well-drained soil which has been deeply spaded and enriched. Deeply planted corms do not require as much staking. When the plants are a few inches high, begin to spray for thrips, their deadly enemy. Check extension service for recommendations.

Corms should be lifted in the fall. The top part should be cut off closely, the withered old corm removed, and the new corm stored in a frost-free location over the winter. Dust with an insecticide-fungicide before storing. If bulbs are left in the ground, they will come back for two or three years, but with fewer and smaller blooms.

Gladioli come in many beautiful colors. Seed and garden stores as well as catalogues offer a wealth of selections. Try the exciting miniature gladioli. Their tiny colorful spikes are most attractive and useful for flower arrangements.

LILIES

True lilies (genus *Lilium*) are spectacular, hardy perennials which provide years of bloom with a minimum of care. Daylilies, canna lilies, and water lilies are not true lilies. Properly planted, lilies will multiply, but can be left undisturbed for years.

Lilies make excellent, long-lasting cut flowers and most are very fragrant. They are available in a variety of sizes, flower shapes, and all colors except blue. By planting different varieties, bloom time may be extended from May until August or September. Bulbs are labeled early, midseason, or late, according to the time of bloom.

Purchasing—Order lilies by mail from a reputable bulb dealer or purchase firm, healthy bulbs from local nurseries. Buy American bulbs as they are grown from seed and are disease-free. Bulbs ordered from colder climates will bloom in the South two to four weeks earlier than the date given in the catalog, depending on the weather. Many lilies can be forced to bloom inside in the winter. Dealers sell precooled bulbs accompanied by instructions.

Where to Plant—Lilies may be planted in raised beds or separate mounds in the flower border with shallow-rooted annuals, perennials, and low growing shrubs which do not compete with them for food and light. The Asiatic hybrids may be planted in full sun or part shade in all regions. In areas with daily summer temperatures of 85°

to 90° and over, plant lilies of the other divisions where they will be protected from hot afternoon sun. This is especially important with Oriental hybrids and most of the species. Good air circulation is necessary to prevent fungus. Avoid low areas where water stands. Lilies prefer their heads in the sun and their feet in the shade.

When to Plant—Although a few lilies may be planted in the spring, mid-November is the preferred time for most varieties. Plant Madonna lilies in August or September. Lilies must be planted immediately upon arrival because they have no dormant period. It is best to have the bed prepared before the bulbs arrive.

Soil Preparation—Good drainage and deep soil preparation are essential. Lilies must have a loose, humus-rich soil that drains excess water rapidly. Prepare the soil to a depth of 12″ to 18″, mixing 1 part humus, 1 to 2 parts good soil, and 1 part clean, sharp sand. Humus can be well-rotted compost, decomposed leaf mold, or crumbled, dampened peat moss. Add a good handful of bone meal or commercial bulb food per square yard. Most lilies prefer a slightly acid soil. However, Madonna lilies need a rather heavy, limey soil.

Planting—Before planting, gently shake each bulb in a paper bag with a good bulb dust which contains an insecticide and a fungicide. Scoop out a generous hole, spread the roots out and place the bulbs on a mound of dirt 12″–18″ apart depending on their size. Cover small bulbs with 3″–4″ of soil, larger ones with 4″–6″. Firm the soil to remove air pockets and then water thoroughly.

Mark each bulb with a small stake or label to avoid breaking brittle new spring growth. A taller stake can be substituted later without the danger of spearing the bulb. In summer tie the tall stems loosely and naturally to the stake.

Mulch the beds with leaf mold, compost, or peat moss for winter protection. In the summer, roots should be kept cool with a light mulch or a shallow-rooted ground cover.

Fertilizing—Lilies are heavy feeders. Apply 6—12—12 as soon as the shoots emerge in the spring, and continue with smaller supplementary feedings every 3-4 weeks during the summer. Water thoroughly after fertilizing. Never allow the fertilizer to touch the stems or leaves as it will burn the plant.

Watering—Lilies need moist, not soggy soil. Let the hose trickle slowly until the soil is wet to a depth of 6″. Overhead sprinkling will encourage disease.

Transplanting—Lilies do not like to be disturbed. Transplant in the fall only when they have become overcrowded. Move Madonna lilies in the summer after blooming. When transplanting, dig, divide, and replant at once. Change the bulbs to another location or reinforce the old soil with fertilizer and humus. The small bulblets may be removed and planted. They will produce flowers in two or three years.

Pests and Diseases—Modern hybrid lilies have been bred for disease resistance. Proper planting and sanitation should prevent most problems. Get rid of faded flowers, and in the fall remove and destroy the stalks and foliage after they have yellowed.

A fungicide, such as Manzate, will control Botrytis leaf spot (a yellowing and withering of foliage during damp weather). A standard rose spray used at 10-day intervals will destroy aphids. Mix liquid fertilizer with the spray for extra benefit.

There is no cure for virus disease, recognized by mottled, distorted leaves. Dig and destroy the diseased plants. Replace the soil where the bulb grew. Never plant new lilies among those which have shown any signs of disease.

General Health—Lily bulbs will be weakened if the plants are allowed to go to seed; therefore cut faded flowers promptly before the seed pods form. In cutting flowers, leave one-third of the stem or the bulb will deteriorate.

Recommended Lilies

In the past only wild species of lilies were available for the garden. Modern growers have developed vigorous new hybrids far superior to their ancestors. Therefore, except for a few species listed below, the new hybrids are recommended. Lily classifications are based on origin and flower form.

Asiatic Hybrids—Earliest to bloom and easiest to grow; sun or part shade; 2′–4′ tall; flowers upright, outward-facing, or pendant. Colors: vivid reds and oranges, a few pastels. Recommended varieties: Enchantment, Firecracker, Corsage, Ming Yellow, Hornback's Gold, Sutter's Gold.

Martagon Hybrids—Bloom May–June. Numerous 3″–4″ flowers in Turk's cap form (pendant flowers with recurved petal tips); 3′–6′ tall. Colors: white, yellow or orange to purple. Afternoon shade. Recommended variety: Paisley Hybrids.

American Hybrids—Bloom June, early July; 4″–6″ blooms, 4′–7′ tall; reflexed flowers. Colors: Yellow, orange, dark reds. Recommended varieties: Bellingham Hybrids, Sunset.

Trumpet Hybrids—Fragrant, bloom July, early August; 6″–10″ flowers, 4′–6′ tall. Colors: white through yellow to pink and copper.

Asiatic Hybrids—Earliest to bloom—May—Easiest to grow; sun or part shade; 2′-4′ tall; flowers upright, outward-facing, or pendant. Colors: vivid reds and oranges, a few pastels. Recommended varieties: Enchantment, Firecracker, Corsage, Ming Yellow, Hornback's Gold.

Flower shapes: trumpet, bowl-shaped, pendant, sun-burst. Full sun, but part shade prolongs bloom in warm areas. Recommended varieties: Black Dragon, Pink Perfection, Thunderbolt, Gold Showers, Heart's Desire.

Oriental Hybrids: Extremely fragrant; bloom late July, August; flowers to 12″ across, 2′–8′ tall. Colors: White, white with gold, pink, crimson. Flowers bowl-shaped, flat-faced, or recurved. A little more difficult to grow, but very showy. Must have afternoon shade. Recommended varieties: Empress of India, Red Band, Imperial Gold, Imperial Silver, Imperial Crimson, Jamboree, Sprite.

True Species

Lilium auratum (gold-band lily)—Fragrant; blooms late June; 5′–6′ tall. Color: White with yellow band.

L. candidum (Madonna Lily)—Fragrant; blooms June; 2′–4′ tall. Color: White.

L. longiflorum (Easter Lily)—Fragrant; blooms June or early July; 2′–3′ tall. Color: White

L. regale (Regal Lily)—Fragrant; blooms July or early August; 3′–4′ tall. Color: White

L. speciosum & varieties—Blooms August, September; 4′–7′ tall. Colors: white, red, pink.

L. superbum (Turk's Cap)—Blooms July and August; 6′ tall. Color: Orange spotted with purple

L. tigrinum (Tiger Lily)—Blooms July or August; 2′–4′ tall. Color: black-spotted orange.

TULIPS

In the Mid-South, tulips bloom April–May with dogwood and azaleas. Many bulb catalogues list the relative time of blooming of different varieties. Since bloom date will vary by as much as two weeks even in the tall varieties, it is important to know. By planting early, midseason, and late varieties, the blooming sequence can be extended for over a month to six weeks.

There are tulips for any desired color scheme. For the best effect, tulips should always be planted in groups of twelve to twenty-four of one kind instead of in rows, unless a formal look is desired. In planting a border some prefer a rhythmic repetition of the same variety, which gives a dramatic landscape effect. Others enjoy working out transitions from one color to another.

A simple but very effective compromise is to choose two favorite varieties, one early and one later blooming. Alternate the two in groups throughout the border, giving two distinct seasons of bloom.

Most tulips do not naturalize well, and will not thrive under deciduous trees, as will daffodils and some other bulbs.

Culture—Start with plump, healthy bulbs from reputable sources. In the deep South, avoid late bloomers, as they cannot tolerate prolonged heat. Most tulips prefer sun. Good drainage is essential. The soil should have a pH of 6.5 for best results.

Dig an area large enough to take care of the number of bulbs desired to a depth of 10 inches. Remove soil. In bottom of the hole place about 2″ to 3″ of compost, 1″ of sand, and scatter a handful of 0–20–20 or bone meal. Work this into the bottom level, mixing thoroughly. Firm the soil, then set bulbs on top of this level, spacing them about 6″ apart. Back fill and firm soil. Water well, as this helps settle the soil and initiate root development. A general rule of thumb is to plant tulips (depending on bulb size) with the top of the bulb 3″–6″ below the soil level.

Do not plant bulbs before November 15. Bulbs planted earlier sprout too soon and risk damage by cold weather. In a large garden change location of tulips each year for best results and reduced chance of disease spread. Carrying tulips over in the Mid-South is not recommended.

Early Season Varieties

Fosteriana—Very large blossoms which open with the daffodils, and are of dwarf habit.

Kaufmanniana—4″–8″ tall, produce large flowers with pointed petals which open horizontally, and therefore, are often called the "water lily tulip."

Mid-season Varieties:

Darwin Hybrid—Grow 22″–30″ tall. Fragrant, large and spectacular. Weather resistant.

Mendel—16″–26″ tall, good growers which survive wind and rain.

Triumph—16″–26″ tall and produce large flowers. They are good to fill the gap between early and late tulips.

Late Season Varieties:

Cottage—16″–24″ tall, self-colored flowers with long, rather pointed petals. They vary greatly in form and color.

Darwin—22″–30″ tall, large, self-colored, deep-cupped flowers on long stems, and are very showy.

Double Late—18″–24″ tall, blossoms similar to peonies, good for cutting. Need some protection from a hot sun.

Greigii—8″–12″ tall, have long-lasting blossoms and bloom very late.

Lily-Flowering—18″–26″ tall, have striking blossoms with long, pointed, curved petals.

Parrot—20″–28″ tall, produce slightly reflexed flowers with streaked or feathered petals. They often have heavy heads.

Rembrandt—20″ tall, petals which are streaked, flushed, striped or veined with contrasting colors, often white. Some catalogues list both *Bybloemen* (rose and mauve stripes against a white ground) and *Bizarre* (dark brown stripes with yellow) as Rembrandt.

FORCING SPRING BULBS FOR INDOOR BLOOM

Forcing bulbs is accomplished by artificially controlling light, water, and temperature in order to bring the bulbs into early maturity with a root system sufficiently developed to support the flower.

Tulips and daffodils force in soil while hyacinths, crocus, snowdrops, scilla and many more of the minor spring bulbs force successfully in rocks and water as well as in soil. Paper whites and many other bulbs can be forced in the same manner.

The important thing to understand is that the root system must be well-developed before the bulb will produce good flowers. If rooting out-of-doors has not been successful, leave the pots of bulbs in the soil where they are and let them mature in their normal season. If the roots look weak and thin when planting indoors, discard and replant, or wait until next fall. Order top quality bulbs, as inferior bulbs are often disappointing. If bulbs arrive before the planting season, store them in a refrigerator until time to plant.

PLANTING IN POTS FOR OUTDOOR ROOTING

A 6″ clay pot will hold 6 tulip bulbs, or 3 hyacinths, or 15 crocus bulbs. A light soil is absolutely essential for good drainage. A mixture of ⅓ garden loam, ⅓ peat moss, and ⅓ sand will insure this. No fertilizer is necessary as bulbs contain their own food. Do not use soil in which bulbs have been grown previously. Pots must be scrubbed clean and soaked overnight before planting. Bulbs like to sit snug. Do not try to reforce bulbs again.

Pots must have good drainage holes covered with broken clay, flat stones, or plastic screening to prevent clogging. A handful of sand on top of this will keep slugs out if the clay becomes dislodged.

Fill pots half full of soil mixture and place bulbs firmly but gently with tips 1″ below the top of the pot. Place tulip bulbs with their flat sides facing the side of the pot. Cover with ½″ soil and top with ½″ sand to keep slugs from spoiling the foliage when it appears. Label pots carefully, noting color, variety, and date of planting; then soak thoroughly. The pots are now ready to be buried.

Bury the pots in a convenient place near water in case of a prolonged dry spell. The loose soil of a flower bed, a vegetable garden, or a cold frame makes digging a trench easy. Trenches must be deep enough for the pots, allowing for a 2″ cover of either sand, soil, straw, leaves or brush. Good drainage in the trench is essential as bulbs will rot if left standing in water for the 12 weeks necessary to develop the root system. If the trench holds water, an inch or two of gravel or sand may be necessary in the bottom.

In the Mid-South timing the flowering of bulbs is difficult. A too-warm November, December, and/or January will certainly make a difference, but the rule is that after 12 weeks the pots will have roots coming through the hole in the bottom and the top sprouts will be 1″ to 3″ tall. Taking a pot out of the trench to examine it does not hurt it at all. If it is not ready, put it back and recover it. When the signs of a mature root system are seen, the pots can be brought into a warm place. For staggered bloom, check labels to select colors desired and note removal dates for the following year.

When brought in, place the pots in a 50°–65° area. At this point invert an empty clay pot over the bulb pot. The light coming through the hole in the bottom of this pot will draw the flower out of the soil. Regular watering is necessary during this period. When the flower stem is 4″ or 5″ tall the covering pot must be removed. The ½″ of sand on top of the soil can be brushed off. Too high temperatures at any time will shorten the life of the flower.

PLANTING IN ROCKS AND WATER

When planting bulbs in rocks and water for forcing many different kinds of containers can be used, but added pleasure comes from selecting those that compliment the color, the size, and the form of the bulbs selected. A notable example of this is the "crocus pot" that is designed very functionally for the successful forcing of crocus, while also showing to perfection the flowers when in full bloom. The container should be at least three times the depth of the bulb to allow room for good root growth without running the risk of having roots force the flower out of the container into a grotesque shape. Dense planting is best only for small bulbs. Hyacinths grow faster in rocks and water than in soil as they make massive roots and require large containers. The water in the container should cover the rocks and it should touch only the bottom of the bulb. Any kind of rock will do, but smaller rocks are easier to set evenly than are large ones.

ROOTING INDOORS

Place planted containers or pots in a cool, dark cellar, a garage, refrigerator (lights off), shed, or any place where they will not freeze. Check the soil for dampness and do not let dry out. If left in the dark too long, the foliage will grow long and unattractive, but if the bulbs are brought in when sprouts are 2″ to 3″ high with well-developed roots, the flowers and foliage will develop to a desirable height. At this point place bulbs in a warm room, 65°–70°, and watch them come into full bloom.

If the bulbs are planted in soil, the best method for forcing the roots is outdoor planting in trenches, but they will also force using the indoor method under optimum conditions.

Amaryllis

Plant with ⅓ to ½ of the bulb protruding above the soil line, preferably in a clay pot. Water thoroughly once, and then sparingly until growth starts. Then increase water and fertilizer (giving bottom heat if possible) and place in a sunny spot. Stake if necessary.

Feed and water all summer to prepare bulbs for forcing next winter. About August or September store cool and dry. A dormant period is necessary to prepare for forcing. In October–November bring into a warm place, fertilize, and water.

Daffodil, Hyacinth, and Tulip

When purchased, precool in icebox in small-holed sacks, and keep dry. Hyacinths and tulips need 12 weeks cold storage, daffodils need 15 weeks or more. The longer the storage, the longer the stems.

In the second week of December soak pots for several hours or overnight. Place flat side of tulip bulb toward edge of pot, and cover top of bulbs with 1″ of soil. Water well. Sink the pot in the ground and cover with 6″–8″ of dirt, leaves, sand, or mulch, and mark spots with stakes. If no rain, water occasionally. In late January check to see if roots are well formed and leaves are just appearing. Bring into the house and clean pot. Cover pot with an inverted pot for two days to straighten stems and acclimate growth. Place in a sunny window and water occasionally. Expect blooms 2nd, 3rd, or 4th week in February, lasting approximately 3 weeks if kept cool.

Lily-of-the-Valley

Refrigerate for 2–4 weeks. Plant pips straight up and cover tops with 1″ of soil. Blooms about 3–4 weeks after potting. Will grow in average room temperature.

LENGTH FROM PLANTING TO BLOOM TIME

Amaryllis: 6–8 weeks in soil
Crocus: 6–7 weeks in water
Freesia: 10–11 weeks in soil
Hyacinth: 8 weeks in water
Lily-of-the-Valley: 4 weeks in soil
Daffodil and Tulip: 8 weeks in soil
Scilla: 8 weeks in soil
Paper Whites: 6–7 weeks in water

BULBS

Heights of flowers and time of bloom will vary depending upon variety planted, location in the garden, section of the country and climate.

B—Bulb T—Tuber
C—Corm TR—Tuberous Root
R—Rhizome

COMMON NAME SCIENTIFIC NAME	KEY	HEIGHT	COMMENTS
Allium Giant Onion *Allium giganteum*	B	3′–4′	Flowers 4″ across, excellent cut flowers. Plant in spring or fall. Use any garden fertilizer after growth appears; sun. *Bloom:* July. *Color:* lavender.
Golden Garlic, Lily Leek *A. moly*		6″–18″	Showy clusters 2″–3″ flowers. Culture same as above. *Bloom:* May–June. *Color:* yellow.
Amaryllis Belladonna Lily *Amaryllis belladonna*	B	2′	Leaves appear in spring and die back before fragrant flower appears. Sun, well-drained soil. Plant bulb 9″ deep, fertilize with 5–10–5 when foliage appears. Also makes a good pot plant. Not hardy. *Bloom:* late summer. *Color:* white, pink, red.
Amaryllis (Hippeastrum) *See* "Container Plants."			
Anemone *Anemone blanda*	T	3″–6″	Daisylike flowers 2″ in diameter. Soak tuber overnight, cover with 2″ soil. Sun or partial shade. Bulbs must be replaced each year. *Bloom:* April–May. *Color:* blue.
A. coronaria	T	8″–12″	Poppylike flower, brilliant clear colors with black center, good cut flower. Recommended strains: de Caen and St. Brigid, see catalogues. Plant in fall, treat as above. *Bloom:* April–May. *Color:* white, red, blue.
Aspidistra Cast Iron Plant *Aspidistra elatior*	T R	To 2½′	Large handsome glossy evergreen leaves, favorite leaf of flower arranger. Partial shade, will stand heat, dust, poor light, bad soil. Also variegated variety. *Color:* inconspicuous flower.
Atamasco Lily *See* "Wild Flowers, Shady Garden."	B		

BULBS

COMMON NAME SCIENTIFIC NAME	KEY	HEIGHT	COMMENTS
Autumn Crocus *See* Colchicum.			
Aztec Lily Jacobean Lily *Sprekelia formossissima*	B	12″–18″	Flowers are 4″ long. Plant in April, dig in fall; store in peat. *Bloom:* May. *Color:* red.
Begonia, hardy *Begonia grandis* *(B. evansiana)*	T	1′–3′	Flowers 1″ or less. Semituberous. Part shade, self-sows, winter mulch. *Bloom:* August thru fall. *Color:* pink red.
Begonia, tuberous *B. tuberhybrida*	T	upright 12″–18″ trailing 12″–18″	Large showy flowers, many varieties. Partial shade; will not tolerate hot nights, store in fall. *Bloom:* Summer. *Color:* all colors but blue and green.
Bletilla Hardy Orchid *Bletilla striata*	R	1′–2′	Leaves have prominent lengthwise pleats; long lasting cut flower and pot plant. Partial shade, heavy winter mulch; plant spring or fall 4″ deep. *Bloom:* 6-week period in early summer. *Color:* pink purple.
Brodiaea *Brodiaea*	C	6″–18″	Many varieties. Sun, thrives in any soil that is not wet or heavily manured, winter mulch. Good cut flower, good for naturalizing. Plant 4″–6″ deep in fall. *Color:* blue purple. *Bloom:* late spring.
Butterfly Lily *See* Ginger Lily.	R		
Caladium *Caladium hortulanum*	T	6″–24″	Grown for decorative heart- or spear-shaped leaves, many varieties. Good for bedding or outdoor pots. Dig and store tubers in fall; replant 1″ deep in April when soil and temperature are warm day and night. Tubers must be started inside in March. Partial shade. *Bloom:* all summer. *Color:* variegated foliage, red, pink, white, green.
Camass Quamash *Camassia quamash*	B	12″–18″	Spikes of starry 1¼″ flowers. Plant early fall, 3″–4″ deep in clumps 9″ or more. Sun to partial shade, tolerates wet areas. *Bloom:* early spring. *Color:* blue to white.

BULBS

COMMON NAME SCIENTIFIC NAME	KEY	HEIGHT	COMMENTS
Canna *Canna*	R	2½′–6′	Many varieties. Foliage green or bronze. Sun, does best in rich soil. Plant anytime. *Bloom:* early summer to frost. *Color:* white to yellow to pink to scarlet.
Chionodoxa Glory-of-the-snow *Chionodoxa luciliae*	B	6″	White and pink varieties available, naturalize for best effect. Sun. Plant in clumps 2″–3″ deep. Keep moist. *Color:* blue. *Bloom:* February-March.
Colchicum Autumn Crocus *Colchicum autumnale*	C	8″	Flowers appear before foliage. Plant 2″–3″ deep in August, sun to partial shade, leave undisturbed. *Bloom:* September–October. *Color:* pink, lavender, white.
Crinum Lily *Crinum*	B	2′–3′	Many varieties. Fragrant lilylike 3″–6″ flowers, straplike leaves. Sun or partial shade; fertilize and mulch heavily; plant bulb high, Not hardy in North. *Bloom:* July–August. *Color:* white, pink, red.
Crocus *Crocus*	B	to 5″	Many varieties, sizes, and bloom times. Sun or partial shade; plant 2½″ deep. Naturalize, first splash of spring. *Bloom:* February–March. *Color:* purple, lilac, white, yellow and striped.
Daffodil *Narcissus*	B	3″ to 2′	Many varieties; *see* special article. *Bloom:* February–mid-April. *Color:* white, pink, yellow, orange, red, and combinations of above.
Dahlia *Dahlia*	T	1′ to 7	Many varieties. *See* special article. *Bloom:* September-October. Miniatures bloom all summer. *Color:* all colors.
Daylily *Hemerocallis*	TR	12″ to 4′	Many varieties, *see* "Popular Plants." *Bloom:* summer. *Color:* all except blue.
Fairy Lily *see* Atamasco Lily.			

BULBS

COMMON NAME SCIENTIFIC NAME	KEY	HEIGHT	COMMENTS
Foxtail Lily Desert-candle *Eremurus himalaicus*	TR	to 3′	3′–4′ spike of tiny flowers; good cut flower lasting to 3 weeks; impressive in garden. Sun; plant September to December in deep rich sandy loam with cow manure; leave undisturbed. *Bloom:* June. *Color:* white.
E. robustus		6′–8′	Same as above. *Bloom:* June. *Color:* pink.
E. "Shelford Hybrids"		8′	Same as above, plant 4″ deep. *Bloom:* June. *Color:* orange.
Fritillaria Crown Imperial *Fritillaria imperialis*	B	2½′–4′	Large clusters of flowers at top of 2½′ stem. Sun; good rich soil. *Bloom:* April. *Color:* orange yellow.
Guinea-hen flower *F. mealeagris*		12″–15″	Flower is checkered red with veins of purple. Sun, rich soil; plant in fall. *Bloom:* April. *Color:* red, purple, white.
Galanthus *see* Snowdrop.			
Galtonia Summer Hyacinth *Galtonia candicans*	B	1′–4′	20–30 fragrant, bell-shaped flowers; culture same as gladiola but can be left in ground with winter mulch in Zone 5–7. Tender; north of Zone 5 should be lifted: Will multiply. Sun. *Bloom:* June–July. *Color:* white.
Giant Onion *see* Allium.			
Gladiolus *See* special article.			
Glory-of-the-snow *See* Chionodoxa.			
Grape Hyacinth *Muscari botryoides*	B	4″–7″	Several varieties, also white, can be naturalized. Sun, plant in fall. *Bloom:* March. *Color:* deep blue.
Hardy Orchid *See* Bletilla.			
Hippeastrum *See* Amaryllis.			

BULBS

COMMON NAME SCIENTIFIC NAME	KEY	HEIGHT	COMMENTS
Hyacinth Common Hyacinth *Hyacinthus orientalis*	B	8″–12″	Very fragrant. Sun, plant 5″ deep in fall, water freely. Single and double varieties; can be forced in pots. Plant new bulbs each year. *Bloom:* April. *Color:* white, pink, blue, yellow, orange, lavender.
Roman Hyacinth *H. romanus*		6″–12″	Fragrant, good for rock gardens. Plant in fall; not hardy above Zone 6. Plant new bulbs each year. *Bloom:* March. *Color:* white, blue.
Iris *See* special article.			
Jack-in-the-Pulpit *See* "Wild Flowers, Shady Garden."			
Jacobean Lily *See* Aztec Lily.			
Jonquil *See* Daffodil.			
Leucojum *See* Snowflake.			
Lily *See* special article.			
Lily-of-the-Valley *Convallaria majalis*	R	8″	Very fragrant, tiny bell-shaped flowers, also a pink variety. Divide in fall; sun or partial shade. Pips can be forced in winter, cover with 1″ soil.
Lycoris Golden Spider Lily *Lycoris africana*	B	1½′	Foliage appears and dies back before bloom. Leave undisturbed. Sun; plant 3″–4″ deep. *Bloom:* Sept.–Oct. *Color:* yellow.
Spider Lily *L. radiata*		1′–2′	Straplike foliage dies back before flowers appear. Same as above. *Bloom:* Aug.–Sept. *Color:* coral red.
Resurrection Lily Amaryllis halii *L. squamigera*		2′–3′	Fragrant, hardy. Sun to semishade. Very desirable. Plant 5″ deep. *Bloom:* August. *Color:* rosy lilac pink.

BULBS

COMMON NAME SCIENTIFIC NAME	KEY	HEIGHT	COMMENTS
Montbretia *Tritonia*	C	18″	Several varieties. Resembles gladiolus, good for cutting. Plant 1″ deep at any time; sun. *Bloom:* August. *Color:* orange to scarlet.
Narcissus *See* Daffodil.			
Oxalis Wood Sorrel *oxalis violacea*	B	8″–10″	Leaves are shamrock-shaped. Use in border or rock garden. Invasive. *Bloom:* June–Sept. *Color:* pink.
Peruvian Daffodil Spider Lily *Hymenocallis narcissiflora*	B	2′	Clusters of very fragrant flowers; blooms a few weeks after planting, must lift bulbs in fall. *Bloom:* July–August. *Color:* white.
Peruvian Lily *Alstroemeria aurantiaca*	TR	2′–3′	Many varieties, minimum of 5 peduncles per stem, good cut flower. Can be potted. Sun to partial shade; good drainage; plant 6″–9″ deep. *Bloom:* June–July. *Color:* orange with red stripes.
A. ligtu		2′–4′	Many varieties, 6–7 peduncles per stem. Sun to partial shade; good drainage. Good for cutting. Neither hardy in cold climate. *Bloom:* June–July. *Color:* pastel.
Quamash *See* Camass.			
Rain Lily *See* Atamasco Lily.			
Scilla Squill Spanish Squill *Endymion hispanicus* *(Scilla hispanicus)*	B	18″	Bell-shaped flowers on spike 20″ high. Sun to partial shade, rock garden, plant in fall. *Bloom:* April. *Color:* white, blue, pink.
Siberian Squill *S. siberica*	B	3″–4″	Dainty, good for naturalizing. Sun to shade; plant in fall. *Bloom:* April. *Color:* deep blue.
Snowdrop *Galanthus nivalis*	B	4″–6″	Sweet scent, nodding blooms. Needs no fertilizer; can be naturalized; hardy. *Bloom:* March. *Color:* white.

BULBS

COMMON NAME SCIENTIFIC NAME	KEY	HEIGHT	COMMENTS
G. nivalis flore pleno		4″–6″	Double. *Bloom:* March. *Color:* white.
Snowflake Summer Snowflake *Leucojum aestivum*	B	12″	Green tipped white bell-like flowers clustered on stalk; can be naturalized. *Bloom:* April. *Color:* white with green.
Spring Snowflake *L. vernum*		To 12″	Same as above. *Bloom:* February–March. *Color:* white.
Springbeauty *See* "Wild Flowers, Sunny Garden."			
Star-of-Bethlehem *See* Wild flowers, "Sunny Garden."			
Sternbergia *Sternbergia lutea*	B	6″–12″	Glossy flower on 4″ stem; crocus-like shape. Sun; good for dry areas; winter mulch; do not disturb; plant in late spring to early summer. *Bloom:* September. *Color:* yellow.
Summer Hyacinth *See* Galtonia.			
Tuberose *Polianthes tuberosa*	B	3′–4′	Very fragrant, good cut flower. Sun; plant in spring after danger of frost, feed monthly with 5–10–5 fertilizer, store in fall. *Bloom:* July–August. *Color:* white.
Tulip *See* Special article.			
Wood Sorrel *See* Oxalis.			
Wood Hyacinth *see* Scilla.			
Zephyranthes *See* Atamasco Lily.			

Popular Plants

AZALEAS

In spring azaleas and dogwoods turn a southern garden into a mass of bloom and a blaze of color. By planting a selection of varieties, one may have azaleas in bloom for two months or more. The plants are literally covered with a profusion of flowers, ranging in color from soft to brilliant hues of white, yellow, orange, pink, crimson, and purple. The flowers are single, double, or hose-in-hose (one flower inside another) forms and may be solid, striped or flecked. Azaleas are among the most important plants in the garden. They are hardy and long-lived, require a minimum of care, and are inexpensive to maintain.

Color—Plan carefully when choosing colors. Many of the vivid colors may clash when planted together, and too much of one strong color may be overpowering. Intersperse bright colors with whites or other evergreens or blend with soft pastels. Azaleas may be planted while in bloom to help in arranging pleasing color combinations. Fortunately, it is simple to correct mistakes because azaleas are easy to transplant.

Landscaping—Ranging in size from 12″ dwarfs to 8′ giants, both evergreen and deciduous azaleas afford numerous landscaping possibilities. The evergreen varieties provide a strong accent in the garden all year long. They are prized for their lovely form and foliage as well as their spectacular bloom. Many have nice fall foliage (reds and pinks). The native deciduous azaleas, which may grow as tall as small trees, are valued for their light, airy, and often fragrant flowers and for the interesting structure of their bare branches. The new hybrids are striking, colorful specimen plants in sunnier areas.

Azaleas are most attractive in naturalized planting in open wooded areas or under deciduous trees. Informal, free flowing mass plantings are very effective, with low growing varieties placed in front of taller ones. Azaleas enhance more formal plantings equally well. As their own form is very desirable, they should be left to grow naturally and should never be sheared or mounded. Dwarf varieties, such as the Satsukis, may be allowed to grow together to form a dense high ground cover under a large deciduous tree. Azaleas may be used as specimen plants, as edging for flower borders, walks, and terraces, as loose, natural hedges or screens, and as foundation plantings (avoid colors which might clash with the color of the building). The dark foliage of broadleaf evergreens and conifers makes a good background for azaleas. Together they provide a pleasant combination of color and texture in the garden.

Companion Plants—Companion plants for azaleas should be shade-tolerant and acid-loving. The classic choices for an azalea garden are dogwoods, hollies, camellias, and evergreen ground covers such as pachysandra, ajuga, liriope, or vinca minor. Spring bulbs and wild flowers add small touches of color and ferns soften the area. Cut-leaf Japanese maples match the native azaleas in airiness and elegance of form.

Container Plants—Certain varieties of azaleas make excellent Bonsai, while others are good greenhouse plants. A potted azalea received at Christmas should not be planted outside until the other azaleas have finished blooming. Check the variety before planting outside for most florists' azaleas are greenhouse plants only.

Planting

Azaleas may be planted successfully in fall, winter, and spring, whenever the soil is workable. Fall planting is best, for this gives more time for the plant to become established. Spring planting, while azaleas are in bloom, makes it easier to arrange colors, but the new growth will have started, and is apt to wilt. Spring planting demands extra care in watering. Azaleas will not tolerate full sun. Filtered sunlight is best. They will not bloom under large shade trees unless the tree's branches are thinned to allow light to come through.

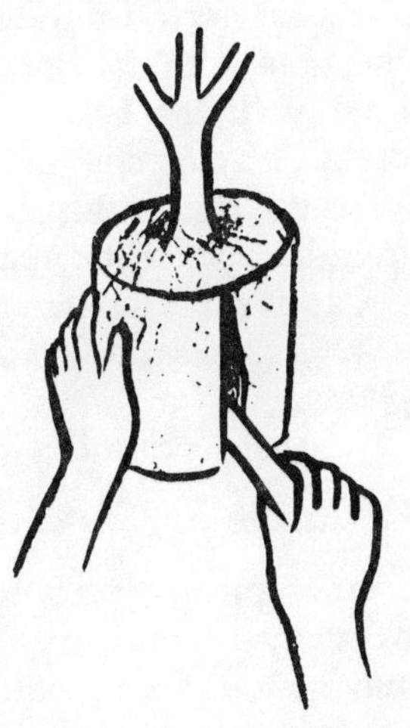

Azaleas grown in containers become root bound very quickly, and if planted in this condition, the plant will die within a year. This can be corrected by vertically scoring the roots with a sharp knife in six to eight places and opening the ball so the roots will spread into the soil. With balled and burlap plants, cut away the top third of the burlap after placing the ball in the ground. Since azalea roots are right at the surface of the soil, heavy ground covers, such as ivy, will smother them and compete for moisture and plant food.

Soil for azaleas must be made from scratch. Otherwise the plants will grow for a year or two and then deteriorate. Save time by doing it right in the beginning. The hole should be three times the width of the ball. Soil should be dug out to a depth of 18″. Save the top 6″ of soil and discard the rest. Make a mixture of ⅓ top soil, ⅓ humus, and ⅓ clean, sharp builder's sand. Fill the hole to just below ground level with this mixture and tamp firmly. Remember that this loose soil will settle between 2″—3″, so allow for this by setting the plant at least 3″ above the surrounding level. After putting the plant in place, scatter

wet peat moss around the ball to stimulate root growth. Finish filling the hole with soil mixture, add about 3″ of mulch, and soak thoroughly. If the bed is on a slope or is very well drained, use the discarded clay soil for a levee at the drip line of the leaves. This will keep the mulch in place. Discard and replace the soil around house foundations for it contains lime and mortar.

Caution: (1) Beware of too-deep planting.

2. Over-accumulation of mulch and fallen leaves can smother plants.

3. Azaleas cannot grow in a heavy clay soil.

Fertilizing and Mulching

Once properly planted, the care of azaleas is very easy. Fertilize twice a year, immediately after blooming and six weeks later, or they may be fed monthly after blooming through August. Use a specially prepared azalea-camellia fertilizer available at seed and garden stores. Follow directions.

The purpose of mulching is to conserve moisture, prevent weeds and improve general appearance. Remove some of the old mulch before feeding and then replace with fresh mulch. Pine needles, shredded pine bark, leaf mold, or shredded oak leaves make the best mulch. Peat moss will crust over, tending to smother the roots, and to shed water. Never use woody materials or leaves that have not decayed. Never let mulch get too deep on old plants.

Acidity

Iron is available to plants in an acid soil of pH 5.0–6.0. Azalea leaves should be rich green; if they begin to turn yellow with dark green veins, the plant needs iron. A quick but temporary way to add needed iron is with a liquid spray of iron sulfate or chelated iron. Spray plant and ground. Follow package directions. For permanent results apply sulfur and aluminum sulfate to the soil to increase acidity.

Caution: If the soil becomes too acid, it locks up all the plant food. Therefore, do not add iron until definitely needed. Have the soil tested.

The first stage of magnesium deficiency is similar to iron chlorosis. The leaves turn yellow. Later reddish purple blotches appear on the leaves which then turn brown on the tips and edges. Spread epsom salts (magnesium sulphate) generously around the plant, or apply as a foliage spray (2 tablespoons per gallon of water).

Watering

The proper soil for planting is essential, but no less important is the watering, for azaleas grow only when they are watered. When planted in very porous soil, the water can run straight through and draw the oxygen down behind it, making a stronger root growth. Except during protracted spells of dry weather, a good watering once a week should be sufficient through June. In July and August more water is needed, as that is the period when the buds are developing, and it takes water to produce buds. During September and October, if dry weather prevails, water only enough to keep azaleas from wilting, so as not to promote new growth which might be damaged by an early freeze. Plants should go into freezing weather well-watered, so check and water if needed during dry spells in winter.

Pruning

Prune azaleas while in bloom for the house, or as soon as bloom is over, as new buds start to form about a month later. Cut back to the point of origin any overvigorous shoots which have to be shortened for shape. Cut out weak undernourished branches at any time for it is better to sacrifice a few poor blooms than to have an unsightly plant. When pruning to improve the appearance of old leggy azaleas, do not remove more than one-third of the branches per year.

Propagation

Azaleas may be propagated by seeds, cuttings, layering, division, and grafting. Leave the seeds and grafting to the experts, but cuttings and layering are easy. Take the cuttings in the spring, insert them directly in the azalea bed where they can stay or in a sand box or cold frame. Remove after roots form. Transplant to a partly shaded location, mulch, and keep moist. To layer, slit a branch at a joint or scrape the bark off one side of the branch. Cover with dirt and mulch. Place a stone or brick to hold it in place until roots form. Cut from parent, replant, and water thoroughly until roots form. An old plant which has made new roots near the surface from being planted too deep may be divided and replanted as several plants.

Diseases

Leaf Gall (Fungus)—Malformed, enlarged, thick, fleshy leaves, pale green changing to velvety grayish white—a problem in wet seasons. Hand pick galls and destroy. Spray plant and ground at first sign of trouble with a fungicide such as Captan or Zineb.

Petal Blight (Fungus)—Flower petals spotted, turning soggy and brown. Attacks large flowered and mid-to-late season plants. Spray flowers and soil three times per week with a fungicide such as Thylate or Zineb. The following spring drench soil just before buds show color with a fungicide such as Truban. Spray again with a fungicide when flowers are open.

Pests

Dormant oil spray in February is good protection against pests. *See* "Sprays."

Lace Bug—Leaves grayish green with dark spots on underside. Spray with an insecticide such as Malathion at 7 to 10-day intervals.

Red Spider Mite—Leaves appear stippled and off-color, turning brown. To check for red spider mite: hold a white paper under a branch and shake. Minute red spiders will drop onto paper. Spray with an insecticide such as Malathion, Diazinon, Kelthane, or an oil-based spray at 7-day intervals on underside of leaves.

Scale—White, cottony scales in forks of twigs and main stems. Spray with an insecticide such as Malathion or Diazinon at 7-day intervals. For indoor plants: remove with cotton swab and rubbing alcohol.

White Fly—Adults fly from the leaves like dandruff when disturbed. Leaves become mottled yellow and have black sooty mold which grows on sticky honeydew secreted by the insect. Spray with an insecticide such as Malathion 3 times at 10-day intervals.

Varieties

Since azaleas come in such a vast number of varieties, it is impractical to list them except by groups. Some are deciduous, the majority evergreen. Some are low and spreading, some are tall and spreading, and some are dominantly upright. In the following lists (E) indicates bloom time from late March to late April, (M) mid-April to mid-May, and (L) mid-May to mid-June.

Evergreen Azaleas

Back Acres—Double or single flowers of substance and texture. Multiple color forms such as solids and white or nearly white centers and colored margins; heat and cold resistant foliage; mid-season to late blooming: very desirable.

White—White Jade—flat-faced white, green in center.

White Centers with Colored Margins—Margaret Douglas–white to pink centers, salmon margins; Marion Lee–white center, pink margin

Pink—Debonaire–light pink; Saint James–white throat, peach margin; Tharon Perkins–pale salmon (E)

Red—Pat Kraft–dark red, very late; Target–scarlet

Glenn Dale Hybrids—Over 400 varieties cover the entire blooming season from April to June. Large flowers, wide range of color, stripes, flecks, and variegated margins and throats. Attractive, glossy, dark green foliage, hardy, heights from low and compact to tall.

White—Bold Face (M), Delight (E), Everest (L), Geisha (E), Glacier (M), Helen Close (M), Martha Hitchcock (M), Moonbeam (L), Treasure (M), Wavelet (L)

Shades of Salmon, Pink and Red—Allure (E) pink, Aphrodite (M) rose pink, Aztec (L) rose red, Copperman (L) orange red, Crinoline (L) rose pink, ruffled margin, Fashion (M) orange red, Glamor (M) rose red, Grace Freeman (M) violet pink, Greeting (M) salmon, Wildfire (E) scarlet

Shades of Purple and Violet—Chanticleer (L) purple, Dauntless (L) purple, Muscadine (M) rose purple, Sarabande (L) purple, Zulu (M) purple

Very Dwarf (late May, early June)—Eros–orange red, Pearl Bradford–rose pink, Sagitterius–Salmon pink, Sterling–rose pink

Indicas (Southern Indian Hybrid)—Large flowers, wide range of color; tall and fast growing, open growth pattern; finished blossoms fall to ground; bloom early to mid-season; tender plants, apt to be damaged by cold.

Alba maculata (M) white speckled with chartreuse
Formosa (M) violet red
George Lindley Tabor (M) white flushed with purple
Indica alba (M) white, fragrant
Mardi Gras (M) white with pink stripes
Pride of Mobile (M) light to deep pink

Kaempferi Hybrids—tall, rather slender growth and profuse blooms in April–May. Blooms rarely damaged by frost. Hardier than Kurumes with slightly larger flowers. Good used as tall accents among Kurumes.

Alice (M) salmon red
Cleopatra (M) lilac rose
Fedora (M) deep pink
Wilhelmina Vuyk (E) white
Willy (M) bright pink

Kurumes—Masses of bloom; dense dark green spring foliage; large range of colors. Hardier than Indicas. Excellent for greenhouse forcing, container plants, and Bonsai. Blooms April–May. Varying in height, some slow growing, most reach 4′–6′, generally upright.

White Flowers—

Apple Blossom—white variegated with pink

H. H. Hume—hose-in-hose

Snow

Shades of salmon pink or red—

Christmas Cheer—brilliant red

Coral Bells—shell pink, hose-in-hose

Glory—pink

Hexe—crimson red, hose-in-hose

Hino-Crimson—crimson

Hinode-giri—vivid red

Pink Pearl—salmon rose, hose-in-hose

Salmon Beauty—salmon pink, hose-in-hose

Sherwood Red—orange red

Satsuki Hybrids—Generally large single flowers, many different colors and forms. Shiny, dark green leaves. Tolerates more sun, but needs protection from afternoon sun. Very late blooming, May and June. Most grow low and spreading, thus excellent for foreground planting as well as Bonsai. For low edging, use very dwarf Gumpo.

Gumpo—White, light pink, or salmon rose

Gunrei—variegated white with pink

Macrantha—pink or salmon red, medium height

Waka-bisu—salmon pink, hose-in-hose, medium height

Deciduous Native Azaleas

In general they require more sun. Flowers are trumpet shaped in terminal clusters, many are fragrant. Mature plants can reach 8′ or more. Difficult to find.

Flame—(the Flame Azalea of the Great Smoky Mountains) *Rhododendron calendulaceum*–flowers orange red, red, or clear yellow. May–June.

Florida—*R. austrinum*–golden flowers in late March and early April. Fragrant.

Oconee—*R. flammeum*–flowers orange, red, to strong pink, yellow, and salmon. Early to mid-April.

Piedmont—*R. canescens*–flowers white to deep pink. Late March. Fragrant.

Pinxterbloom—*R. nudiflorum*–flowers white, light pink, or deep violet. April. Honeysuckle fragrance.

Plumleaf—*R. prunifolium*–flowers red, orange red, to orange. Very late blooming. Foliage appears before flowers. Must have shade.

Swamp—*B. viscosum*–spicy, fragrant white flowers. Hybrids may be pink to salmon, yellow. Mid-May to early June.

Sweet—*R. arborescens*–flowers white, fragrant. May–June.

Deciduous Hybrid Azaleas

Very desirable. Large spectacular clusters of bloom, many quite fragrant. Require more sun than evergreen azaleas.

Ghent Hybrids—Palest yellow through varying shades of apricot and flame. Single and double flowers bloom early to midseason. Plants tend to be leggy. They do not require as much acidity as other azaleas.

Knaphill—Clusters of large flowers in colors from pinks, creams, and near whites to reds and oranges. April–May.

Exbury	Ilam
Slocock	Knaphill

Mollis Hybrids—Less hardy than the Ghent azaleas, possibly more heat resistant. Colors are yellow, orange, to orange red, and growth is upright. They tolerate less acid soil (lime lightly). Late midseason bloom.

Mucronulatum—Very early lavender flowers which bloom with forsythia. Tender. May be killed back by a late spring freeze.

CAMELLIAS

Camellias are beautiful, shiny broad-leaved evergreen shrubs that grow naturally as undershrubs in woodlands where they have the protection of trees. The two best known types are the Japonicas and the Sasanquas, but there are several other popular species and hybrids. In recent years new varieties of *Camellia reticulata,* often referred to as Chinese Reticulatas or hybrids, have been introduced. These, while not as widely known or used, are a worthwhile and highly pleasing addition to the camellia family.

Camellias, with their outstanding foliage and flowers of many forms and variations of white, pink, and red, may be successfully grown outdoors in the milder climates. They are used for background planting, for foundation planting with other broad-leaved evergreens, as specimen plants, and the sasanqua varieties for hedges and espaliers. The sasanquas are easiest to grow outside in the Mid-South. Their combined blooming times provide a period extending from September through March. *Gibbing* (see p. 164) is also a factor in determining the period of bloom.

When to Plant

Container-grown plants may be set out at any time during the growing season. Those balled in burlap should be planted during the winter season, October through March. Keep roots and leaves moist before planting. Water well after planting until plants become established.

Too-deep planting is the principal cause of failure with camellias. They should be planted in loose soil which will settle a couple of inches as water is added. Allow for this by setting the top of the ball 2″ or 3″ higher than surrounding ground level. Pack soil firmly in bottom of hole before planting to minimize settling.

Where to Plant

Partial shade is best. Camellias prefer filtered sunlight. If planted near foundations or walls, test soil often for alkalinity and, if needed, adjust soil pH *(see soil below)*. Do not plant against walls without shade or tree protection, as the heat from the wall will be detrimental. Avoid locations where there are heavy surface roots from trees. The north or east side of a house or garden is satisfactory when protection is given from the hot midday sun. Camellias must have good drainage. If necessary, dig the hole much deeper and put in coarse gravel or rocks to allow the excess water to drain away.

Soil Requirements

The soil should be slightly acid and rich in organic material. Preparation and requirements of the soil are the same as for azaleas. To increase acidity, bring the soil pH to between 5.5 and 6.5 (*see* "pH Factor in Soil").

Watering

Water thoroughly once a week if there is no rainfall. Also lightly sprinkle the foliage during the hot summer months (not in midday). Lack of sufficient moisture during August and September will cause bud drop. The natural habitats of these plants are areas of heavy rainfall, so it is important to water each time to a depth of several inches. Camellias should also be well watered going into winter.

Pruning

Camellias respond to pruning and shaping. They can be pruned in the cutting of blooms or, when needed, *immediately* after the blooming period. Prune different varieties accordingly. Remove dead and weak, spindly growth whenever found. Use regular tree paint on any large pruned stems. On plants with heavy bud crops, *disbudding* results in larger and better flowers.

Mulch

The ground should never be cultivated around the roots of the plants as the root system is close to the surface. Mulch to conserve moisture and keep down weeds outdoors. Use 2″ of any of the following materials: oak leaves, pine needles, wet peat moss, or shredded pine bark mulch. In the slat house, use only a light mulch, such as a sparse covering of pine needles.

Fertilizing

Fertilize twice a year—once in March and again early in June. Use especially prepared azalea-camellia fertilizer which may be purchased at seed stores. Follow directions on container. Water thoroughly; soil should be moist when plants are fertilized. *Do not overfertilize camellias.*

When leaves get yellowish instead of rich dark green, the trouble is usually not enough acidity. This generally occurs in late summer. *See* "Azaleas: Acidity."

Pests and Diseases

Camellias are remarkably free from pests and diseases. The following is for use only if needed. Follow directions on container.

Scale—For scale on underside of leaves, spray with an oil-base spray or an insecticide such as Malathion. Do not use oil spray when temperature is above 80° or below 40°.

Aphids—Appear on growth of new leaves in spring and may be controlled with an insecticide such as Cygon or Malathion. Apply on both sides of leaves.

Leaf Gall—Pick off and dispose of deformed or thickened leaves. Damp weather increases this trouble and dry weather stops it. Spray with a fungicide such as Captan or Zineb.

Chewing Insects—Use an insecticide such as Malathion or Isotox.

Spider Mites—Cause surface of leaves to lose color in a speckled pattern. Use a miticide such as Kelthane. Spray top and underside of foliage.

Flower Blight—Caused by *Sclerotinia camelliae.* It is a fungus disease that forms in the base of blossoms and affects only them. Blossoms turn brown, the petals have a veined appearance, and the rotted tissues become soggy. The infected flowers should be removed, and disposal made of all fallen blossoms and leaves. Highly effective also is the use of a fungicide known as PCNB, sold under various trade names such as Terraclor and Fungiclor. Apply to all of the soil surface in winter or early spring before blooms appear.

Ants—A dust such as Chlordane sprinkled around base of plants will control ants which spread aphids.

Because of the susceptability of camellias to extreme cold many gardeners prefer growing camellias under glass or in a slat house *(See pg. 57)*. Many more varieties can be grown and the blooms enjoyed and exhibited far more successfully with this protection. However, early and late blooming varieties may be grown satisfactorily in the garden.

The use of Gibberellic Acid, called *Gibbing,* is now widely recommended and used by camellia growers on the buds of plants grown both outdoors and indoors. This treatment extends the blooming season and makes possible a larger number of blooms.

To Gibb: remove small pointed leaf bud near a flower bud (flower buds are round) leaving a tiny cup. Put one drop of acid into the cup and mark the branch with a string. Stagger the process over several weeks for extended bloom. Flowers from buds so treated are generally of better texture, larger, and longer lasting.

Varieties

The latest edition of camellia nomenclature, adopted as *The Official Nomenclature Book of The American Camellia Society,* lists approximately five thousand varieties with descriptions and information on each. Consult local nursery about the varieties adaptable to local conditions.

Camellia japonica—Japonicas produce unbelievably beautiful flowers in white through shades of pink and red, and combinations of these colors, from September to May. Consider the blooming period and include in the collection early (fall), midseason (winter)—not recommended outdoors—and late (spring) bloomers if the climate is not too severe.

Camellia sasanqua—A very good shrub for the garden. Its graceful form, profusion of bloom and dark green foliage, and ability to thrive in sun or shade make it an excellent plant. Blooms earlier than japonicas—September through December. Very useful in cold climates because the flowers come early and are usually finished before the worst part of winter.

Camellia reticulata—Natural growth is more open than japonicas. They prefer more sunlight and can stand heat. Well adapted for containers.

Helpful Hints

To keep a camellia bloom put 1 teaspoon water in the bottom of a brandy snifter or a glass bowl. Place bloom in snifter and cover the top with a glass plate or plastic wrap. Keeps longer.

CHRYSANTHEMUMS

No plant has gone through greater changes in the last few years than the chrysanthemum. Hardiness, increased earliness of bloom, and greater size have been bred into the varieties that bloom outdoors. All varieties come in white and shades of yellow, pink, lavender, red, orange, and bronze. For named varieties check catalogues.

Where to Plant

Chrysanthemums may be planted almost anywhere in the garden. They will flourish in full sun or in partial shade. If grown in partial shade, they will become leggy and lose lower leaves. They will survive more neglect than any other family of plants, making them a good choice for the gardener who goes away in the summer. Although they will tolerate neglect, they repay bountifully for extra care.

Propagation

Chrysanthemums may be grown from divisions from last year's growth or preferably, from rooted cuttings which are much freer from disease. Second year mums are not as productive. For maximum garden display start cuttings in April. Cut the tip of a strong shoot straight across, 4″ long, removing the leaves from the base of the stem. If cuttings are from last year's growth, choose shoots farthest from the center of the plant. Treat the cuttings with a rooting hormone. Clean sand or a mixture of sand and pulverized peat moss makes a good rooting medium. Root in cold frame or in flats in a shady place. Firm sand around the cuttings, and keep moist. Cuttings will root in about three weeks. When well rooted, plant them in desired location.

Culture

Mums need lots of fertilizer and water. Before planting prepare the soil by spading in about a 3″ layer of well-rotted or dehydrated manure or compost to which superphosphate has been added. For specimen blooms give an additional feeding of ⅓ cup commercial fertilizer (6–12–12) per plant about July 15th, and repeat this about August 15th. Do not fertilize after buds show color. Keep well watered.

Pinching Back and Disbudding

When growing mums to get long stems for picking do not pinch back. To double the crop of flowers and provide bushy plants pinch back. When plants are 6″–8″ tall, pinch out the tip of each stem, including the top set of leaves. Soon new growth will appear. Pinch out new shoots each time they grow 6″. Stop pinching about July 15th.

Do not remove buds from the pompoms and bunch varieties. With larger varieties to obtain specimen blooms rather than many smaller ones, remove side buds, leaving four to six lateral stems to a plant.

Keep any additional lateral stems pinched off until August. When small clusters appear at the end of the stems and each bud is about the size of a pea, remove all but one or the number of flowers desired.

Diseases and Pests

Leaf spot—Use a fungicide, such as Manzate (Maneb).

Cucumber beetles in fall—Use an insecticide, such as Sevin or Malathion. This may have to be applied weekly during the blooming period.

Types

Arctic Hybrids—These are a very beautiful strain of border mums, making a spreading mound of large, single daisylike flowers on stems about 14″ long. They bloom over a long period and are very hardy.

Azaleamums (Cushion Mums)—These have the advantage of early and continuous bloom but many of them have the unpleasant habit of retaining their faded blooms, which spoils the effect.

Button—Blossoms less than an 1″ across, tightly petaled, hardy and late flowering.

Harvest Giants—Vigorous plants produce large 5″–6″ fully double flowers in late summer or early fall.

Pompom—Blossoms about 1½″ to 2″, bloom in clusters on long stems throughout the fall.

Spider or Fuji—Spreading flat-headed flowers.

Spoon—Spreading flat-headed tubular petals with end flaring into shape of a spoon.

DAYLILIES

There is no more adaptable flower in the garden than the daylily (hemerocallis). It has no insect enemies, will grow in almost any soil,

will bloom in either full sun or partial shade, and can be planted anytime the ground is not frozen.

Although June is the month when the majority of daylilies are at their peak of bloom, there are some varieties that start blooming in late April or May, others during July and some (known as rebloomers) that will flower occasionally until late September. Some varieties remain open at night and are good for flower arrangements.

Daylilies are available in an almost endless variety of colors, size, and shapes of flower heads and heights, and some are fragrant. Colors of new hybrids range from reds, mahoganies, oranges, pinks, browns, melons, golds, lemon yellows, greenish yellows, to almost white. *Caution:* Our native roadside orange daylily should not be planted near hybrids because they will crowd them out.

Heights range from 12″ to over 4′. Flower heads range from 1½″–9″ in diameter. Although a single flower lasts only one day, each stalk will produce blooms for 2 to 5 weeks, depending on the variety and weather conditions.

Daylilies make a good background for lower plants. Planted among daffodils the new foliage hides the dying daffodil leaves. Remember when placing daylilies, the flower heads turn toward the strongest light. Daylilies multiply vigorously. Allow room for the spreading foliage.

Planting

Do not plant too deep. There should be only 1″ of soil on the top of the roots. Make a small mound in the center of a generous hole and place 3 to 5 plants on top of the mound with the roots spreading down and around. Fill in the hole with soil. A good mixture is 2 parts soil to 1 part sand and 1 part humus, with a little cottonseed meal or 6–12–12.

Daylilies prefer a slightly acid soil. Although daylilies bloom and multiply in spite of neglect, they do respond to a light fertilizing. When new growth first appears, sprinkle lightly with 6–12–12, or superphosphate. Do not let fertilizer touch the foliage. A thorough watering a few weeks before blooming will increase the size of blooms. If old established plants appear to need a little fertilizer, feed lightly four to six weeks after the peak of bloom with a low nitrogen fertilizer (4–8–12). A too-rich soil produces foliage at the expense of blooms. Mulch new plants sparingly. Old plants need no mulch. Daylilies will survive near drouth conditions as well as damp areas. Watch for slugs in wet conditions. To preserve next year's bloom, do not remove yellow foliage in fall until dead. To divide an overgrown clump, dig up with a fork, cut into smaller pieces with a sharp shovel, and replant.

Daylilies vary in cost from one to one hundred dollars; the price generally reflects the supply and the number of plants since the speciment was first introduced—not the quality of the plant. For help in choosing varieties, daylilies may be seen and purchased in some local gardens while in full bloom, or selected and orders placed for later delivery. The local chapter of the American Hemerocallis Association can supply the names of commercial growers in the area. There are also a number of outstanding commercial growers who publish mail order catalogs (usually advertized in garden magazines). Varieties change frequently and new hybrids are introduced yearly.

GARDENIAS

The gardenia is an evergreen shrub which has extremely fragrant white flowers, shiny green leaves, and can grow up to 5′. It is a semihardy plant which does well in the greenhouse and may also be grown in the garden in Zones 7, 8, and 9.

Gardenias need protection during severe winters as extreme cold will split the bark causing the plant to die. Northern exposure is recommended as morning sun will burn the leaves after frost. Bloom time ranges from spring to summer depending on variety.

The culture is the same as that of camellias—acid soil and lots of humus. Gardenias need some sun for setting of buds. They are subject to white fly and scale. *See* "Sprays."

Varieties:

August Beauty—smaller leaf and flower, reblooms in fall
Gardenia Fortunei—hardiest of large flowered
Myster—least hardy of large flowered
G. *radicans*—dwarf

IRISES

Irises constitute a vast genus with hundreds of species and thousands of hybrids. This enormous number of iris varieties offers a broad range of colors, bicolors, and blends, with new introductions made each year. Irises are one of the best perennials for spring and early summer bloom. Their often fragrant flowers are desirable for arrange-

ments while their spiked foliage remains attractive all summer.

Bearded

The bearded iris is the most common garden iris. It requires well drained, slightly sweet soil, and six hours of full sun a day. It is propagated by division of rhizomes (a rhizome is a rootlike underground stem producing roots from its lower surface and leaves or shoots from its upper surface.) Bloom period is spring and early summer.

Dwarf Bearded

Height 4″–6″. These irises are profuse bloomers with perfectly formed miniature replicas of the bearded iris. They bloom in late March and April, and are ideal for low borders and rock gardens.

Intermediate Bearded

Height 15″–18″. These irises are similar to the tall bearded and are prolific bloomers. They flower slightly later than the dwarf varieties.

Tall Bearded

Height 32″–42″. These irises offer an unlimited choice of color. Their showy flowers are effective in the perennial garden as accent plants or in a display bed. Their bloom time is May; however this may be extended by a selection of early, mid- and late-season varieties.

Crested (Iris Cristata)

Height 4″–6″. Their small blue and white flowers with touches of yellow and orange appear in late March or early April. They are very effective for a wild flower or rock garden and grow well in semishade.

Beardless

These irises require a well-drained but more acid and moist soil than the bearded varieties. They are propagated by division of rhizomes, and bloom from late spring to early summer.

Siberian

Height 2½′–3½′. These irises have grasslike foliage and slender stems with flowers of whites, blues, and purples. They bloom in May to early June. They require a well-drained, acid soil with plenty of compost, and full sun. They need watering in early spring and at bloom time. Rhizomes should be planted 1″–2″ deep.

Spuria

Height to 2′. Their culture is same as for Siberian. They have a wide range of colors and are good for cutting. Spurias should be mulched in late fall with well-rotted manure and the clumps left undisturbed for years.

Japanese

Height to 2½′. These irises require rich acid soil kept constantly moist from spring through bloom time. Plant 2″ deep in part shade. Their large flat flowers range through shades of blues, pinks, purples, lavenders, to white.

Louisiana

Height 2′–3′. These irises are varieties derived from species native to the marshes of Louisiana. Their culture is almost opposite to that of bearded. They require fertile acid soil with an abundance of moisture and sun. Rhizomes must be protected from the sun with mulch. Their flat showy flowers offer a broad range of color.

Bulbous

These true perennial bulbs should be planted in the fall. They bloom in the spring and early summer. They are propagated by natural bulb division.

Dutch—Height 1½′ to 2′. Plant 4″ deep in slightly sandy, well-drained soil where they will receive several hours of sun a day. The arch-like flowers range in shades of blue, yellow, lavender, purple, and white. Bloom time is April.

Spanish—Height 1½′–2′. These irises bloom a few weeks after the Dutch irises. Colors range from blues, yellows, oranges to bronzes.

English—Height 1½′–2′. They are more difficult to grow than the Dutch and Spanish irises. They require moist, heavier soil, and less sun. Their colors are blues, pale lilacs, reddish purples, and white. Bloom time is June or July.

General Culture of Bearded Iris

Plenty of sun and good drainage. Raise bed if possible.

Soil requirements: Slightly sweet soil. If soil is acid, add lime.

Preparation of soil: Soil should be worked to a depth of 10″–12″; add bone meal and superphosphate, mixed with a helping of 5–10–10. If soil is exceptionally heavy, add sand. Mix several inches of soil and compost at the bottom of the hole, and allow for settling.

Planting: Early July through August. For best effect plant three rhizomes of the same variety in a clump. Dig a hole about 5″ deep, leaving a mound in the center. Place the rhizomes on the mound with the fans facing outward, spreading the roots on each side. Arrange the soil around the rhizomes leaving the top halves exposed. Firm the soil around the roots. Too-deep planting will prevent bloom. Iris will not tolerate mulch as sun is needed on rhizome to prevent rot.

Watering: Water after planting, and fairly frequently for two weeks until new root system is established. Watering will be needed only during dry spells.

Fertilizer: Iris will thrive without feeding, but will respond to a light sprinkling of 5–10–10 or bone meal around the rhizome in early spring and again 1 month after blooms fade. Do not overfertilize or overwater.

Dividing: For largest blooms, clumps should be divided every three or four years. Division may be done from early July through August. Break or cut apart at joints of healthy rhizomes and discard old ones. Wash with a hose and expose newly cut surface to the sun for several hours. Replant 8″–12″ apart with the leaf fan facing the same direction. Cut fan back to about 4″.

Diseases and Pests

Irises are quite resistant to diseases and pests. However, to prevent problems, beds should be kept clean of grass, dead foliage, and debris at all times. Old bloom stalks should be removed after bloom period.

Crown rot attacks the base of the plants, causing the leaf fans to disintegrate and fall over. Use a fungicide such as Terraclor. Follow directions carefully.

Soft rot (rhizome deterioration). Scrape out all of the infected tissue and dispose of it carefully. Cut scraped area on a slant, expose to sun, and pour a bleach such as Clorox over the wound.

Fungus leaf spot. Brown spots appear on leaf and often cause the entire leaf to turn brown and die. Remove dead and infected leaves and destroy. Spray plants and surrounding ground with a fungicide, such as Zineb or Captan. If this does not control it, generously dust plant and ground with a fungicide such as Terraclor.

Borer. This is a worm that hatches from eggs laid on old blossom stalks, debris in bed, etc. The borer eats its way through the leaf fan to the heart of the rhizome. Small holes and a wet appearance on the leaf may be an early indication. Kill worm if possible, clean bed, and dispose of debris. Spray plants and bed with a systemic poison such as Cygon. Follow directions very carefully. Consult local garden centers for all remedies.

PEONIES

Peonies are a handsome addition to the garden. They are a long lived, elegant flowered perennial which blooms in May. The fragrant flowers are excellent for cut material but when cutting, leave at least three leaves below the cut for the strength of the plant. For larger blooms for cutting, remove all but one bud per stem. Peonies range in color from white and pale yellow through shades of pinks and reds.

They prefer a cold climate but can be grown in the Mid-South. Success depends largely upon these factors—plenty of moisture, good drainage, deep preparation of soil, full sun, and a pH of 6.0–6.5. Late bloomers sometimes do not open well because of heat. Peonies usually take 3 to 5 years to mature to blooming size.

Planting

Peonies should be planted in the fall, late September to November for best results. Prepare a hole to a depth and width of 21″. Mix soil with compost and two handfuls of bone meal or milorganite. Avoid fresh manure. Plants should be set so the eyes are even with or 1″ below the soil. Allow soil to settle to avoid too deep planting. Plant in full sun or partial shade. Do not plant near large trees because of root invasion. Correctly planted they may be left undisturbed for many years.

When the leaves turn brown in the fall cut the stems to the ground. Gather up the debris and burn to prevent disease. Tree peonies should not be cut back. Do not mulch in winter because peonies should be allowed to freeze.

Diseases

Blight—Young shoots wilt and die or tips turn brown and die. Remove immediately all infected parts and burn. Spray with bordeaux mixture or a fungicide such as Manzate several times in the spring. Carefully remove all mulch in the spring. Cut all tops in the fall and destroy. This sanitation helps control blight and leaf spot. Continually remove all diseased parts. Crown rot is best controlled by good drainage.

Division

Divide in fall. Discard any soft roots and remove all old dirt. Wash off plant with a hose. With a sharp knife cut through the crown in sections of from 3 to 5 eyes, as new roots come from the eyes. Roots are very brittle. Avoid replanting where disease has occurred.

Fertilize

Peonies are heavy feeders. Put a cupful of bone meal or milorganite around each plant in March, August, and October, and a top-dressing of wood ashes in February. The size of the bloom may be increased by applying a commercial fertilizer such as 0–20–20 after buds have formed in the spring and also by disbudding in April.

Varieties

Chinese *(Paeonia lactiflora)*—Single, Japanese (or Anemone) peonies are beautiful in the garden because heads do not bend down in the rain. They are also good cut flowers. Doubles are lovely but need staking because of the weight of the flower heads.

Tree *(Paeonia suffruticosa)*—Single and semidouble, have woody growth above the ground, and do not die back in the fall.

ROSES

The rose is the queen of flowers. They come in all colors and many are fragrant. Rose bloom reaches a zenith during May and June, and again in August to early fall. However, many varieties bloom intermittently all summer. Points of absolute agreement among rose growers are:

1. They must have good drainage; a raised bed is best.
2. They require at least 8 to 10 hours of sun. Full sun is best.
3. They must be fertilized and watered.
4. They require disease and insect control.
5. They require pruning and mulching.

How to Make a Rose Bed

Pick a well-drained, sunny location. Prepare the bed in fall and let it rest until spring. Remove sod and dig 24″ deep. Mix 1 part coarse builder's sand, 1 part compost, 1 part well-rotted manure, and 1 part top soil. Roses prefer a heavy soil, mostly clay.

The pH should be 6.0 to 7.0. To raise acidity use a mixture of 3 buckets peat moss and 2 cups cottonseed meal or add powdered sulfur according to directions. If the soil is too acid, add ground limestone at a rate of 4 pounds per 100 square feet.

Planting

Buy roses from reputable nurseries. Members of the American Rose Society rate roses on a scale from 1 to 10. Look for these ratings on the tag that accompanies the rose bush. Two year old, field grown roses with at least 3 canes are preferred. Avoid spent greenhouse or waxed stem roses. If roots are dry, soak for several hours in a pail of water before planting.

Roses require firm planting. Dig a hole 2′ wide and 1½′ deep. Make a mound of soil in the center, placing the roots over it. Trim all roots which are damaged or too long for the hole without bending. Plant so that the graft is at least 1″ above ground level. Replace about one half of the soil and tamp firmly with hands as it is added, taking care not to injure the roots. Add water to settle the soil and finish filling the hole. Then mound 6″ of soil over the bud union to keep it from drying out and to protect it from a late cold snap. When new growth is about 1½″ long wash the excess soil away gently with a hose. Roses need good air circulation and plenty of room for roots to spread.

When to Plant

Roses may be moved in late November or December, but the preferred planting time is late February through March. Do not plant dormant plants after April 15th or plants in cans after May 15th.

Cultivating

Good housekeeping is the secret to good roses. The soil should be loosened after every heavy rain to keep from forming a crust. Remove and destroy all fallen leaves and petals. Cut off all dead flowers as soon as they fade. Seed heads should not be allowed to form.

Disbudding

Disbudding develops one full size flower to a stem from roses that bloom in clusters. Remove all but the dominant, central flower bud from each cluster. This makes the flower grow larger. On hybrid teas, remove any bud below the terminal bud for specimen blooms. Remove the largest and smallest bud from a floribunda cluster for specimen clusters.

Pruning

Pruning is an all year job. In fall, after the first frost, cut back all long growth to keep the wind from rocking plants loose in the soil. In February cut back all dead wood, crossed canes, and weedy growth. Suckers (fast-growing shoots growing from below the graft) should be removed completely by breaking them off below the soil where they are connected to the trunk. Remove about ½ to ⅓ of last year's growth. Roses may be cut back very lightly in early July to promote fall bloom.

Keep the center of the bush open by removing blind shoots, crossed canes, and branches with yellow, sick leaves. Cut off lower leaves about 8″ from the ground to let in air and make it easier to water. Do not prune strong roses as hard as weak ones. Paint cut ends with tree paint to prevent the invasion of stem borers.

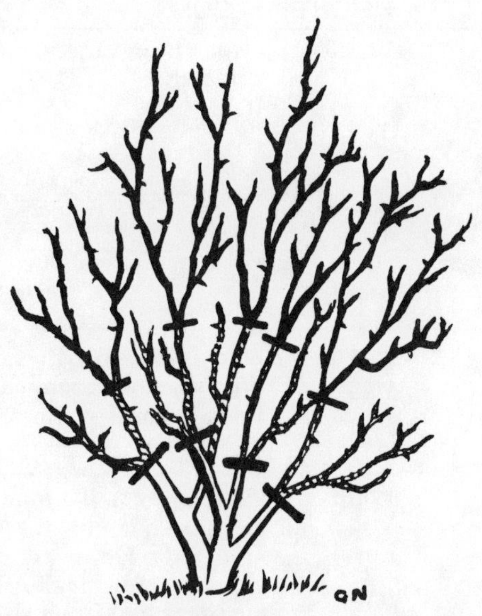

On large-flowered climbing roses prune out old, dead, and diseased wood. Remove the spent flowers. Climbing roses are vigorous growers in full sun and may need to be kept in bounds.

Cutting Roses

Remember that cutting roses helps in the pruning of the plant. Each correct cutting produces more roses. Always cut roses at a 45° angle toward the center of the rose bush. Cut ¼″ above an outward-ing facing leaf which has 5 or 6 leaflets. Cut first year roses with short stems because foliage is needed for plant growth.

Water

Water roses twice a week if it does not rain. Thorough soaking is better than frequent sprinklings. Water in the morning and avoid wetting the foliage in the afternoon to prevent black spot.

Winter Protection

Cover rose bushes with 6″ or 7″ of soil in fall. After the first hard freeze, cover the soil with a layer of leaves held in place by evergreen branches, wire netting, or other light material. Do not do this too soon.

ROSES

NAME	HEIGHT	BLOOM
Climbing	10′–50′	Depends on variety, many bloom all summer.
Floribunda	2′–4′ average	Blooms are somewhat smaller than hydrid tea, single, semi-double or double. Usually borne in clusters. Most bloom all summer.
Grandiflora	8′–10′	Blooms prolifically from spring to frost. Produces quantities of flowers like a floribunda. Flowers usually clustered, but sometimes single. They often have the shape and larger size of the hybrid tea.
Hybrid Tea	2½′–7′ but most are 3′–5′ tall	Flowers are double, often fragrant on long, straight stems. Long lasting blossoms good for cutting. Most beautiful of all roses.
Miniature	4″–13″	Some have solitary flowers. Others bear clusters of flowers. Most are not fragrant. Many bloom all summer.
Old Fashioned	3′–10′, depending on variety	Very fragrant. Often blooms in early summer, generally only once.
Polyantha	3′–4′	Clusters of small blooms. Blooms in spring and intermittently during summer. Very few are fragrant.

COMMENTS	PRUNING
Train horizontally for more profuse blooms. Climbing roses do not climb naturally. They must be trained and tied to supports. Unsupported climbers are hybrid teas, Floribundas and Grandifloras.	Remove all dead or weak wood. In summer as soon as flowers fade, shorten laterals (flowering stems originating from main canes) to 3½″ to 6″. Be sure to cut to a twig containing 5 or 6 leaves. Varieties which bloom only once should have some of the older, dark canes cut back to the base. Do not let seed pods form on climbers.
Hardy, prolific bloomer. Used as an informal hedge. Compact bush good in the perennial border. Most are low growing.	Remove twiggy interior growth. Keep 6 to 8 canes and try to leave the bush open with enough room for flower clusters to develop.
Tall vigorous bush which is extremely hardy. Use as tall hedge or background plant.	Allow grandifloras to grow to their full size. After pruning in February, their cane height is about 3′ to 4′ and may support as many as 8 structural canes.
Should be in a bed for roses alone.	Keep 3 to 6 strong, good canes. Canes should be well spaced to allow good air circulation. Remove old nonproducing canes at the bud union.
Natural dwarfs; good for edging in beds, and rock gardens, and as house plants. Hardy. Need 6 hours of sun, but some shade is desirable. Plant a little below nursery level (they have not been grafted) to promote root development.	Maintenance varies with the variety. Most miniatures should be pruned to within 2″ of the ground in February.
Hardy, little maintenance, not as beautiful as newer varieties. Hard to find.	Similar to hybrid tea.
Very hardy, small leaves on compact plant. Can resist some drought conditions.	Cut polyanthas back by one-third.

ROSES

NAME	HEIGHT	BLOOM
Shrub	6′–8′	Many are single. Most are fragrant. Not as much color variety as others. Older varieties bloom only once. New varieties bloom all summer.
Tree Roses	Up to 5′ depending on type	Depends on variety.

Fertilizer

February: Mulch the bed with well-rotted manure or compost 3″ thick. Try to use manure which is free from nut grass. *March or April:* Lime the bed with a commercial agricultural lime. *During Growing Season:* once or twice a month put commercial rose food around each bush, using the recommended amount. Work in lightly and water. Then spray every 2 weeks with a commercial rose spray containing a fungicide and insecticide. Do not fertilize new bushes until after they have bloomed. Alternatively, a timed-release rose fertilizer containing a systemic insecticide to control chewing insects may be applied to the soil in early spring and repeated every 6 weeks or so until August 10. When using a time-release fertilizer a foliar feeding should be added in March and repeated each month if needed until August 10. This method saves time, but follow directions carefully because systemics are dangerous and fertilizers burn. Do not overfertilize. Water roses deeply to enable the fertilizer to enter the soil and reach the entire root system. *July:* Apply 3″ mulch (cow or horse manure or compost is best). Stop feeding roses in August. *November:* Repeat mulch.

Pests and Sprays

One can simplify rose care by using one of the commercial rose

COMMENTS	PRUNING
Tough, tolerates poor soil, good for hedges. Disease resistant.	When young, prune only to shape, When mature, cut twiggy growth and very old, dark canes. Shorten other canes by one-third in February.
Man-made grafted plants. Hybrid tea and grandiflora are most popular types. They are good for formal gardens and are very elegant. Trunk must be wrapped or painted with water base paint to protect from hot summer sun. In winter, partially uproot the plant, lay it on its side and cover with soil, held in place by evergreen branches. They must be planted with a support stake. Place stake on hottest side (south or west).	Remove any growth from the trunk which is below the upper bud union.

sprays or dusts especially formulated for roses. These contain 3 or 4 fungicides and insecticides to control most common rose diseases and pests. If using a commerical rose dust instead of a liquid, be sure to apply it early in the morning while the dew is still on the roses. Spray with a dormant rose spray containing lime sulphur in November before mounding with soil for winter protection and again in February. The February spray is essential.

Pests and Fungus

Aphids and Chewing Insects: Make a spray of 1 tsp. liquid dishwashing soap per gallon of water or use an insecticide such as Malathion. *Black spot:* Leaves have black, rounded spots. Pick off infected leaves and burn. Spray once a week with a fungicide such as Maneb or Benomyl. *Crown gall:* When the plant has not flourished, digging will reveal large spongy growths at the soil level. Remove soil from the hole and replace it. Throw away plant and soil. *Mildew:* Leaves and shoots have whitish covering. Use a fungicide such as Benomyl or sulfur. *Stem borers:* Watch for holes at the end of the stem. Cut off stem past the borer and burn it. Paint the end with tree paint. *Thrips:* Nearly invisible; flowers are malformed and buds turn brown and do not open. Spray flowers with an insecticide such as Malathion.

The Flower Border

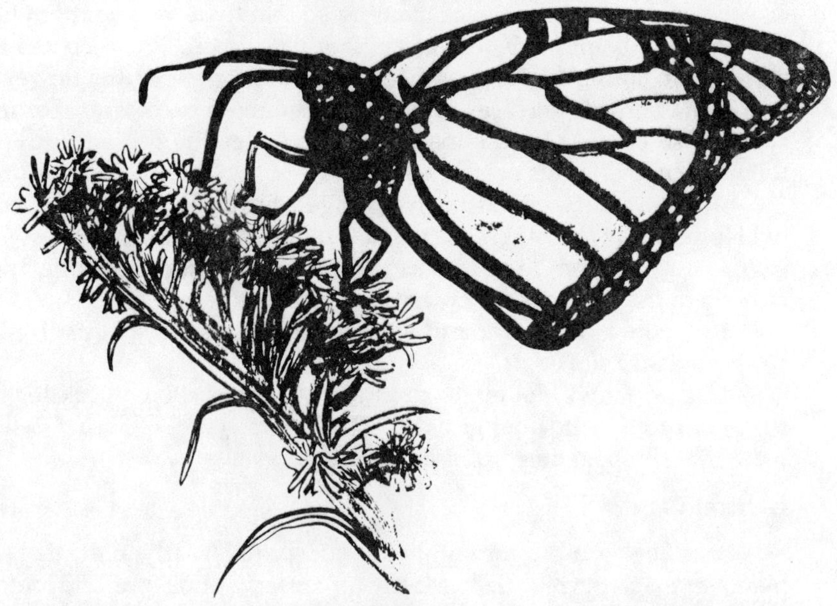

Perennials form the backbone of the flower border. The term perennial is somewhat misleading, since in some areas many of them die back in the late summer to reemerge the following year.

In order to have an interesting border which is seldom without bloom, plant long blooming, easily managed perennials with the addition of well chosen annuals, biennials, and a few bulbs for variety. Consider the following suggestions in planning an attractive flower border:

1) Provide a strong background: a shrubbery border, a wall or fence, or the side of the house.

2) Plan the area on paper first. Consult the following charts for color, height, bloom time, and spacing.

3) Emphasize the reliable perennials such as peonies, iris, daylilies, lilies, phlox, and chrysanthemums. Let annuals and other perennials play secondary roles. A few plants with short bloom time but spectacular flowers, such as oriental poppies, should also be considered. In limited spaces omit perennials whose foliage disappears completely after flowering and those which are rampant growers.

4) Plants should be placed in groups of three or more, repeated at rhythmic intervals throughout the border. In general, place taller flowers at the back.

5) Make the border wide enough (suggested width, 5′–6′) to accommodate several depths of planting so that there will be room for one group of plants to bloom as another dies down. Allow spaces to walk in the border to stake, trim, etc. without trampling the flowers. In narrow borders one-season plantings are more successful. For instance, use peonies for the main show and edge the bed with tulips followed by marigolds or periwinkle.

6) Choose plants with attractive foliage which look good in and out of bloom. Leave the others for the cutting bed.

7) Plan color from front to back, starting in the front in spring and moving to the back of the bed as the season continues.

8) Keep the border neat and sharply edged with the plants firmly supported and staked.

9) Cut off faded blooms to promote new ones. Pinch back leggy stems to promote bushier growth.

10) *See* "Propagation" for seed planting.

General Care

Water—Soak ground throughly (do not sprinkle) early in the day so plants are dry by nightfall. Mulch to conserve moisture and deter weeds.

Fertilize—Too much nitrogen causes luxuriant foliage and few blooms. When preparing the bed dig in 3–4 oz. of 0–20–20 per 100 square feet. For established beds give each established clump a handful of 5–10–5 once in early spring and again 4 to 6 weeks later. Alternate using organic and chemical fertilizers. In general use natural fertilizer (compost, dried cow manure, fish emulsion, bone meal) for long-range care, commercial fertilizers for quick pickups.

Cultivation—Cultivated perennials grow faster. Cultivate shallowly once in early spring and again 4–6 weeks later. Use a forklike tool with tines. Cultivate to a depth of 1″ to 2″ between groups of plants and individual plants.

Pest and Disease—A garden that is not overcrowded, that is clean of debris and infected plants, and is properly fed and watered is relatively troublefree. If problems arise, use products which control specific insects and diseases (*See* "Garden Care"). Avoid powerful broad spectrum insecticides that destroy beneficial as well as harmful insects. *Read all labels and follow directions carefully.*

HELPFUL HINTS

1. Designing and making beds and borders: For straight lines follow a string stretched between stakes. For irregular lines and curves, outline the bed with a hose, and then dig along its edges.

2. Mark all dormant plants and bulbs with a stake or label to avoid injuring or digging them up when working the bed.

3. How to kill nut grass: Remove all plants from infected bed. Cover with two layers of black plastic. Leave for 2 years or 2 summers. For faster results, use a weed killer such as Roundup. Follow directions carefully. Do not use close to shrubs or trees.

4. Rule of Thumb: Bloom in the spring, divide in the fall. Bloom in the fall, divide in the spring.

5. Rooting: Place several willow branches in water for 2 days. Remove. Willow water encourages cuttings to root.

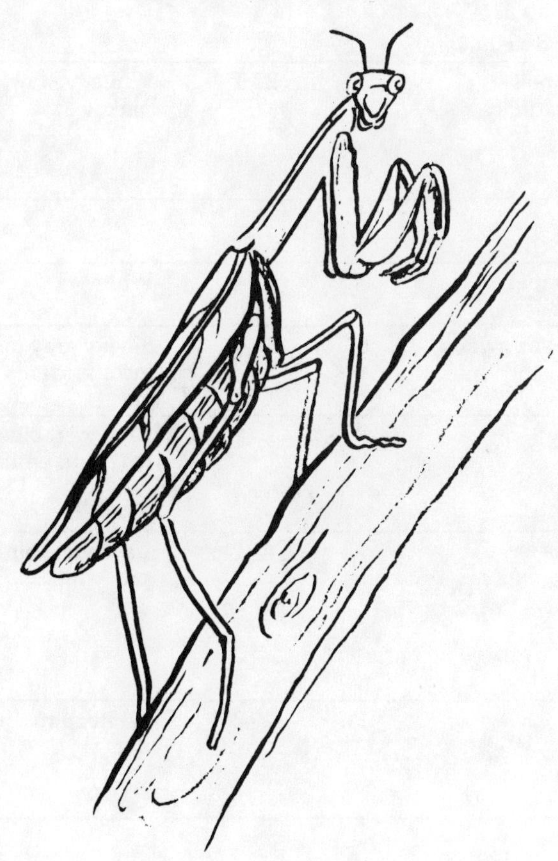

ANNUAL, BIENNIAL AND PERENNIAL FLOWERS

KEY
Annual—A plant that lives for one year or season.
Biennial—A plant that produces roots and leaves one year and blooms the following year, then dies.
Perennial—A plant lasting for more than two years' growth.

COMMON NAME SCIENTIFIC NAME	KEY	HEIGHT	COLOR
African Daisy *See* Daisy	A		
Ageratum *Ageratum*	A	3″–2′	Blue, pink
A. houstonianum	A	3″–2′	Blue (pink or white less common)
Ageratum, hardy Mist Flower *Eupatorium coelestinum*	P	1½′–3′	Blue
Alyssum, sweet *Lobularia maritima*	A	2″–9″	White, yellow, lavender, pink
Anchusa *See* Bugloss	A		
Angel's trumpet *Datura inoxia*	A	1′–4′	White
Artemisia (Wormwood) *Artemisia*	P	3′–4′	Silvery gray foliage; rather inconspicuous white flowers
Aster, hardy *Aster*	P	1′–5′	Lavender, blue, pink, rose, and white
Aster, China *Callistephus chinensis*	A	8″–2½′	Lavender, pink, red, purple, white
Astilbe *Astilbe*	P	2′–3′	White, pink, red, lavender

SPACE APART	BLOOM TIME	COMMENTS
8″–12″	all summer	Sun. Well-drained soil. Good cut flower.
6″–9″	all summer	Start seeds indoors 6–8 weeks before last frost. Sun, but tolerates partial shade. Also dwarf variety.
1½′–2′	late summer to late fall	Sun; will tolerate partial shade. Any soil. Native to eastern U.S.
6″–8″	summer to late fall	Sun; tolerates partial shade. Any soil. Shear to prolong bloom. Sow seeds early spring outdoors, inside 6–8 weeks before last frost. Rock garden, edging, hanging baskets.
2′	summer	Sun. Rich, rather dry soil. Opens at night; rank. Fragrant. Self-sows.
12″–18″	mid to late summer	Sun or partial shade. Any soil. Needs moisture, good drainage. Valued for feathery, aromatic foliage.
8″–18″	all summer	Sun. Average soil, not too rich. Sow seeds or set out plants of named varieties in early spring. Divide most varieties every other spring.
12″	Sept.–Nov.	Sun to part shade. Moderately rich alkaline soil. Work wood ashes into soil. Choose wilt-resistant varieties. Start in cold frame or indoors 6 weeks before last frost. Use insecticide for leaf hoppers. Good cut flower.
15″–18″	May–June	Partial shade; tolerates sun. Rich moist soil with humus. Multiplies rapidly. Divide spring and fall every two years.

ANNUAL, BIENNIAL AND PERENNIAL FLOWERS

COMMON NAME SCIENTIFIC NAME	KEY	HEIGHT	COLOR
Baby's-breath *Gypsophila paniculata* (P)	P/A	2′–3′	White, pink
G. elegans (A)		12″–18″	White, pink
Bachelor's button *See* Cornflower	A		
Balloon Flower *Platycodon grandiflorus*	P	1′–2½′	blue, white
Balsam *Impatiens balsamina*	A	6″–2′	White, salmon, pink, red
Baptisia *See* False Indigo	P		
Beard-tongue *Penstemon*	P	12″–18″	Pink, red, white
Bee Balm Bergamot *Monarda didyma*	P	2′–3′	Red, rose pink
Begonia *Begonia semperflorens*	A	6″–9″	Pink, white, red
Begonia, hardy *B. grandis (B. evansiana)*	A	18″–24″	Pink
Bellflower (P) *Campanula*	P/B	10″–18″	White, blue, lavender, purple
Bergenia *Bergenia cordifolia*	P	12″ up	Pink, white
Black-eyed Susan *See* Daisy, Black-eyed Susan	A/P		
Blanketflower *Gaillardia*	A/P	18″ (A) 8″–2′ (P)	Yellow, red, orange, bicolored

SPACE APART	BLOOM TIME	COMMENTS
18″–24″	June–July	Sun. Alkaline soil, not too rich. Good cut flower.
8″–12″	June–July	Same as above.
12″	June–October	Sun or partial shade. Good drainage. Easily grown from seed sown in garden in early spring.
6″–12″	June–October	Sun. Rich, light, moist soil. Often self-sows. Sow seeds in garden after last frost.
12″–15″	June–July	Sun. Acid soil with humus. Good drainage. Sensitive to winter moisture. Good cut flower.
12″	May–June	Sun or partial shade. Moist, well-drained soil with humus. Remove faded flowers to prolong blooming. Attracts bees and hummingbirds. Good cut flower.
6″–8″	all summer until frost	Partial shade. Rich moist soil. Buy young plants in spring. Bring in house for winter bloom. Cuttings will root for summer bloom.
6″–8″	August–November	Partial shade. Showy, red-lined foliage, small flowers. Will bloom where nothing else will.
10″–12″	early summer until frost, depending on variety	Sun or partial shade. Almost any well-drained garden soil. Large family, great variations in size. For border or rock garden. Reliable.
12″–15″	March–April	Partial shade. Any soil. Decorative foliage, clusters of flowers on nodding stems. Leave undisturbed.
8″ (A) 10″ (P)	early summer to frost	Sun. Light sandy soil. Tolerates dry conditions. Easy to grow, true perennial. Large daisylike flowers. Good cut flower.

ANNUAL, BIENNIAL AND PERENNIAL FLOWERS

COMMON NAME SCIENTIFIC NAME	KEY	HEIGHT	COLOR
Blazing-star Gay-feather *Liatris*	P	18″–3′	White, purple
Bleeding-heart *Dicentra spectabilis*	P	2½′–3′	Pink
D. eximia		1′–2′	Pink
Bluebells *Campanula rotundifolia*	A/P	2′–3′	White, blue
Browallia *Browallia*	A	12″–18″	Blue, white
Bugloss *Anchusa*	B/P	3′–4′	Blue
Butterfly weed *Asclepias tuberosa*	P	18″	Orange, yellow
Calendula Pot Marigold *Calendula officinalis*	A	12″–15″	Yellow, orange
Candytuft *Iberis sempervirens*	P	6″–9″	White
Globe Candytuft *I. umbellata*	A	7″–12″	White, lavender, pink
Canterbury-bells *Campanula medium*	B	2′–3′	White, blue, pink
Cape Forget-me-not *Anchusa capensis*	B/A	18″	Blue
Cardinal flower *Lobelia cardinalis*	P	2′–3′	Red
Carnation *Dianthus caryophyllus*	A/P	1½′–2′	White, yellow, orange, pink, lavender
Chinese-lantern *Physalis alkekengi*	A	1′–2′	Orange pod
Christmas rose *Helleborus niger*	P	12″–15″	White to greenish

SPACE APART	BLOOM TIME	COMMENTS
12″–15″	mid to late summer. June–August	Sun. Ordinary garden soil. Several varieties.
12″–18″	spring	Partial shade to shade. Good garden soil.
8″	spring, summer	Same as above. Native
12″–15″	early summer to fall	Sun. Dependable.
8″–10″	June to frost	Sun, partial shade. Moderately rich soil. Pinch for compact growth. Easy to grow, self-sows. Bring inside and cut back for winter bloom. Buy young plants or start indoors 6–8 weeks before last frost. Prefers cool nights.
12″–15″	April	Partial shade to sun. Very hardy. Cut back for fall bloom.
8″–12″	June–July	Sun. Any soil. Endangered species. Do not transplant from the wild.
12″	summer	Sun. Fertile soil. Cool growing weather; will not tolerate heat.
12″	April–May	Mounds of tiny flowers. Sun. Nice evergreen plant for edging beds. Prefers cool nights.
12″	spring–summer	Sun or partial shade. Same as above.
12″–18″	June–July	Partial shade. Rich soil. Keep faded blooms pinched off for new bloom.
12″–15″	May	Partial shade. Flower clusters; self-sows.
12″	summer	Partial shade. Moist soil. Endangered species.
12″–18″	early summer–fall	Sun. Good cut flower. Prefers cool nights. Dwarf varieties for bedding plants.
2′	summer	Sun; partial shade. Good for drying.
12″–15″	late winter–early spring	Partial shade. Rich, moist soil. Should not be disturbed once established.

ANNUAL, BIENNIAL AND PERENNIAL FLOWERS

COMMON NAME SCIENTIFIC NAME	KEY	HEIGHT	COLOR
Chrysanthemum *See* "Popular Plants"	P		
Cleome *Cleome*	A	3′–5′	Pink, white, lavender
Cockscomb *Celosia cristata*	A	1′–3′	red, yellow, magenta, orange
Coleus *Coleus blumei*	A	6″–2′	Multihued leaf
Columbine *Aquilegia*	A/P	2′–2½′	Many colors and hybrids
Coneflower *Rudbeckia*	A/P	2′–2½′	Yellow, with dark center
Coreopsis *Coreopsis grandiflora*	A	1′–3′	Yellow
Coralbells *Heuchera sanguinea*	P	12″–18″	Dainty pink, red, white, lime green
Cornflower Bachelor's-button *Centaurea cyanus*	A/P	2′	True blue, pink, rose, white
Cosmos *Cosmos*	A	3′–4′	Lavender, pink, white, yellow, orange
Daffodils *See* "Bulbs"			
Dahlias *See* "Popular Plants"			
Daisy *Chrysanthemum leucanthemum*	P	2′	White
Daisy, English *Bellis perennis*	B/A	6″	White, pink
Daisy, Gloriosa *Rudbeckia gloriosa*	A/P	2′–3′	Yellow, gold, orange, mahogany
Daisy Black-eyed Susan *Rudbeckia hirta*	A/P	24″	Yellow with black or brown center

SPACE APART	BLOOM TIME	COMMENTS
10″	June–October	Sun. Rank. Self-sows; good cut flower. Several varieties.
8″–12″	summer	Sun. Compact or feathered head. Good for drying; dry by hanging upside down.
8″–10″	summer	Partial shade. Plant for foliage; unattractive flower, keep pinched off. Good bedding plant.
To 2½′	spring	Partial shade. Moist sandy loam. Feathery foliage, good cut flower. Do not overmulch.
12″–15″	midsummer to midfall	Sun. Several varieties.
12″	summer	Sun. Rank. Good for cutting. Many varieties, including dwarf.
18″	spring	Sun. Good garden soil. Neat edging plant.
12″–18″	summer	Sun. Pick to continue bloom; good for cutting.
12″	July–November	Sun. Poor soil. Good for cutting; keep picked.
12″	May–June	Sun. Field daisy. Good cut flower. Reproduces rapidly.
8″	spring	Sun or partial shade. Will not tolerate extreme heat. Good for border. Seed in fall for spring bloom.
12″–15″	July–September	Sun or partial shade. Cut to encourage bloom. Single and double.
12″	summer	Sun. Many varieties; good cut flower.

ANNUAL, BIENNIAL AND PERENNIAL FLOWERS

COMMON NAME SCIENTIFIC NAME	KEY	HEIGHT	COLOR
Daisy, Shasta *Chrysanthemum maximum*	P	1′–2′	White
Daisy, Transvaal or Gerbera *Gerbera jamesonii*	A	18″	White, pink, salmon, red, violet
Delphinium *Delphinium*	P	3′–4′	Blue, white, pink
Dollar plant Silver dollar, Honesty *Lunaria annua*	B	2′	Pink, white
Dusty-miller *Centaurea gymnocarpa*	P	1′	Silver foliage
False Dragonhead *Physostegia virginiana*	P	2′–4′	Pink, white
False Indigo *Baptisia australis*	P	3′	Blue
B. tinctoria		2′–3′	Yellow
Flax *Linum*	P	18″	Blue
Flowering Tobacco *Nicotiana alata grandiflora*	A	12″–18″	White to scarlet and off shades
Forget-me-not *Myosotis scorpioides semperflorens*	B	8″	Blue, pink, white
M. sylvatica		8″–24″	Blue, pink, white
Four-o'clock *Mirabilis jalapa*	A	2′–3′	Multi
Foxglove *Digitalis*	B	2′–3′	White, pink, purple, yellow
Funkia *See* Plantain Lily	P		

SPACE APART	BLOOM TIME	COMMENTS
12″	June–October	Sun. Many varieties. Large clumps need dividing.
2″–12″	all summer	Sun. Not hardy in cold winters.
12″	summer	Sun. Will not tolerate heat; prefers cool nights. See Larkspur for substitute, also Baptisia. Treat as an annual in the Mid-South.
1′	late spring, early summer	Sun. Grown for flat translucent center of seed pods; good for arrangements.
10″	summer	Average soil. Sun. Grown for attractive foliage. Border plants.
15″–18″	late summer–early fall	Sun or shade. Flower spikes 8″–10″. Easily grown.
2′–3′	mid-spring	Sun or partial shade. Can be substituted for delphinium and lupine in hot climates. Pinch faded flowers to extend bloom time.
2′	midspring, early summer	Sun, partial shade. Lupinelike bloom.
12″	May–October	Sun, partial shade. Several varieties; prefers cool nights.
12″–18″	May–June	Sun to partial shade. Well-drained soil. Do not divide. Dwarf "Nicki Series" excellent.
9″–12″	summer	Sun, partial shade. Cool and damp climate. Clusters of tiny flowers.
9″–12″	summer	Same as above.
12″	summer	Sun. Rich, well-drained soil.
18″	early summer	Sun or partial shade; shade in hot areas. Tall spike flowers. Plant seed in July, leave in cold frame until February. Worth the trouble it takes to grow.

ANNUAL, BIENNIAL AND PERENNIAL FLOWERS

COMMON NAME SCIENTIFIC NAME	KEY	HEIGHT	COLOR
Gas plant *Dictamnus albus*	P	2′–3′	Pinkish to purple, white
Geum *Geum*	P	12″ plant 18″ flower stem	Bright orange, red, yellow
Gladioli *See* "Bulbs"			
Globe Thistle *Echinops sphaerocephalus*	P	5′	Bluish gray
Gloriosa Daisy *See* Daisy, Gloriosa			
Goatsbeard *Aruncus*	P	2′–3′	White, pink
Hollyhock *Alcea rosea*	A/B	5′–9′	White, yellow, pink, red, lavender to near black
Hosta *See* Plaintain Lily			
Impatiens *I. sultana*	A	Up to 18″	White, pink, red, magenta, salmon
Jewels-of-Opar *Talinum paniculatum*	A	2′	Tiny, orange buds. Tiny hot pink flower on spike
Jupiter's beard *Centranthus ruber*	P	2′–3′	White, pink, red
Lantana Polecat geranium *Lantana montevidensis*	A	12″–15″	Orange, pink, yellow, red, white
Larkspur *Consolida*	A	1′–3′	White, blue, lavender, pink
Lenten Rose *Helleborus orientalis*	P	12″–15″	White, lavender, green

SPACE APART	BLOOM TIME	COMMENTS
3′–4′	early summer	Sun. Best if left undisturbed. Shiny dark green leaves, lemon scented. Flower spikes 10″–12″ mature in 3 years. Good cut flower, seed pods attractive in dried arrangements.
12″	midspring to midsummer	Sun. Good garden soil. Several varieties.
2′	summer	Sun. Globular flower heads; dark green, prickly leaves. Long-lived, heat and drought tolerant.
18″–24″	early summer	Sun, partial shade. Rose family.
1′	summer	Sun. Rich soil. Single, double, fringed or ruffled flowers. Plant seed in open ground in June or July for following year's bloom.
6″–10″	summer	Shade; New Zealand variety tolerates sun. Reseeds. Can be repotted to hold for following year and winter blooms.
18″	all summer	Partial shade. Any soil. Good filler for arrangements. Self-sows.
12″–15″	early summer–midfall	Sun or partial shade. Good for cutting; cut to encourage blooms. Fragrant flowers. Dependable.
12″	summer	Sun. Rank. Good for training into standard in container; bring indoors before frost. Good for border. Many varieties, some trailing. Subject to white fly.
8″–12″	spring–early summer	Sun. Prefers cool evenings. Annual species of delphinium.
18″	early to mid spring	Partial shade, moist neutral humusy soil. Evergreen.

ANNUAL, BIENNIAL AND PERENNIAL FLOWERS

COMMON NAME SCIENTIFIC NAME	KEY	HEIGHT	COLOR
Lily *See* "Bulbs"			
Loosestrife *See* Lythrum			
Love-in-a-mist *Nigella damascena*	A	12″	Deep to pale blue, white, pink
Lythrum *Lythrum*	P	2′ up	Pink magenta
Marigold *Tagetes*	A	6″–3′	Orange, yellow, brown
Mexican Sunflower *Tithonia rotundifolia*	A	to 6′	Rich orange
Nasturtium *Tropaeolum majus*	A	8″	Yellow to mahogany
Nicotiana *See* Flowering Tobacco			
Painted-tongue *Salpiglossis sinuata*	A	2′–3′	Red, purple, blue
Pansy *Viola*	B	6″–8″	Multi
Peony *See* "Popular Plants"	P		
Periwinkle *Catharanthus roseus*	A	to 18″	Pink, white

SPACE APART	BLOOM TIME	COMMENTS
8″	summer	Sun. Good for cutting. Feathery foliage.
18″	summer	Sun. Newer varieties avoid old magenta color.
12″	summer to frost	Sun. Many varieties. Heat tolerant, dependable.
3′	summer to frost	Sun. Good cut flower, var. "Torch" recommended.
8″	summer	Sun. Prefers cool evenings. Pick to encourage bloom. Does not like to be transplanted. Soak seeds before planting.
1′	summer	Sun, partial shade. Leaves rich, velvety texture, subtle shades. Good for cutting.
8″	early spring to midsummer	If pansies are being grown from seed, plant in cold frame or seed bed in late August. Let them remain there until late October, then transplant to their permanent location in the garden. Pansies like a well-drained soil, rich in humus. To bloom well they must have some sun, but will last longer in the spring if they are shaded for part of the day. A light dose of commercial fertilizer, once during the winter and again in early spring, greatly increases the vigor of the plant. Good plants may be purchased locally and planted out in the garden any time from October to March when the weather permits. Mulch lightly when starting. Bloom will be prolonged if picked frequently.
8″	summer to frost	Sun to part shade. Any soil. Good bedding plant.

ANNUAL, BIENNIAL AND PERENNIAL FLOWERS

COMMON NAME SCIENTIFIC NAME	KEY	HEIGHT	COLOR
Petunia *Petunia*	A	To 1′	All colors
Phlox *Phlox divaricata*	P	12″	Lavender, blue
P. drummondii	P	6″–1½′	Pink to scarlet yellow, lavender, white
Garden Phlox *P. paniculata*	P	1′–4′	Magenta, white, blue
Moss Phlox, Moss Pink, Ground Pink *P. subulata*	P	6″	Magenta, white, blue
Pink Sweet William *Dianthus barbatus*	P	1½′–2′	Pink to yellow
China Pink *D. chinensis*	A	6″–12″	Pink, scarlet to white
Plantain lily *Hosta* or *Funkia* *Hosta ventricosa*	P	18″–24″	Pale or deep blue
H. decorata		18″–24″	Lavender to white
H. fortunei		18″–24″	Lavender
H. minor alba		10″	White
H. plantaginea grandiflora		18″–24″	White
H. variegata		18″–28″	Lavender
Poppy *Papaver orientale*	P	24″–30″	Flamboyant pink, scarlet to orange
Portulaca Purslane *Portulaca grandiflora* (Moss Rose)	A	6″	Red, pink, white, orange
Queen Anne's Lace *See* "Wild Flowers"	P		
Rattlebox *Crotalaria*	A	18″–24″	Yellow
Red-hot-poker *Kniphofia uvaria*	P	2′–3′	Orange to yellow
Rose, *See* "Popular Plants"	P		

SPACE APART	BLOOM TIME	COMMENTS
10″	summer	Sun. Indispensable bedding flower; keep pinched back.
12″	early spring	Partial shade.
8″	summer	Sun. Grows in masses, good ground cover for lilies. Self-sows.
2′	summer	Sun
6″–8″	early spring	Sun. Creeping
12″–18″	summer	Sun. Well-drained alkaline soil. Clove-scented flowers.
8″	summer	Sun. Well-drained alkaline soil. Clove-scented, single or semidouble flowers.
12″–24″	September	Partial shade. All subject to slugs.
12″–24″	August–September	Shade. Green leaves with white border.
18″	June	Partial shade.
18″–24″	August	Partial shade.
18″–24″	August	Partial shade. Fragrant.
18″–24″	July	Green and white variegated foliage.
12″	May	Sun. Plant seeds in fall; difficult to transplant. Good drainage essential.
6″–12″	all summer	Warm, sunny location. Plant in masses in dry spots where nothing else will grow. Flowers close at night.
12″	late summer	Sun. Rich soil. Spike flowers resembling lupine; good for cutting. Needs long growing season; plant seeds and do not disturb.
1½′–2′	summer–fall	Sun. Well-drained soil. Attracts hummingbirds.

ANNUAL, BIENNIAL AND PERENNIAL FLOWERS

COMMON NAME SCIENTIFIC NAME	KEY	HEIGHT	COLOR
Salvia Sage *Salvia farinacea*	P	3′	Azure, white
S. splendens	A	18″	Red, purple
Scabiosa Pincushion flower *Scabiosa caucasica*	P	to 2′	Blue, lavender
Sedum Stonecrop *Sedum spectabile*	P	2′	Ivory, pink to red
Snapdragon *Antirrhinum majus*	A	6″–4′	Every color but blue
Spider flower *Cleome spinosa*	A	5″	Pink, white, orchid
Stokes' Aster *Stokesia laevis*	P	12″–18″	Blue, lavender, white
Sunflower *Helianthus annuus*	A	12′–15′	Yellow
Sweet pea *Lathyrus odoratus*	A	8″–10″	Pastels
Sweet William *See* Pinks			
Torch-lily *See* Red-hot-poker	P		
Tulip *See* "Bulbs"			
Verbena *Verbena*	A	10″	Pink, red, blue, lavender, purple
Violet *See* "Wild Flowers"			
Wishbone flower *Torenia*	B	8″–10″	Blue
Yarrow *Achillea*	P	3′	Yellow, pink, white
Zinnia *Zinnia*	A	6″-3′	Multi

SPACE APART	BLOOM TIME	COMMENTS
18″	summer	Sun. Good for cutting. Var: Blue Bedder, White Bedder.
12″	summer	Sun. Red attracts hummingbirds.
8″	summer	Sun. Fertile, well-drained soil. Remove faded flowers for extended bloom.
18″–24″	late summer to fall.	Sun. Also see "Ground Covers." Many other varieties.
6″–12″	summer	Sun. Good soil. Likes cool evenings. Good for cutting. Three heights, tall must be staked. Single and double versions; see catalogues.
2′	summer	Sun. Good cut flower, pungent. Profuse seeder.
12″–15″	summer	Sun. Well-drained soil. Good for cutting. *See* Wild Flowers.
2′	summer	Common sun flower. Super bird food.
8″	summer	Sun; prefers cool evenings. Rich soil. Dwarf or climbing varieties; climbers must be supported.
12″	summer	Sun. Fertile soil. Profuse bloomers; good bedding plant.
10″	summer	Sun. Good for bedding; used to replace pansy. Self-sows.
12″	summer	Sun. Pungent; good for drying. Several varieties.
8″	summer	Sun. Good cut flowers; many varieties; see catalogues. Water at ground level to avoid mildew.

Herbs and Vegetables

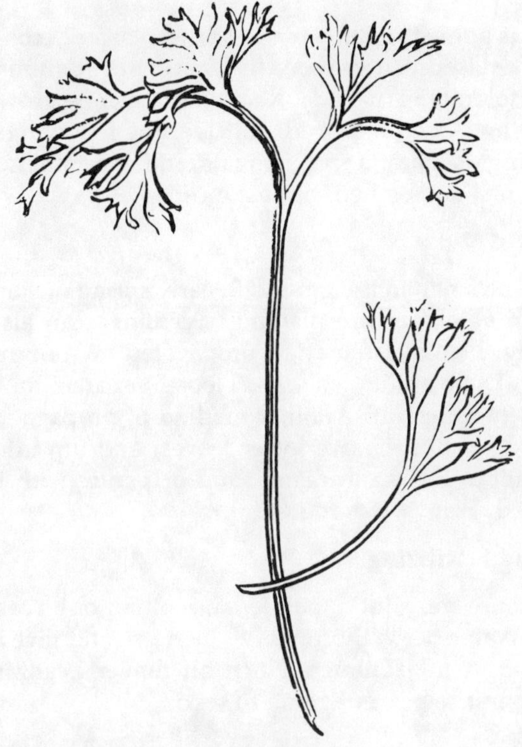

HERBS

Botanists consider any plant that dies to the ground after the growing season an herb. In ancient times any plant that was not a tree or a bush was called an herb. Today herbs are considered any small useful plant that is nonwoody. They can be perennial, biennial, or annual. Until this century herbs were extensively used for medicinal purposes. Today they are also used for food seasoning, scents, decorative appearance in a flower border, cosmetics, dyes, and insect repellants. Both "herb" and "erb" are acceptable pronunciations.

Cultivation

Soil should be porous, slightly sandy, and on the neutral side. An ideal mixture is 4 parts top soil, 3 parts vermiculite or perlite, 1 part peat moss or compost, and 2 big handfuls of agricultural lime. Most herbs like a midsummer application of 5–10–5 fertilizer (¾ lb. per 100 square feet).

Drainage is a must for all herbs. For this reason herbs planted on a slope or in a raised bed grow well. Most herbs require full sun, but several will tolerate part shade. Many herbs can be grown indoors.

When laying out an herb bed, consider the following: accessibility for harvesting, separation of annuals and perennials, height and width of plants, and esthetic appearance.

Planting

Seeds can be sown in the ground in early spring or started inside in flats about 6 weeks before planting. Seedlings can also be bought commercially. Plants also may be propagated by root division in the early spring. Dig plant up, shake soil loose, separate roots and divide into thirds, then replant. Another method of propagation is tip cutting. Cut a 4″–6″ tip, remove lower leaves, and dip into a hormone rooting solution. Set tip in damp sand or perlite with the base leaf joints covered. Plant when rooted.

Watering and Fertilizing

Herbs require very little maintenance, thus one reason for their popularity. Water herbs thoroughly when dry and give them a feeding of 5–10–5 in midsummer. Pinch off flower heads for a bushy, robust plant and to prevent going to seed.

Pests

Herbs are generally pest free. However they sometimes get red spider mites and white fly. Infected plants can be sprayed with tepid soapy water.

Harvesting

For fresh uses pinch back tip of plant at any time or for clump plants (parsley and chives) cut whole spears (leaflets) from the outside of the clump at ground level.

It is very important to harvest herbs when the plants are richest in essential oils. The time to harvest plants to be used for their leaves and flowering branches is early in the morning and just as the buds are about to open, or after the first one has unfolded its petals. Wash and dry the branches, strip the leaves from the stems, place the leaves loosely on a shallow screened tray, and put in a shaded room. Stir them every morning so all will be exposed to air. In three or four days they should be dry and ready to be packed in airtight glass jars.

Seeds of herbs are collected as soon as they are ripe and before they fall to the ground. They too should be washed, dried, and packed away for future use.

Herbs can be frozen. Gather them as for dried, rinse dirt off, pat dry, and blanch leaves or freeze as is.

Recipe for Potpourri

Two quarts rose petals and buds (red holds color better)—sweet smelling varieties only should be used. Put them on sheets of paper in any airy room to dry, which should take about 24 hours. Sprinkle with a thin layer of salt—some prefer to add a little benzoic acid to the salt.

Dry and add sweet geranium or lemon verbena leaves, a few bay leaves, lavender, heliotrope, mignonette, garden pinks, violets, and other sweet smelling flowers, and any sweet smelling herbs such as rosemary, basil, marjoram, anise, etc. More salt should be added at this time.

Always keep in mind that roses must predominate.

Add a spice mixture of the following:

1 ounce:	*¼ ounce each of:*	*⅛ ounce each of:*
Violet sachet powder	Powdered cloves	Crushed coriander
	Powdered mace	Cardamon seeds
	Powdered cinnamon	Powdered gum storax
	Powdered allspice	Powdered gum benzoin

Mix the flowers thoroughly with the spice mixture. A drop or so of essence of roses will enhance the fragrance. Leave the potpourri in a tightly covered crockery jar for several weeks, stirring occasionally. When ready for use, put in bowls to give a delicious scent to the room.

Recipe for Pomander Ball

Oranges, lemons, or apples, whole cloves, and orris-root powder provide the essential ingredients for delightfully fragrant Pomander Balls.

Prick the fruit with a cooking nail or small knitting needle and insert a whole clove. Continue the procedure until the fruit is entirely covered with cloves.

Pour a small amount of orris-root powder in a plastic bag, put the fruit into the bag, add more powder, then close the bag and shake it until the fruit is evenly and completely covered with the powder.

Place the individual fruit on a fresh square of cheesecloth and tie with a ribbon. Make a loop at one end of the ribbon so that it may be hung in a clothes or linen closet, or it may be placed in drawers.

Orris-root, which has the fragrance of fresh violets, may be purchased at pharmacies.

HERBS

KEY
A—Annual
B—Biennial
P—Perennial

COMMON NAME SCIENTIFIC NAME	KEY	HEIGHT	COMMENTS
Anise *Pimpinella anisum*	A	2′	Sow fresh seeds in May, do not transplant, thin plants to 9″ apart. Fresh leaves and seeds for seasoning.
Basil *Ocimum basilicum*	A	6″–20″	Pinch out tips for a bushy plant. Leaves green or dried for seasoning. Easily grown from seeds or cuttings. Var. "Dark Opal," purplish foliage.
Bee Balm *Monarda didyma*	P	2′–3′	Scarlet flowers attract hummingbirds; pungent odor. Hang dried stalks in linen closet.
Borage *Borago officinalis*	A	1½′–2′	Blue or purple flowers; attracts bees. Young tender leaves used for seasonings, imparts flavor of cucumber.
Caraway *Carum carvi*	A, B	2′	White or pinkish flowers. Sow seeds where plants will remain for two seasons; seeds produced second summer. Seeds and tender leaves used for seasoning.

HERBS

COMMON NAME SCIENTIFIC NAME	KEY	HEIGHT	COMMENTS
Chervil *Anthriscus cerefolium*	A	18″–24″	Thrives in shade, rich soil. Used like parsley; one of French "fines herbs."
Chives *Allium schoenoprasum*	P	10″	Sun. Blue purple flowers, onion scented. Plant in flower beds to discourage aphids; can be potted indoors for winter use. Dig and divide every 2 to 3 years.
Dill *Anethum graveolens*	A	2′–4′	Sun. Yellowish green flower. Sow early spring, does not transplant well. Young leaves and seeds for seasoning.
Garden Sage *Salvia officinalis*	P	2′	Sun. Aromatic leaves used dried for cooking. Propagates from cuttings. Cut back to half its height each spring.
Garlic *Allium sativum*	P	2′	Sun. Plant segments 8″ apart and 2″ deep; do not confuse with wild garlic. When leaves turn yellow, dry in sun, hang in kitchen.
Horseradish *Armoracia rusticana*	P	to 15″	Plant 4″ deep; best treated as annual. Harvest in fall.
Lavender *Lavandula angustifolia*	P	2′–3′	Full sun; light, limy, well-drained soil. Fragrant, used in sachet.
Lemon Balm *Melissa officinalis*	P	2′	Sun or part shade. Moist soil. Lemon scented, used in seasonings. Winters well.
Lemon Verbena *Lippia citriodora*	P	12″	Sun, moist soil. Terminal white flowers, lemon scented foliage. Shrub in South, pot plant in North; move to greenhouse in winter.
Mint *Mentha* Apple Mint Curly Mint Orange Mint Peppermint Pineapple Mint Spearmint	P	1′–2′	Rich damp area, some shade as leaves lose color and flavor in full sun. Suggestion: plant in tubs to confine creeping roots. Pinch off blossoms for a bushier plant and to prevent reseeding.

HERBS

COMMON NAME SCIENTIFIC NAME	KEY	HEIGHT	COMMENTS
Marjoram (Sweet) *Majorana hortensis*	P	2′	Keep pruned to 7″ or 8″ in hedge or ball, keep well mulched. Used for seasonings.
Oregano *Origanum vulgare*	P	2½″	Full sun, well-drained soil. Leaves for seasoning. Pinch off blossoms for bushier plant.
Parsley *Petroselinum*	B	6″–8″	Partial shade; medium rich soil. Can be easily transplanted; soak seeds before sowing. Curly and fern leaved varieties. Treat as annual.
Rosemary *Rosmarinus officinalis*	P	15″	Sun, garden soil, good drainage. Dark, needlelike leaves. Propagate from cuttings.
Sage *See* Garden Sage			
Savory (Summer) *Satureja hortensis*	A	14″	Sun. Pinch tips for bushier plants. Propagate from cuttings or root division. Aromatic, good for seasoning. Cut and dry branches by hanging upside down.
Savory (Winter) *Satureja montana*	P	14″	Same as above.
Tarragon *Artemisia dracunculus*	P	18″	Sun. Mulch in winter; do not fertilize. Propagate from cuttings or root divisions. Plant 18″ apart. Good for seasoning.
Thyme *Thymus vulgaris*	P	8″	Sun, light, sandy, limy soil. Small leaved. Keep well clipped to prevent woody growths. Can be potted and put in sunny window during winter. For drying, cut before or at flowering time; hang upside down. Propagate from seeds or cuttings.

VEGETABLES

Vegetables are a delight to the eye and a joy to the palate. Whether growing in containers, a small plot, or several acres, good gardening fundamentals must be observed.

Planning the Garden

Choose a slightly sloping, well-drained spot with a minimum of six hours of sunlight (full sun preferred). Leafy vegetables tolerate more shade than root crops. Raised beds are also desirable.

Plant cool and warm crops in different sections. The cool crops should be harvested by midsummer and can be replanted for a fall garden. Rotate crops each year to reduce plant disease. Arrange rows so taller plants will not shade shorter ones.

Soil Preparation

Soil should be tilled to a depth of 6″ to 7″. Never work soil where too wet. To test soil roll a handful into a ball. If it doesn't crumble easily, it is too wet to work.

Organic material (compost) is used to open up clay soils and improve drainage. In sandy soils, organic material holds moisture and nutrients. Be sure to add enough to comprise ⅓ of soil mixture.

Liming and Fertilizing

The soil pH should be 6.0–6.8. Consult local county extension agent for information on soil testing. Check the pH every 3 years. It is best to add lime in the fall and mix it into the soil. Only finely ground lime may be applied in the spring. Vegetables require a complete fertilizer, such as 6-12-12 or 13-13-13. It should be applied in the spring and worked into the soil before planting. Do not overfertilize vegetables. Manure, which adds organic material, can be used to supplement chemical fertilizer. Green manure will burn.

Planting

Seeds—Consult package for proper spacing and planting depth. Do not sow too deeply or too thickly. Keep soil moist until seedlings emerge. Let plants reach 1½″–2″ before thinning to the recommended spacing. Crowded plants will not produce well.

Transplants—Broccoli, cabbage, cauliflower, eggplant, pepper, tomato, and a few others are usually transplanted rather than direct seeded. Select small, stocky healthy plants. Plant on a cool day or in late afternoon. Water in with ½–1 pint of starter solution per plant (1 tablespoon 10–50–10 per gallon of water). Set plants at the depth they grew or slightly deeper. See "Propagation."

Water and Mulch

Vegetables require 1″ to 1½″ of water per week. Soak thoroughly, as shallow waterings cause shallow root growth. Water early in the day so plants will dry before night.

Mulch to conserve moisture and reduce weeds. Apply 2″–4″ of organic mulches, such as straw, grass clippings or compost, around the established plants. Do not use grass clippings to which herbicides and heavy metal chemicals have been applied. The best inorganic mulch is black plastic (*See* Black Plastic Gardening).

Staking and Training

English peas, sugar snap peas, tomatoes, cucumbers, and pole beans may be trained on a stake, wire cage, or fence.

Weeds

Shallow hoe cultivating is the only safe method of weed control. Do not use herbicides in the home garden. Use mulches to reduce weeding.

Insects, Diseases

Select disease-resistant varieties. Check local garden center or local extension service center for suitable spray or dusts. Many sprays are unsafe for vegetable gardens. Follow directions carefully.

Harvesting

Frequent picking increases yield.

Black Plastic Gardening for Vegetables

Advantages—(1) No soil preparation required. May be laid over any grass except Bermuda. (2) Hastens soil warming in spring by 10°. Promotes earliness in warm season crops. (3) Planting unhindered by spring rains. (4) Less insect damage. (5) Clean vegetables.

Disadvantage— Because of increased soil temperature, not well suited for cool season crops.

Method—(1) Six weeks before spring planting, sprinkle 15 pounds of 6–12–12 per 1,000 square feet. Lime if necessary. (2) Spread 6 mil. 20′ × 40′ black plastic. Secure plastic with boards, bricks, or earth. (3) At planting time cut X-shaped holes large enough to accommodate the mature plant and plant seeds or sets. Root crops not recommended. Beans, cabbage, corn, eggplants, melons, squash, and strawberries do especially well. Leafy vegetables are recommended. (4) Water under plastic in summer and mulch on top of plastic to keep roots cool (if desired). (5) After growing season, store plastic for the next year.

HELPFUL HINTS

If rabbits are eating vegetables, dust with red pepper or blood meal. Dogs, however, are attracted to blood meal.

To ripen green tomatoes, place tomatoes in a plastic bag with a cut ripe apple. Tie securely. They will turn red soon.

Strawberries like a pine needle or straw mulch.

Do not plant cucumbers near melons. The melons will taste of cucumber.

To prevent cut worm damage to seedlings, surround each plant with a plastic cup from which the bottom has been removed.

VEGETABLES

NAME	PLANTING DATES	INCHES BETWEEN PLANTS	COMMENTS
Asparagus Plants	February	18	Plant 2 year old roots in a separate bed. Remove and set aside top 6″ of soil. Work in 2″ of rotted manure and a sprinkling of 5-10-5 to a depth of 6″ or more. Spread roots, cover with reserved soil. Mulch. Feed with 5-10-5 in spring before growth starts. Harvest for only 1 week the first year, 2 weeks the second. Do not cut back foliage until frost.
Beans, Lima Bush	May 1–June 15	3–4	Require warmer growing conditions than snap beans. *Planting to harvest:* 65–75 days.
Beans, Lima Pole	May 1–June 15	3–4	Require support. *Planting to harvest:* 80–90 days.
Beans, Snap Bush	April 15–June 20	3–4	Tenderer than pole beans but not as much yield. Make successive plantings for longer season. *Planting to harvest:* 60–65 days.
Beans, Snap Pole	April 15–June 20	3–4	Provide support. *Planting to harvest:* 60–65 days.
Beets	Early March	2–3	Thin to improve size. Alkaline soil. *Planting to harvest:* 55–65 days.
Broccoli Plants	March 1–April 1	18	Begin insect control soon after transplanting. Harvest before flower develops. Hot weather reduces yield. *Planting to harvest:* 60–70 days.
Brussels Sprouts Plants	Feb.–March	12–18	Hot weather reduces yield. To reduce disease do not plant in the same spot each year. *Planting to harvest:* 90–100 days.

VEGETABLES

NAME	PLANTING DATES	INCHES BETWEEN PLANTS	COMMENTS
Cabbage, Spring (Plants)	Late Feb.–March	18	Begin insect control early. Do not plant in the same spot each year. Reduce moisture near maturity to prevent splitting heads. Cabbage prefers cool weather. *Planting to harvest:* 62–75 days.
Cabbage, Fall (Plants)	July 5–Aug. 15	24	Begin insect control soon after planting. *Planting to harvest:* 80–90 days.
Cantaloupe	May 1–15	24	Requires bee pollination. Spray only in late afternoon. Do not plant near cucumbers as they assimilate the taste. Late plantings subject to mildew. *Planting to harvest:* 80–100 days.
Carrots	March 1–April 1	2–3	Avoid heavy soil. Thin to improve size. *Planting to harvest:* 75–85 days.
Cauliflower Plants	March 1–April 1	18–24	Begin insect control early. Too much heat prevents proper maturation. Tie leaves overhead to blanch when curd is visible. *Planting to harvest:* 60–70 days.
Collards	March or July	12	Begin insect control early. *Planting to harvest:* 65–75 days.
Corn, Sweet	April 1–June 1	8–12	For pollenization plant 3 rows or more in blocks. Successive planting for continued harvest. *Planting to harvest:* 80–95 days.
Cucumber	May or June	12 if trellised	Requires bee pollination. Spray only in late afternoon. Trellising increases quality and yield. Do not plant near melons. Burpless varieties available. *Planting to harvest:* 50–55 days.
Eggplant Plants	May or June	24	Requires high temperatures. *Planting to harvest:* 75–80 days.
Kale	Feb. or Aug.	12	Begin insect control early. *Planting to harvest:* 60–90 days.

VEGETABLES

NAME	PLANTING DATES	INCHES BETWEEN PLANTS	COMMENTS
Lettuce, Leaf (Loose-leaf)	Feb.–April	4–6	Plant shallow. Requires moist soil to germinate. Becomes bitter and bolts in hot weather. Fall crops possible. *Planting to harvest:* 40–50 days.
Lettuce, Head (Bibb, Boston)	Feb. or Sept.	12–15	Plant shallow. Requires moist soil and light to germinate. *Planting to harvest:* 60–70 days.
Okra	May 5–20	18	Soak seed overnight before planting. Plant only after soil warms to 70°F. Dwarf varieties available. *Planting to harvest:* 50–60 days.
Onions	Feb. 1–Mar. 31	2–3	Withstands heavy frost. Soil should be loosened to produce larger bulbs. For storage harvest when stalk falls over. *Planting to harvest:* 30 days for bunch, 90 days for storage.
Parsley (Biennial)	May or July	2	Soak seeds overnight before planting. Do not let go to seed. *Planting to harvest:* 90–100 days.
Peas, English	Feb. 1–Mar. 20	2–4	Staking and early planting increase yield. Very cold resistant. Does not tolerate heat. *Planting to harvest:* 80–90 days.
Peas, Sugar Snap	Feb. 1–Mar. 20	2–4	May exceed 6′ in height. Plant early. Edible pods require stringing. Very cold resistant. Does not tolerate heat. *Planting to harvest:* 70–80 days.
Pepper, Bell (Plants)	May or June	18	Temperatures above 90°F. cause blossom drop. Do not plant near hot peppers. *Planting to harvest:* 70–80 days.
Pepper, Hot (Plants)	May or June	18	Temperatures above 90°F. cause blossom drop. *Planting to harvest:* 60–70 days.
Potatoes, Irish	Mar. 5–20	8–12	Cut potato into pieces 3–7 days before planting. Seed pieces must have an eye. *Planting to harvest:* 90–120 days.

VEGETABLES

NAME	PLANTING DATES	INCHES BETWEEN PLANTS	COMMENTS
Radish	Feb. 15–Apr. 15	1–2	Fall crops possible. High temperatures and dry soil reduce quality. Good plant for children to grow. *Planting to harvest:* 21–30 days.
Spinach, Spring	Feb. 5–15	3–4	Very cold resistant. Climbing variety available. *Planting to harvest:* 45–50.
Spinach, Fall	Sept. 10–20	6–8	*Planting to harvest:* 40–50.
Squash, Summer (yellow, zucchini)	May–June	12–24	Requires bee pollination. Spray only in late afternoon. Later plantings possible with rigid insect control. Plant 5 seeds in hills of soil, thin to three plants, or plant in row. First flowers generally drop. *Planting to harvest:* 45–55 days.
Squash, Winter	May or June	24–36	Spray only in late afternoon. First flowers generally drop. Let mature on vines until skins are extremely hard. *Planting to harvest:* 90–110 days.
Tomato Plants	April 15–June 15	24	Mulching aids disease control. Lime soil to reduce blossom end rot. Leggy plants will root along stem if buried 2″–3″ below soil surface. Provide support. Feed once a month with 6–12–12 fertilizer scattered in a circle well away from stem. Water copiously. See pg. 213 for cutworms. Remove suckers between stem and stalk. *Planting to harvest:* 70-80 days.
Turnip, Greens	March or Aug.–Sept.	3	Scatter seeds. *Planting to harvest:* 30–40 days.
Watermelon	May 1–31	48	Spray as for cucumbers and cantaloupe. For large gardens. *Planting to harvest:* 80–90 days.

The Shady Garden

The plants which flourish most successfully in the shady garden are our native mid-South woodland species. A variety of broad-leaved evergreens which bloom, berry, or have attractive leaf coloration are the backbone of the easy-maintenance garden. Planted in groups they form an evergreen background.

Ground covers can be used as carpeting to prevent excessive evaporation and weed growth. Ferns, wild flowers, and bulbs can be tucked under and around trees and shrubs. Spring, summer, and fall-flowering plants will provide seasonal variety.

Most shade-loving plants need deeply prepared soil, rich in humus, with coarse sand for drainage. Do not clean up the natural mulch layer unless small bulbs and plants are being smothered, and then do as little as possible. This keeps weeds from being a problem.

Colorful perennials and annuals are good in the foreground if the sun can reach them. See special articles on bulbs and ferns.

PLANTS FOR SHADE

Flowering Trees

Dogwood
Fringe Tree
Hawthorn
Horse Chestnut
Magnolia glauca
Redbud
Red Buckeye
Sourwood

Blooming Broad-Leaved Evergreens

Abelia
Andromeda floribunda
Andromeda japonica
Azaleas
Camellias
Mountain Laurel
Leucothoe
Rhododendron
Tea Plant

Broad-Leaved Evergreens for Foliage

Acuba
Anise
Boxwood
Cherry Laurel
Cleyera
Euonymus (Shrub)
Holly
Mahonia

Deciduous Blooming Shrubs for Partial Shade

Deutzia
Forsythia
Hydrangea (Shade-tolerant varieties)
Kerria (Single and double)
Magnolia stellata
Mock orange
Saint-John's-wort
Sweet Shrub
Viburnum
Winter Sweet

Ground Covers

Ajuga
Foamflower
Epimedium
Euonymus
Ferns
Goutweed
Ivy
Lily-of-the-Valley
Liriope
Mondo
Pachysandra
Vinca Major
Vinca Minor
Violets

Perennials for Interest and Color

Ageratum
Astilbe
Bugloss
Beebalm
Begonia (Hardy)
Daylilies
Foamflower
Forget-me-not
Hosta
Jacob's-ladder

Bleeding-heart (Wild)
Bleeding-heart (Old Fashioned)
Candytuft
Columbine
Coneflower
Coralbells
Lilies
Liriope
Lythrum
Oxalis
Phlox

Annuals

Caladium
Impatiens
Flowering Tobacco
Pansy
Wishbone Flower

HARDY FERNS

Hardy ferns, as opposed to tropical ferns, are a wonderful addition to any shady garden, especially the wild flower garden. There are about 10,000 species in the world but only the easiest to grow and the most common are listed.They are available at many nurseries throughout the country. Do not dig ferns in the woods unless they are threatened by the bulldozer.

Ferns are one of a few nonblooming plants, others being mushrooms, club mosses, equisetum, liverworts, and lycopodium. Although most native ferns die back after frost, there are a few that are evergreen.

Ferns reproduce by spores. Spores appear in two forms: 1) a fertile stem of all spores, like the sensitive fern, and 2) a frond similar to the fern frond, such as the ostrich, and lady ferns, but with spore cases on the underside of it. Identification of the family, genus, and species is done by examining the arrangement of the spore cases. Some are along the edges in a row, or in circles, or in other patterns. A magnifying glass reveals that great variety of design of the spore cases. Do not confuse the spore cases with scale.

Ferns should be planted in the same ecological situation as their native habitat. Many grow in limestone areas and should have lime added annually. In acid areas most prefer acid soil, especially in hardwood areas (see charts for soil pH). Do not rake fallen leaves from the fern bed. The fiddleheads (new growth) force their way through the heavy leaf fall and raking may break them.

Watering should be frequent in drouth periods and fertilizing is up to individual choice. Mainly ferns thrive on their own. Be very cautious of using nitrogen fertilizers which will burn the fronds. Ferns do not need superphosphate because they do not bloom.

Ferns are very fragile and the stems are brittle. Keep dogs out of them. Usually they are beautiful in the spring and summer. To renew the fern foliage for fall cut back in late July and August. Shear close to the rhizome and cut off all broken stems and scruffy fronds as low as possible, using sharp scissors.

HARDY FERNS

KEY
Once Cut—frond is cut into simple leaflets
Twice Cut—frond is cut into simple leaflets, which are also cut.
Thrice Cut—frond is cut into simple leaflets which are cut and cut again.

COMMON NAME SCIENTIFIC NAME	KEY	HEIGHT	WIDTH OF FROND	COMMENTS
Beech Broad Beech Fern *Thelypteris hexagonoptera*	2	24″	14″	Triangular frond, spore cases scattered in margin. Semimoist, open spots in rich woods, acid soil.
Long Beech Fern *Thelypteris phegopteris*	2	12″	8″	Triangular frond; bottom pair of leaflets turn down, 12 pairs in all. Shaded moist bank, acid soil.
Bracken *Pteridium aquilinum*	2	to 3′	18″	Leaflets on long coarse stem, spore cases on narrow lines near margin. Crisp brown erect growth after first frost. Invasive. Sun or shade; any soil.
Christmas Fern *Polystichum acrostichoides*	1	2′	4″	Hardy evergreen, abundant in most areas, spore cases top third of fertile frond. Shade; alkaline soil.
Cinnamon Fern *Osmunda cinnamomea*	2	3′	6″	Fertile frond is separate with cinnamon-colored spore cases. Hardy. Moist; shade; any soil.

HARDY FERNS

COMMON NAME SCIENTIFIC NAME	KEY	HEIGHT	WIDTH OF FROND	COMMENTS
Climbing Fern *Lygodium japonicum*	2	climber	4″–6″	Vinelike growth. Grows well potted and trained on a form. Sterile leaflet different shape from fertile leaflet. Moist shade; acid soil. Dies back in winter except in greenhouse.
Fragile Fern *Cystopteris fragilis*	3	1′	4″	Delicate appearance, bright green spring growth, first to appear. Spore cases dotted on underside of fertile frond, wrapped in tip of frond. Damp, rich, acid soil; shade.
Goldie's Fern *Dryopteris goldiana*	2	3′	12″	Golden green color; 12 alternating leaflets, spore cases on back of darker frond. Moist rich acid soil; cool woods.
Grape Fern *Botrychium virginianum* "Rattlesnake"	3	10″	12″	Deciduous, fertile frond rises from juncture of sterile frond. Shade, moist or dry acid soil.
Hay-scented Fern *Dennstaedtia punctilobula* "Boulder Fern"	2	16″	5″	Delicate foliage; sterile and fertile fronds similar, spores contained in tiny cups under fertile fronds. When crushed it smells like hay. Partial shade, dry acid soil.
Holly Fern *Polystichum lonchitis*	2	2′	5″	Shiny serrated leaflet, dies back in winter. Spore cases dotted under fertile subleaflet. Moist, alkaline soil; shade.
Interrupted Fern *Osmunda claytoniana*	2	2½′	5″	Fertile fronds are interrupted in the center by four or more pairs of leaflets bearing spore cases that later turn brown. Rocky dry soil; sun or part shade. Alkaline soil.
Japanese Painted Fern *Athyrium goeringianum*	3	18″	5″	Delicate silver-splashed green frond; prefers leaf mold in soil. Not native to U.S. but does well with other ferns. Herringbone pattern under fertile frond leaflet. Acid soil.

HARDY FERNS

COMMON NAME SCIENTIFIC NAME	KEY	HEIGHT	WIDTH OF FROND	COMMENTS
Lady Fern *Athyrium filix-femina*	3	2½′	10″	Delicate. Grows in circular clusters; spore cases curved or horseshoe-shaped on underside of fertile frond. Moist acid soil, partial shade. Propagates easily.
A. filix-femina rubellum	3	2½′	10″	Same as above but with dark red stems
Maidenhair Fern *Adiantum capillus-veneris* "Southern"	2	to 12″	3″	Delicate and feathery. Slightly pendulous, shiny black stems similar to Northern but without the whorls, fanshaped leaflets, spore cases wrapped under leaflet. Shade, moist, prefers lime.
A. pedatum "Northern"	2	20″	10″	Circular or horseshoelike fronds borne on slender erect dark stalks, leaflets bluish green. Spore cases wrapped under leaflet. Shade, moist alkaline soil.
Maidenhair Spleenwort *Asplenium trichomanes*	1	7″	1′	Evergreen sterile fronds lie on surface year round, fertile fronds bright green and erect. Withers in winter. Good drainage is essential, shade, alkaline soil.
Marsh Fern *Thelypteris palustris*	2	18″	6″	Spore cases in curled up leaflets. Grown in open marshy places, often in full sun, alkaline soil.
Narrow-leaved Spleenwort *Athyrium pycnocarpon*	2	3′	6″	Tall slender pale green fronds. Spore cases under fertile leaflet on fertile frond. Neutral soil, open sunny spots or open woodlands, plenty of moisture.
Ostrich Fern *Matteuccia struthiopteris*	2	4′–5′	14″	Brown fertile fronds shorter than graceful green plumelike sterile fronds. Can be grown in cultivation for a large specimen. Shade or partial shade; low wet open woodlands; acid soil.
Rattlesnake Fern *See* Grape Fern				

HARDY FERNS

COMMON NAME SCIENTIFIC NAME	KEY	HEIGHT	WIDTH OF FROND	COMMENTS
Resurrection Fern *Polypodium polypodioides*	1	to 7″	2″	Grows like ivy on trees or dead stumps; lives without soil. In dry weather it looks dead, revives with rain. Spore cases under tip of leaflet on fertile frond, fronds short. Partial shade.
Royal Fern *Osmunda regalis*	2	1′–5′	12″	Coarse fronds with fertile tips containing spore cases. Partial shade, acid soil, wet lands; will grow in water.
Sensitive Fern *Onoclea sensibilis*	2	2½′	12″–14″	Invasive. Fertile frond is a separate stalk containing small, brown, round beads. Can be used in flower arrangements. Part shade, damp, acid soil.
Woodfern *Dryopteris marginalis* "Leatherleaf"	2	15″	6″	Many varieties. Evergreen, rich blue green leathery fronds; spore cases on margin of leaflets. Shade, any woodsy soil, good drainage.
D. spinulosa	3	30″	8″	Many varieties. Variable size fronds; spore cases on margin of leaflets. Shade, damp, acid soil.
Woodsia *Woodsia obtusa* "Blunt-lobed"	3	15″	4″	Evergreen. Fronds hairy underneath, commonest and largest woodsia. Spore cases underside of fertile leaflet. Part shade, neutral moist soil, needs protected location.
W. ilvensis "Rusty"	2	6″	1″	Small coarse fronds growing in tufts; leaflets rusty underneath in dry weather; spore cases underside of fertile leaflet. Moist, neutral soil, partial shade, good drainage.

WILD FLOWERS

Often gardeners are not aware that many prized garden plants are actually wild flowers. Some are considered weeds, but on the other hand, the definition of a weed is a plant out of place. Our southern native species (a species is a plant which maintains its form without

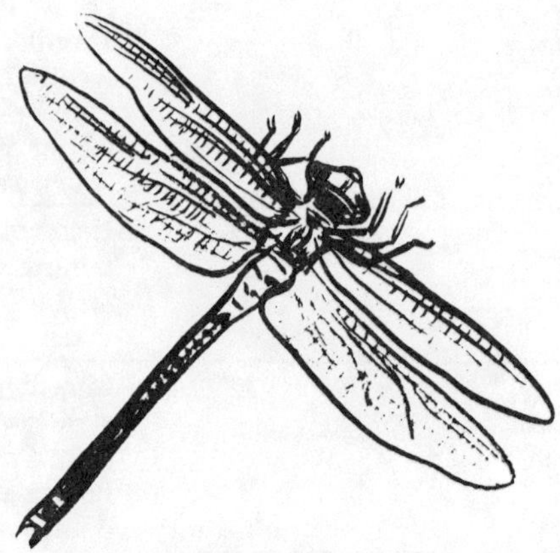

help from man) number over 6000. Many are alien, that is, brought in from other parts of the world and settled here, even hybridizing themselves with the native ones. Only the wild flowers that are the most showy and adaptable to gardens have been selected for coverage.

Growing wild flowers in the garden can be an act of conservation, to help prevent species from extinction. Growing them from seed is the most practical method, as many are extremely difficult to transplant. Digging them from their native habitat is NOT an act of conservation. However many plants are available from reliable nurseries. Also many are easily shared by generous gardeners.

The most important factor in growing wild flowers is to plant them in a soil and climate similar to that of their native habitat. Therefore attention must be paid to soil pH, leafmold, moisture, amount of sun, shade, and dormancy. Naturally a flower coming from a sunny, dry, or sandy spot will not thrive in a damp, shaded area, and conversely, a succulent shade lover will not grow in the hot sun. Some wild flowers will not bloom as handsomely in too-rich a soil, for they will go to foliage at the expense of the blooms. Others adapt to good garden care and increase in size and color. Individual preferences will have made themselves evident in most cases, and experimentation will show the way with others. This article serves merely as a guide. More detailed information can be found in libraries or from books listed in the bibliography section.

WILD FLOWERS FOR THE SHADY GARDEN

KEY
A—annual
P—perennial

COMMON NAME SCIENTIFIC NAME	KEY	COLOR	HEIGHT	DESCRIPTION AND BLOOM TIME
Alumroot *See* Coral Bells				
Atamasco Lily (Rain Lily, Fairy Lily, or Zephyranthes) *Zephyranthes atamasco*	P	white pink	12″	Grassy leaf, funnel-shaped flower to 3″; spring-summer; leaf mold.
Baneberry Cohosh *Actaea alba*	P	white	2′–3′	Racemous flower, poisonous white berry; spring; leaf mold.
A. rubra		white	2′–3′	Red berry, same as above.
Bellwort Merrybells *Uvularia grandiflora*	P	yellow	18″	Bell-like flower; spring; leaf mold.
U. sessilifolia		greenish yellow	12″	Same as above.
Bottle Gentian Closed Gentian *Gentiana andrewsii*	P	blue	12″–20″	Flower never opens; August–October; leaf mold.
Cardinal flower *Lobelia cardinalis*	P	red	2′–4′	Spike flowers, 6″–12″; summer; moist, partial shade.
Carolina Lily *Lilium michauxii*	P	Orange red	1′–4′	August–September; leaf mold.
Celandine Poppy Wood Poppy *Stylophorum diphyllum*	P	bright yellow	12″–18″	2″ flower; spring; rich moist soil.
Columbine *Aquilegia caerulea*	P	blue	1′–3′	Spring; semishade, good garden soil.
A. canadensis		yellow & orange	1′–2′	Same as above.
Coralbells Alumroot *Heuchera americana*	P	white or green	18″–24″	Low foliage; May–July; acid soil, partial shade.
H. sanguinea		coral	18″	Low foliage, spike flower; spring–summer.
Crinum Lily Swamp Lily *Crinum americanum*	P	white	2½′	Fragrant; summer into fall; damp, leaf mold; leave undisturbed. Part shade.
Dutchman's-breeches *Dicentra cucullaria*	P	white	8″–10″	Spring; leaf mold; prefers foothills or mountains.

WILD FLOWERS FOR THE SHADY GARDEN

COMMON NAME SCIENTIFIC NAME	KEY	COLOR	HEIGHT	DESCRIPTION AND BLOOM TIME
Fairy-wand *Chamaelirium luteum*	P	white	2′	Low foliage, raceme flower; early summer, moist rich soil.
False Solomon's seal *Smilacina racemosa*	P	creamy white	to 3′	Tapering spike flower; spring; leaf mold.
Foamflower *Tiarella cordifolia*	P	white	6″–12″	Tiny white spike flower, spring, dies back in summer; leaf mold.
Forget-me-not *Myosotis scorpioides*	P	blue	12″	Clusters of tiny flowers; spring; garden soil, partial shade. Many other varieties.
Greek Valerian *Polemonium reptans*	P	blue	8″–15″	Drooping flower in clusters; spring; leaf mold.
Green Dragon *Arisaema dracontium*	P	pale green	1′–4′	Flower similar to Jack-in-the-pulpit, large spathe with yellow spike center, handsome palmate leaf stalk, cluster of red berries in fall; spring; leaf mold.
Iris *Iris cristata*	P	blue, white	3″–8″	Spring; partial shade, garden soil. Will not bloom in dense shade, likes to be planted near rocks.
I. fulva		tawny orange	2′–3′	Spring; partial shade, damp, hardy.
I. verna		lavender with yellow	2″–6″	Spring; sandy soil; similar to cristata but not crested.
Jack-in-the-pulpit *Arisaema triphyllum*	P	green & brown	12″	Flower followed by rich, red berries; spring; damp leaf mold.
Jacob's-ladder *Polemonium caeruleum*	P	blue	1′	Flowers drooping in clusters; spring; leaf mold. Similar to Greek Valerian.
Lady slipper Moccasin flower *Cypripedium*	P	pink	6″–15″	Spring; acid woods; endangered species.
Larkspur Wild Delphinium *Delphinium tricorne*	P	purple	1′–2½′	Spring; partial shade, rich, damp soil.
Lobelia *Lobelia siphilitica*	P	clear blue	3′	Spike flower; partial shade, moist.

WILD FLOWERS FOR THE SHADY GARDEN

COMMON NAME / SCIENTIFIC NAME	KEY	COLOR	HEIGHT	DESCRIPTION AND BLOOM TIME
Mayapple *Podophyllum peltatum*	P	white	to 18″	Waxy flower borne on double leafed stem; spring; garden soil.
Orchid *Orchis*	P			Many varieties; see wild flower catalogues. Do not dig from the wild.
Phlox Wild Sweet William *Phlox divaricata*	P	lavender	12″	Spring; semishade, garden soil.
Shooting Star *Dodecatheon meadia album*	P	white	12″	Low foliage; spring; leaf mold, good drainage.
D. meadia splendidum		pink	12″	Small flower on top of stem, low foliage; spring; leaf mold, good drainage.
Solomon's-seal *Polygonatum biflorum*	P	creamy white	to 3′	Flowers hanging below leaf axil; spring; leaf mold.
Spider lily *Hymenocallis caroliniana*	P	white	1½′	Fragrant; spring; marsh and bogs, semishade, Zone 7 south.
Squirrel corn *Dicentra canadensis*	P	white	8″–10″	Fragrant; spring; foothills or mountains, leaf mold.
Sweet Cicely *Osmorhiza claytonii*	P	white	2′–3′	Fernlike foliage, small flowers; spring; semishade, garden soil; profuse reseeding.
Trillium *Trillium erectum*	P	dark red	to 12″	Spring; semishade, leaf mold.
T. grandiflorum		white changing to pale pink	to 12″	Early spring; leaf mold.
T. luteum		yellow	8″–12″	Mottled leaf; early spring; leaf mold.
T. sessile		red, purple	to 12″	Mottled leaf; early spring; leaf mold. Many varieties, see catalogues.
Trout lily *Erythronium albidum*	P	white	6″–9″	Early spring; moist, leaf mold.
Dog-tooth violet *E. americanum*		yellow	4″–10″	Mottled leaf; early spring; leaf mold.
Vinca Periwinkle *Vinca minor*	P	lavender, blue and white	6″	Spring; garden soil. Useful as ground cover.

WILD FLOWERS FOR THE SHADY GARDEN

COMMON NAME SCIENTIFIC NAME	KEY	COLOR	HEIGHT	DESCRIPTION AND BLOOM TIME
Violet *Viola*	P	white, yellow, lavender, purple, purple and white		Spring; many varieties.
Virginia Bluebells *Mertensia virginica*	P	blue	to 2′	Buds and fading flowers are pink; spring; leaf mold, lime.
Wild Bleeding-heart *Dicentra eximia*	P	pink	10″–18″	All summer; leaf mold, damp.
Wild Delphinium *See* Larkspur	P			
Wild Geranium Cranesbill *Geranium maculatum*	P	pink	to 2′	Spring; leaf mold.
Wild Ginger *Asarum canadense*	P	maroon	4″	Flower ground level; spring; moist, leaf mold. Good ground cover.
Wild Sweet William *See* Phlox	P			
Wood Sorrel *Oxalis violacea*	P	violet to rose pur- ple	to 10″	Spring and summer; acid soil.

WILD FLOWERS FOR THE SUNNY GARDEN

COMMON NAME SCIENTIFIC NAME	KEY	COLOR	HEIGHT	DESCRIPTION AND BLOOM TIME
Ageratum *Eupatorium coelestinum*	A	bright blue to la- vender	to 2′	Delicate fluffy flower heads; summer; garden soil.
E. perfoliatum (Boneset)		white	2′–3′	Late summer; garden soil.
Angel's-trumpet *Datura inoxia*	A	white	3′–4′	Large trumpet-shaped, fragrant flowers, blooms at night; summer; garden soil.
Bachelor's-button *Centaurea cyanus*	A/P	blue, white, rose, purple, mauve	1′–2′	Summer; garden soil.

WILD FLOWERS FOR THE SUNNY GARDEN

COMMON NAME SCIENTIFIC NAME	KEY	COLOR	HEIGHT	DESCRIPTION AND BLOOM TIME
Baptisia *See* False Indigo				
Beard-tongue *Penstemon australis*	P	lavender	2½′	Many other varieties. Has been hybridized; check catalogues. Spring and summer; garden sandy soil.
P. digitalis		white	3′	
P. hirsutus		pink	3′	
P. tubiflorus		white	3′	
Beautyberry *Callicarpa americana*	P	bluish	4′	Insignificant flower, clusters of purple berries in fall, shrub; summer, garden soil.
Bee Balm Oswego Tea *Monarda didyma*	P	red	to 3′	Summer; ordinary soil.
Wild bergamot *M. fistulosa*		lavender	to 2′	Summer; ordinary soil.
Blackberry Lily *Belamcanda chinensis*	P	orange	1½′–4′	Ornamental black fruit; early summer; rich, sandy soil. Member of iris family.
Black-eyed Susan *Rudbeckia hirta*	P	yellow and brown	3′	Summer; garden soil.
Blanketflower *Gaillardia lanceolata*	A	yellow	18″	Summer; garden soil.
Blazing-Star *Liatris elegans*	P	purple to pink and white	1′–4′	Summer and fall; garden soil. Easily transplanted.
L. pycnostachya		deep lavender	3′	Florescent bloom from top to bottom of spike.
Gay Feather *L. spicata*		purple	4′	Florescent bloom from top to bottom of spike.
Bluebell *Campanula americana*	A	blue	3′–4′	Summer; garden soil.
Blue-eyed Grass *Sisyrinchium angustifolium*	P	violet blue	to 12″	Spring; garden soil; easily transplanted, multiplies.
Blue Sage Blue Salvia *Salvia farinacea*	P	blue	2′–3′	All summer; garden soil.

WILD FLOWERS FOR THE SUNNY GARDEN

COMMON NAME SCIENTIFIC NAME	KEY	COLOR	HEIGHT	DESCRIPTION AND BLOOM TIME
Bouncing Bet *Saponaria officinalis*	P	pink	1′–2′	Spring to fall; garden soil.
Buttercup *Ranunculus*	P	yellow	6″–12″	Summer; garden soil; many varieties.
Butter-and-eggs *Linaria vulgaris*	P	yellow orange	1′–3′	Summer and fall; garden soil.
Butterfly Weed *Asclepias tuberosa*	P	orange	2′–3′	Summer; thrives in garden soil. Good cut flower.
California Poppy *Eschscholzia californica*	A	orange yellow	12″	Summer; poor, dry sandy soil. Will not stand transplanting.
Calliopsis *Coreopsis tinctoria*	A	yellow, yellow and maroon	2′–3′	Summer; very prolific.
Coneflower *Echinacea pallida*	P	pale orchid	to 3′	Long drooping rays; summer; garden soil.
E. purpurea		reddish	3′–4′	Broad coarse oval leaves, summer; garden soil.
Daylily *Hemerocallis fulva*	P	copper orange	3′–4′	Summer, garden soil. Do not plant near hybrid lilies. Propagates by root division.
Dogbane Bluestar *Amsonia tabernaemontana*	P	sky blue	2′–3′	Late spring; damp garden soil.
False Indigo *Baptisia alba*	P	White	3′	Early summer.
B. australis		blue violet	to 4′	Substitute for delphinium in hot climates; 12″ spike of pealike flower; early summer.
B. tinctoria		yellow	3′	Summer.
Fire Pink *Silene virginica*	P	scarlet	1′–2′	Loose clusters of star-shaped flowers; summer; open woods and rocky slopes.
Ginger Lily Butterfly Lily *Hedychium coronarium*	P	white	3′–5′	Fragrant; summer; rich, moist soil. Not hardy above Zone 7; needs protection from western sun.
Indian Pink Pinkroot *Spigelia marilandica*	P	red tube with yellow lining	2½′	Late spring; rich soil. Propagation by root or seed; good for cutting.

WILD FLOWERS FOR THE SUNNY GARDEN

COMMON NAME SCIENTIFIC NAME	KEY	COLOR	HEIGHT	DESCRIPTION AND BLOOM TIME
Iris Larger Blue Flag *Iris versicolor*	P	blue	2′–3′	Early summer; damp soil.
Slender Blue Flag *I. prismatica*		blue	1′–3′	Early summer; marshy.
Yellow Flag *I. pseodacorus*		yellow	4′	Spring; damp.
Lantana Polecat Geranium *Lantana montevidensis*	A	yellow, orange, pink, white	to 3′	Summer; garden soil. Can be trained into standard. Not hardy above Zone 7.
Lupine *Lupinus perennis*	A/P	blue, white, violet, pink	1′–3′	Summer; sandy, poor soil; likes cool nights.
Oxeye Daisy Field Daisy *Chrysanthemum leucanthemum*	P	white with yellow center	to 2′	Summer; any soil. Good for cutting.
Phlox *Phlox drummondii*	P	white to crimson	to 12″	Summer; garden soil. Showy garden escape.
Portulaca Moss Rose *Portulaca grandiflora*	A	all colors except blue	4″–8″	Summer; dry poor soil. Can be used for ground cover.
Primrose Sundrops *Oenothera fruticosa*	P	yellow	1′–3′	Summer; garden soil.
O. missouriensis		yellow	10″	2½″ flower; summer; garden soil.
O. speciosa				See White Evening Primrose
Queen-Anne's-Lace Wild Carrot *Daucus carota*	P	white	to 6′	Summer; good for cutting; dries well.
Rattlebox *Crotalaria spectabilis*	P	yellow	to 3′	Late summer; any soil. Poisonous to cattle.
Salvia *Salvia azurea*	P	true blue	to 4′	Summer; garden soil; good for cutting.
Sedum *Sedum*	P			Many varieties. Good ground cover.

WILD FLOWERS FOR THE SUNNY GARDEN

COMMON NAME SCIENTIFIC NAME	KEY	COLOR	HEIGHT	DESCRIPTION AND BLOOM TIME
Snow-on-the-Mountain *Euphorbia marginata*	A	pale green	3′	Insignificant flower, broad white margins on leafy bract; summer and fall; garden soil. Poisonous milky juice.
Spiderflower Cleome *Cleome spinosa*	A	white, pink, orchid, purple	4′–6′	Summer; any soil; pungent odor; prolific seeder. Thorny stem.
Spiderwort *Tradescantia virginiana*	P	brilliant blue, white	to 2½′	Spring to early summer; any soil; closes at night. Related to Wandering Jew.
Spring-beauty *Claytonia virginica*	P	pink & white	4″	Spring; any soil; bulb.
Star-of-Bethlehem *Ornithogalum umbellatum*	P	white with green stripe	4″–12″	Spring; any soil; bulb. Do not confuse with Spring-beauty.
Stokes' aster *Stokesia laevis*	P	lavender blue, white	to 2′	Late spring; moist garden soil; may need staking.
Sunflower *Helianthus annuus*	A	yellow	1′–10′	Summer; any soil; grow for bird food.
Tansy *Tanacetum vulgare*	P	golden yellow	1′–3′	Flat topped cluster of buttons, fernlike leaf, very pungent; summer to fall; any soil.
Texas Bluebonnet *Lupinus texensis*	P	blue	to 2′	Spring. Grows only in Texas due to certain bacteria in soil.
Turk's-Cap Lily *Lilium superbum*	P	red orange	to 8′	Summer; damp, rich soil.
Vinca Periwinkle *Vinca rosea*	A	white pink magenta	18″	Summer; garden soil; showy.
White Evening Primrose *Oenothera speciosa*	P	pink, white	to 2′	Late spring; tolerates poor soil.
Yarrow *Achillea millefolium*	P	white, hot pink, yellow	1′–3′	Pungent, feathery leaf; summer; any soil.
Yucca Adam's-needle *Yucca filamentosa*	P	white	4′	6′ spike of many bell-shaped flowerlettes, sharp leaves; summer; garden soil, many other varieties.

Container Plants

Successful culture of house plants depends upon choosing the right plant for the right place. Factors to consider are water, light, soil, temperature, and humidity. Watering, soil, and temperature can be controlled but, except for artificial light, the uncertainties of sunshine make light a problem. For this reason it is usually wise to select plants that fit into a home's environment rather than change the environment to fit the plants. Knowing the light and temperature requirements of the plants will prevent any future disappointments.

Too much watering usually results in leaves yellowing and dropping off at the base of the plant. Too little watering results in the edges of the leaves turning brown and the plant wilting. Edges can be trimmed with scissors. Never let the roots stand in water. To tell how moist a plant is, stick a finger ½″ into the pot. Improper drainage should be corrected. If the plant needs humidity, place a tray with pebbles under the pot and keep water in it. The pebbles keep the pot out of the water.

If a plant is fertilized too much, it will quickly outgrow space allotted for it. Since most commercially grown plants have a slow release fertilizer in the soil, do not fertilize immediately after buying. Never fertilize when the soil is dry or the plant is in bad shape. When buying a fertilizer read the labels to determine if it is a slow release fertilizer, a slow growing fertilizer or a fast growing one. Constantly change the types since there are different elements in all brands.

It is very important to clean the foliage of plants regularly. If there is a dust build-up, light will not penetrate. Putting any oil on the leaves will kill plants as then they cannot breathe. Spray the plants outside with a hose or in a tub in the house.

Plants like to be moved outside in the summer. Move them slowly, leaving on a porch or covered area for several weeks to acclimate them. Then, always leave them in part shade and never direct sun.

Spring is the best time to repot, although with house plants any time is a good time if they need it. A general purpose mixture is one part sterilized potting soil, one part peat moss, and one part perlite. It is imperative to have good drainage and a light soil mixture. Always place a piece of shard or nylon screening over the drainage hole and press soil around the plant, being careful not to injure the roots.

Light needs of plants vary, but a general rule is the closer to the window the better. If it is a good sunny window, the plant will have to be turned to keep from being lopsided. Learn which plants tolerate low light before buying.

Artificial light can be used to grow any plant. Incandescent 60-watt bulbs, fluorescent grow lights (one tube of warm white and one of cool white) or a combination of cool white fluorescent with incandescent bulbs (with a ratio of two watts of fluorescence to one of incandescence) are satisfactory. The fluorescent should be placed 6″ away from the plant and will last longer than the incandescent. A plant placed 3′ away from artificial light will receive no beneficial light. Artificial lights should be kept on 12–16 hours a day although the more they are turned off and on, the quicker they burn out. Consider automatic timers.

When buying a plant, choose carefully. Find the strongest one and do not buy a bargain plant. Isolate it from other plants for several weeks since disease or insects might appear. If insects appear, try to find out what kind they are. Use an insecticide intended for house plants.

Read the directions before using as the spray can burn some plants. Also, do not buy a plant that is root bound, one that has brown edges on the leaves, or one with spots. A younger plant acclimates itself to house conditions better than an old one. Plants like attention. The more they receive, the more they respond.

Helpful Hints

1. When to repot plants: new leaves come out smaller than average, plants wilt between waterings, lower leaves yellow, roots appear on surface or through hole in bottom.
2. Soak all terra cotta pots overnight before using because dry pots will absorb water from the soil.
3. Never use dirty pots. Soak in bleach or ammonia water and scrub. Use sterile potting soil.
4. Place sharp pebbles, pot shards, or nylon screening in large pot bottoms for proper drainage. It is safer to underwater than overwater. Water house plants with tepid water. Never use ice cubes. Cold water can damage fine root hairs.
5. When moving a plant or repotting avoid heavy feeding until plant has adjusted to new environment.
6. Plants in clay pots need water more frequently than those in plastic.
7. Never place a house plant in a draft, such as in front of heat ducts or doorways, or on top of the TV because of bottom heat.
8. Smear egg white with finger on trimmed strap leaves to prevent brown edges as it seals leaf tips.
9. In winter place containers of water near heating vents for additional humidity. Mist plants more often in winter.

Plants need more water and fertilizer when they are in active growth or are flowering, less water and no fertilizer when they are resting (dormant). Never let soil in pots dry out completely. When watering dracaena, let water stand overnight so chlorine will evaporate or use rain water to keep leaf tips from turning brown. If planning a trip, water plants thoroughly, enclose entire pot and plant in a clear plastic bag, secure at the top and under pot. It will conserve moisture for 2 weeks or more. Do not place in the sun.

BEGONIAS

Begonias are an enormous family of plants. Some have showy flowers while others are cherished for foliage alone. Begonia leaves may be tiny and delicate or huge, and most are larger on one side of the main vein. Begonia flowers grow in clusters, and their colors range widely. Each flower is male or female but not both. Begonias are grouped by the type of root—bulbous, fibrous, tuberous, or rhizomatous. Begonias for containers and flower beds are covered in this article.

General Culture

Soil—All begonias require a rich, humusy, slightly acid soil with enough coarse sand to drain well. A good potting mixture is 3 parts loam, 2 parts well-rotted manure, 1 part peat, and 1 part vermiculite.

Water—Begonias require lots of humidity which, with more delicate varieties, may mean a daily misting. If the house plant is very dry, submerge it carefully upside down in a pail of water. This also cleans the leaves and allows them to breathe. Never let the sun shine on begonia foliage when wet. Do not overwater begonias as the roots will quickly rot. Good drainage is important.

Location—Begonias do not do well in deep shade. They need light for bloom indoors, so in winter a south window is best. In summer, move outside to an eastern exposure because begonias do not like hot direct summer sun. Begonias thrive under artificial light, and some will pass up their dormancy period in the house. Outdoors good air circulation is necessary to prevent problems from high humidity.

Dormancy—When dormancy approaches, double male flowers may become single. Leaves turn yellow and dry. Rex begonias, especially, may lose all of their leaves and stop growing. Stop fertilizing and give just enough water to keep the plant from completely drying out. Remove it from direct light while resting. Dig and store tubers and rhizomes if planted outdoors.

Fertilizing—Feed with 4–12–4 when the plant begins to produce new growth after its dormant period, and every few weeks while in bloom.

Pruning—Most begonias need some pruning after flowering. Semperflorens, especially, should be cut back at this time for maximum bloom and a more bushy plant. Severely prune all straggly, middle-aged begonias.

Propagation—Propagation is easy. New plants can be grown by rooting stems, rhizomes or leaves, by seeds, by layering, and by dividing old plants or tubers.

Hygiene—Dust tubers and rhizomes with a good fungicide before planting or storing. If insects are a problem, wash leaves in soapy water, and, if necessary, spray with an insecticide. Removing all dead leaves and flowers can prevent many problems. Allowing the soil to dry out before watering prevents rot. Check for slugs.

There are many species and varieties of begonia of which only a few can be mentioned.

Begonia grandis (B. evansiana)

Commonly thought to be tuberous is actually bulbous. *B. evansiana*, the hardiest of all begonias, is a fine, tall ground cover for wooded areas and a filler for crocus, daffodils, and other spring bulbs. The rich veined leaves are attractive in autumn and bloom until frost. Bloomtime starts on established plants in late spring and continues intermittantly all summer.

Culture—In spring plant bulbs 1″ deep in 3″ rich, woodsy loam. Space them 6″–8″ apart. Semishade is best. Water or mist during dry weather. A light mulch of leaves is desirable for winter protection. Mark location so as not to disturb dormant bulbs or new shoots the following season. Spring flowering plants will reappear from the old bulbs, and new plants grow from the bulblets.

Begonia Tuberhybrida

Summer-flowering tuberous-rooted begonia, having large, showy blossoms which often resemble camellias, roses, narcissus, or other flowers. They range in color from white to salmon, pinks, reds, yellows, and oranges. *B. tuberhybrida* are among the effective plants for hanging baskets in the house or cool greenhouse. They are also easy to force during the winter with florescent lights for indoor bloom.

Culture—Outdoor planting is not recommended in the south as *B. tuberhybrida* prefers cool nights (50°–55°) and day temperature not over 75° or 80°. If outdoor planting is attempted, water frequently, and reduce temperature by misting often. Plant in a shady spot which receives not more than 2 hours of early sunshine. Start tubers or seeds in early spring 2 months before 50° nights are expected. Put plants in the potting garden outside when the night temperature reaches 50°, and bring back in the house when it is 75°.

Begonia semperflorens

The wax begonia is the best known of all fibrous begonias. It is most popular as a houseplant, but may be planted in the garden or placed outside in pots for summer decoration. *B. semperflorens* has glossy heart shaped foliage which may be green, bronze or mahogany. This begonia blooms almost all summer till autumn, and off and on throughout the year in the house. Many new varieties have semidouble or double flowers in all shades of pinks, reds, and white.

Culture—B. semperflorens needs more light and less humidity than other begonias. However, during the heat of summer, frequent misting of outdoor plants is necessary; allow soil to dry slightly between watering. Some new varieties are more heat resistant. Part shade.

Begonia Rex

A fibrous type which is primarily a house or greenhouse plant. It bears small pink and white flowers every spring, but is usually grown for its foliage, which runs the gamut of color, texture, and size.

Culture—Rex begonias tend to be delicate but are worth the effort. They need protection from direct sunlight, but plenty of indirect light. They prefer a night temperature of 60°–65°, and a day temperature of 68°–72°. They like moist soil and high humidity, but do not mist hairy-leaved varieties as this breeds disease. Remove flower buds to promote strong leaf growth.

Begonia coccinia

The angel wing begonia ranges in size from under a foot to over 6 feet. These begonias have bamboolike stems and distinct joints. They are grown both for foliage, which may be green, pink, or splotched in a great variety of textures, as well as attractive flower clusters. House plant.

Begonia heracleifolia

The star begonia is a very hardy house plant. It has pink or white flowers and a star-shaped leaf.

Begonia scharffi

Has large clusters of white flowers with pink beards. It is a profuse bloomer, and has large white hairy leaves which point downward. It is tall and shrubby. House plant.

Begonia feastii

The beefsteak begonia has thick, round leaves, green on their upper surface and rusty beneath. It has pale pink blossoms. Place the beefsteak begonia in a north window.

Begonia elatior

The Rieger begonia, a tuberous rooted hybrid. Glossy leaves in many shades of green; flowers white, pink, yellow, orange, red, single and double. Keep slightly dry between waterings. Feed once a month; 4 hours of sun. House plant.

CONTAINER PLANTS

KEY
B—Blooming
F—Foliage
G—Greenhouse

COMMON NAME SCIENTIFIC NAME	KEY	HEIGHT	COMMENTS
African Daisy *Gerbera jamesonii*	B, G	To 1½′	Sun, moist; attractive cut flower. *Color:* shades of scarlet to orange, yellow, white.
African Violet *Saintpaulia*	B	6″	Many varieties. Indirect sun, barely moist. Water with tepid water only. Do not get cold water on leaves. *Color:* white, blue, pink, red, purple; hybrids of many colors.
Agapanthus Lily of the Nile *Agapanthus africanus*	B	18″–24″	Half day sun, cool, keep moist and fertilize only during growing season; likes to be pot bound. *Color:* blue, white.
Airplane plant *See* Spider plant			
Aloe *Aloe*	F	12″	Succulent; best in half day sun or bright indirect light; allow to become dry then water thoroughly; fertilize once a year. Many varieties. First aid plant. Spread jelly-like liquid from broken stem on burns and insect bites.

CONTAINER PLANTS

COMMON NAME SCIENTIFIC NAME	KEY	HEIGHT	COMMENTS
Aluminum plant *Pilea cadierei*	F	To 10″	Dark green and silver quilted leaves, other varieties have different color combinations. Bright indirect light, moist, good for terrariums. Propagate by stem cuttings in early spring.
Amaryllis *Hippeastrum* hybrids	B	1′–2′	Bright indirect light, moist. Fertilize monthly until Sept., then dry off until a month before desired bloom. Blooms: winter-spring. *Color:* pink, white, red, salmon and mixed colors.
Anthurium *Anthurium andraeanum*	B, G	2′–3′	Bright indirect sunlight, warm, moist; fertilize every two weeks. *Color:* orange red to rose and white.
A. scherzeranum	B	12″	Same as above. Some grown for leaves with insignificant flower. *Color:* red, rose, white.
Aralia *Aralia*	F	To 4′	Many varieties, many heights; interesting growth pattern; good for bonsai; noted for feathery foliage. Warm, moist soil, tolerates poor light.
Artillery plant *Pilea microphylla*	F	10″	Warm, moist, filtered light; small succulent leaf, slow growing.
Asparagus Fern *Asparagus setaceus*	F	hanging stems to 4′	Many varieties and leaf forms. Older plants bloom white followed by red berry. Moist, warm filtered light. Not a true fern.
Aspidistra Cast-Iron plant *Aspidistra elatior*	F	15″–30″	Noted for foliage; good for flower arrangements. Will tolerate heat, cold, wet soil or drouth, dust, neglect and dim light; grows best with good care.
Avocado *Persea americana*	F	To 10′	Large seed can be sprouted in water. Coarse leaf. Easy for children to grow. Pinch back to 1 ft.
Azalea *Azalea*	B	12″	Belgian hybrids are popular florist gift plant. *Color:* shades of pink and white.

CONTAINER PLANTS

COMMON NAME SCIENTIFIC NAME	KEY	HEIGHT	COMMENTS
Baby's Tears Mind-your-own-business *Soleirolia soleirolii*	F	¼″	Mosslike creeper grown for delicate foliage; ground cover for bonsai and greenhouse floor. Cool, partial shade.
Begonia *See* special article			
Bird-of-Paradise *Strelitzia reginae*	B, G	2′–3′	Large, striking flower resembling a bird's head. Rich soil, good light. *Color:* orange blue.
Bromeliad *Bromelia*	F, B		Large family of many species and hybrids. Leaves long and stiff forming a rosette, decorative foliage and long lasting brilliant blossoms. Warm filtered light; water in rosette cup. To force bloom place a piece of cut apple in rosette and cover entire plant with plastic until bud appears. *Color:* many showy colors.
Brunfelsia (G) *See* Yesterday-today-and-tomorrow			
Cactus *Cactus*	F	6″–2′	Hundreds of varieties, interesting shapes; check specific cactus books. Succulent, keep moist but not wet. See special article on succulents, including cactus. *Color:* many colors.
Caladium *Caladium*	F	1½′	Noted for foliage; effective all summer in shady garden. Diffused light, water freely, feed lightly. Leave in pots and store in fall. Do not water til spring. Also dwarf variety. *Color:* pink, red, white, green variegated leaves.
Calamondin Orange *Citrofortunella mitis*	B, F	To 3′	Ornamental form and foliage; fragrant bloom; small, orange, acidic fruit; blooms and fruits in cycles. Full sun; let soil dry slightly between waterings; fertilize early spring, early summer, and fall. *Color:* white.
Cape Primrose *See* Streptocarpus			

CONTAINER PLANTS

COMMON NAME SCIENTIFIC NAME	KEY	HEIGHT	COMMENTS
Camellia *See* special article			
Carissa *C. grandiflora*	F, B	3′–5′	Fragrant star-shaped flowers, glossy leathery leaves, scarlet plum-like fruit. *Color:* white.
Carissa Natal plum *C. grandiflora nana compacta*	F, B	18″–24″	Dwarf variety. *Color:* white.
Cattleya *See* special article on Orchids			
Chinese Evergreen *Aglaonema*	F	1′–2′	Several varieties; slow growing. Will tolerate little light and dry conditions, does best with light and moisture; will grow in water.
Christmas Cactus *Zygocactus truncata*	B	12″	Flower borne on succulent stem, blooms Oct.–Feb. Good light, do not overwater. *Color:* white, orange pink to magenta.
Cineraria *Senecio*	B	10″	Daisylike flowers, discard after blooming. Moist; cool. Many varieties. *Color:* every color except yellow.
Clivia Kaffir Lily *Clivia miniata*	B, G	2′	Lilylike flowers, thick evergreen strap-shaped leaves. Likes to be pot bound; let rest in fall without fertilizing, fertilize every two weeks during growing season; indirect light. Keep evenly moist. *Color:* coral, orange, yellow.
Club Moss *Selaginella kraussiana*	F	To 6″	Emerald green, overlapping scalelike leaves; good for hanging baskets, ground cover for bonsai and terrariums. Moderately moist, warm, indirect light.
Coleus *Coleus*	F	To 2½′	Many varieties. Grown for foliage of maroon, green, crimson, yellow, or combination of these colors. Keep pinched back, insignificant flowers. Indirect light, subject to mealy bugs.

CONTAINER PLANTS

COMMON NAME SCIENTIFIC NAME	KEY	HEIGHT	COMMENTS
Columnea *Columnea*	G, F		Vinelike plant, use in hanging containers; velvety foliage, flowers spring into fall. Keep evenly moist; bright indirect light. *Color:* red, yellow, or orange.
Crossandra *Crossandra*	B	To 12″	Gardenialike leaf, blooms year round. Direct sun. Keep evenly moist; fertilize once a month. *Color:* pastel, salmon orange.
Croton *Codiaeum variegatum*	F	3′–5′	Many varieties; foliage in shades from green, yellow, orange, pink, red, and crimson; requires sun to retain color. Fast grower, should be kept pruned. Milky sap poisonous.
Cyclamen *Cyclamen persicum*	B	12″	Florist cyclamen. Petals reflexed and twisted. Cool night temperatures, good drainage, bright indirect light. Also dwarf varieties. *Color:* white, pink, red.
Dieffenbachia Dumb Cane *Dieffenbachia*	F	To 10′	Many varieties; handsome leaves, spotted with white, cream or yellow markings. Moderate light, do not overwater; needs to be cut back when leggy. Poisonous.
Dracaena Corn plant *Dracaena*	F	To 3′	Many varieties, many different shapes and sizes of leaves. Light, rich soil, will thrive in sunless rooms. To water let tap water stand overnight so chlorine can evaporate, or use rain water, to keep leaf tips from turning brown. *Color:* White berries on coral stem.
Dumb Cane *See* Dieffenbachia			
Easter Lily *Lilium longiflorum*	B	2′	Florist lily at Easter time. Can be planted outside and will bloom following summer. *Color:* white.
False Aralia *Dizygotheca elegantissima*	F	3′–5′	Jagged dark green leaflets. Bright indirect light, keep barely moist.

CONTAINER PLANTS

COMMON NAME SCIENTIFIC NAME	KEY	HEIGHT	COMMENTS
Fatsia *Fatsia japonica*	F	4′ up	Bold shiny leaves, can be pruned to desired height; variegated varieties. Half day direct light, barely moist.
Ferns *See* special article			
Fig Weeping fig *Ficus benjamina*	F	6′ or more	Shiny leathery leaves; may lose leaves when moved. Prefers light; keep moist.
Rubber Plant *F. elastica*	F	To 12′	Large shiny dark green oval leaves, will branch when cut back. Semimoist, tolerates much neglect. Also variegated form.
Fiddle-leaf fig *F. lyrata*	F	To 12′	Shiny large, fiddle-shaped, dark green, leathery leaves. Filtered to bright light, heavy, semimoist soil, good drainage; do not overwater.
Creeping fig *F. pumila*	F	Vine	Semihardy outdoors. Small leaf, clinging vine; excellent for topiaries and hanging baskets. Humidity, direct light; susceptible to red spider.
Fuchsia Lady's eardrops *Fuchsia*	B, G	1′–4′	Many varieties, good for hanging container. Protect from hot sun, needs light, water well while blooming then reduce for resting period. Can be grown as standards, prune Jan. to Feb. Subject to white fly. *Color:* red, purple, white, pink.
Gardenia Cape jasmine *Gardenia jasminoides*	B, G	1′–3′	Very fragrant, dark glossy green leaves. Half day sun, moïst soil, high humidity, good drainage, fertilize monthly. Subject to white fly. *Color:* white.
Geranium *Pelargonium*	B	12″–18″	Many varieties, including variegated. Direct sun, dry out between waterings, do not overfertilize, high clay content in soil. Do not let water touch leaves. Pinch back for a bushier plant. Outside, keep in indirect light. *Color:* white, pink, red, coral.

CONTAINER PLANTS

COMMON NAME SCIENTIFIC NAME	KEY	HEIGHT	COMMENTS
Gloxinia *Sinningia speciosa*	B	To 12″	Velvety bell-shaped blooms. Warm, moist; high humidity. Water with tepid water only; do not get water on leaves. *Color:* white, red, pink, purple.
Grape Ivy *Cissus rhombifolia*	F	vine	Shiny green leaves; good for hanging baskets. Bright indirect light, let dry before watering thoroughly.
Hearts-entangled *See* Rosary vine			
Heliotrope *Heliotropium*	B	6″–12″	Fragrant, several hybrids. Half-day sun, moist. Can be treated as tender annual outdoors. *Color:* purple.
Hibiscus *Hibiscus*	B, G	To 4′	Many varieties; prune to keep desired height. Full sun, keep moist. Flower lasts only one day. Move outside in summer. *Color:* white, yellow, red, salmon, orange.
Hoya Wax plant *Hoya*	B	vine	Fragrant; some basket varieties. Half day sun, moist. *Color:* many colors.
Hydrangea *Hydrangea macrophylla*	B	18″–24″	Florist flower; plant outside to enjoy each summer. Sun, moist. Lime for pink flowers, aluminum sulfate for blue, and neutral soil for white. *Colors:* pink, white, blue.
Impatiens *Impatiens wallerana*	B	18″–24″	Partial shade, keep pinched for fullness, requires little care. For blight spray with a fungicide. Some varieties with variegated leaves. *Color:* white, pink, salmon, fuchsia, orange, purple.
Ivy *Hedera*	F	vine	Many varieties. Leaf sizes ½″–6″; shapes: lobed, rounded, wavy, or smooth. Good for topiary and hanging baskets. Half day sun, will grow in water. *Color:* leaves green, variegated, cream, yellow, pink, or white.

CONTAINER PLANTS

COMMON NAME SCIENTIFIC NAME	KEY	HEIGHT	COMMENTS
Ixora *Ixora coccinea*	B	To 4′	Half day sun, moist; can be kept below 2′ by pruning. *Color:* red, yellow
Jacobinia *Justica carnea*	B	1′–3′	Half day sun. Late spring bloom in greenhouse, summer bloom when pots are put outdoors in partial shade. Requires much fertilizer and water. *Color:* rosy-pink.
Jade plant *Crassula argentea*	F	To 3′	Succulent. Fat, thick, oval green leaves, inconspicuous white flower. Slow grower. Half-day sun; let soil dry out before watering.
Jasmine *Jasminum*	B	To 2′	Fragrant; many varieties. Half day sun, moist. *Color:* white.
Jerusalem Cherry *Solanum pseudocapsicum*	B	10″–18″	Flowers followed by cherry-sized poisonous scarlet fruit. Half day sun, let dry before good watering, keep out of drafts. *Color:* white.
Kalanchoe *Kalanchoe blossfeldiana*	B	18″	Many varieties; succulent. Bright light, heavy soil, good drainage, cool nights, drench and then let dry. *Color:* pink, red, salmon, yellow. Discard after blooming.
Kenilworth Ivy *Cymbalaria muralis*	F	vine	Hanging basket, decorative trailer. Semilight, moist. Keep pinched.
Lemon *Citrus limonia* 'ponderosa'	B, G	To 4′	Fragrant flowers followed by extra large lemons. Half day sun, semi-dry between watering, fertilize early spring, early summer, and fall. To control size pinch off new growth any time. *Color:* white.
Lily-of-the-Nile *See* Agapanthus			
Lipstick plant *Aeschynanthus radicans*	B	To 16″	Many varieties. Hanging baskets. Dark green waxy leaves, cut back stems to 6″ after flowering for new growth. Sunny window, warm, humid. *Color:* orange red.

CONTAINER PLANTS

COMMON NAME SCIENTIFIC NAME	KEY	HEIGHT	COMMENTS
Marguerite *Chrysanthemum frutescens*	B	To 3′	Half day sun, moist. Keep pinched for desired height; blooms winter and spring. *Color:* white, yellow.
Mind-Your-Own-Business *See* Baby's Tears			
Miniature Rose *Rosa chinensis 'minima'*	B	6″–12″	Fragrant. Half day sun, moist; fertilize every two weeks; subject to red spider. Blooms year round. *Color:* white, pink, red, yellow.
Monstera Split-leaf Philodendron *Monstera deliciosa*	F, B	vine	Very large plant; old plants have spathelike flower to 1′, large leathery perforated leaves, long cordlike aerial roots. Tolerates any condition except freeze, soil barely moist. Climber and needs support.
Moses-in-the-cradle *Rhoeo spathacea*	F	8″–15″	Dark green swordlike leaves with purple beneath. Bright indirect light, barely moist.
Mother-in-law's-tongue *Sansevieria trifasciata*	F	18″–30″	Toughest houseplant; stiff thick leaves often mottled with white; keep washed or dusted.
Nasturtium *Tropaeolum majus*	B, G	1′–6′	Bush or trailing. Several varieties, some double; check label on seed package. Sun, moist, cool greenhouse. Will not tolerate high heat. *Color:* all colors except blue.
Natal plum *See* Carissa			
Night-blooming Cereus *Hylocereus undatus*	B, G	To 15′	Climber; fragrant flower opens slowly at night, then dies by dawn. *Color:* white.
Norfolk Island Pine *Araucaria heterophylla*	F	To 12′	Pyramidal, very symmetrically branching ornamental. Bright light, barely moist; repot at 3–4 year intervals.

CONTAINER PLANTS

COMMON NAME SCIENTIFIC NAME	KEY	HEIGHT	COMMENTS
Oleander *Nerium oleander*	B, G	To 8′	Dark dull green lance-shaped leaf; cut back after flowering. Bright light; subject to scale and mealy bugs; set outside in summer. All parts very poisonous if eaten. *Color:* apricot, pink, red to white.
Orchid *See* special article			
Palm *See* special article			
Pandanus Screw Pine *Pandanus veitchii*	F	3′–5′	Slow grower. Bright indirect sun, semidry between watering, use charcoal in soil. Do not let water stand in axils as leaf will rot and fall off.
Paper plant *Cyperus papyrus*	F	To 2½′	Umbrellalike foliage at top of stalk. Water copiously. Pots can be sunk in fish pond in summer. To propagate: cut stem and insert upside down in glass of water, roots form from center of leaves.
Peacock plant *Calathea makoyana*	F	To 2′	Red stalks, green leaves with purple and red underneath. High humidity, bright indirect sun; best in terrarium.
Peperomia Radiator plant *Peperomia*	F	To 12″	Many varieties, leaves smooth or wrinkled, striped or variegated. Warm; bright indirect light; keep moderately dry between thorough watering.
Philodendron *Philodendron*	F	vine	Many varieties, green and variegated; will climb or trail; most popular and dependable. Keep cut to desired size. Medium light, moderately dry. Grows in water or soil.
Pickaback plant Piggyback plant *Tolmiea menziesii*	F	12″	Furry leaves bear tiny plantlets at their bases. Easily propagated at any time from leaves bearing plantlets. Moist, fertilize every two months, bright indirect light.

CONTAINER PLANTS

COMMON NAME SCIENTIFIC NAME	KEY	HEIGHT	COMMENTS
Pineapple *Ananas comosus*	F	3′	Spiny edged leaves of grayish to bronze green, gracefully arching. Half day sun, moist. Top of a pineapple with 2″ of pith may be rooted in water, changed frequently; when roots appear plant in potting soil.
Pocketbook plant *Calceolaria crenatiflora*	B	6″–12″	Richly colored pouchlike flowers, often spotted; profuse bloomer in spring. Cool, part sun, discard after blooming. *Color:* yellow, red, orange, bronze.
Poinsettia *Euphorbia pulcherrima*	B	To 4′	Prized for colorful bracts produced around Christmas. Sunny, moist, no drafts. Difficult to bring into bloom following year, due to demanding light requirements. *Color:* red, pink, white; also variegated.
Pomegranate (Dwarf) *Punica granatum 'nana'*	B	2′	Spring and summer flowers followed by reddish fruit. Cool, moist, half day sun, fertilize every 4 months. Attractive as bonsai. *Color:* flame.
Pothos *Epipremnum aureum*	F	vine	Variegated leaves resemble philodendron, and culture same.
Prayer plant *Maranta leuconeura*	F	6″–8″	Dark green leaves with red veins in fishbone pattern, purple undersides; leaves close at night. Bright indirect light; moist, dry side in winter; feed every 2 months from spring to fall.
Rabbit's tracks *M. leuconeura* var. *kerchoviana*	F	6″–8″	Leaves have dark spots resembling rabbits tracks. Culture same as above.
Primula Primrose *Primula*	B	6″	Pastel to strong colors; winter to spring bloom. Must have very cool conditions, part shade, moist. *Color:* All colors.
Radiator plant *See* Peperomia			

CONTAINER PLANTS

COMMON NAME SCIENTIFIC NAME	KEY	HEIGHT	COMMENTS
Rosary vine Hearts-entangled *Ceropegia woodii*	F	Vine to 3′	Purple stems bearing heart-shaped silver speckled leaves with purplish undersides. Bright indirect light, water after moderately dry, feed every two weeks from spring to midsummer only.
Rubber Plant *See* Ficus			
Schefflera Umbrella tree *Brassaia actinophylla*	F	To 6′	Palmate leaf. Half day sun to partial shade, warm, semidry between waterings; cut back to keep bushy. Also dwarf variety.
Screw Pine *See* Pandanus			
Shamrock *Oxalis acetosella*	B	To 12″	3 leaflets. Sun, moist. Symbol of Ireland. *Color:* white, pink.
Shrimp plant *Beloperone guttata*	B	18″	Flowers white, bracts colored in drooping terminal spikes. Sun; rich, well-drained soil; keep trimmed. *Color:* yellow or coral.
Spathiphyllum *Spathiphyllum clevelandii*	F	12″–18″	Lance-shaped dark green leaves, long-lasting flower. Filtered sunlight, moist; tolerates low light. Also dwarf variety. *Color:* white, light green.
Spider plant *Chlorophytum comosum*	F	To 2′	Grasslike arching leaves, small flowers in graceful sprays. Plant produces long wiry stems that terminate in small plantlets, which may be rooted easily. Also variegated varieties. Filtered sun, moist; best in hanging basket, tolerant of house conditions. *Color:* white.
Star Jasmine *Trachelospermum jasminoides*	B	vine	Fragrant star-shaped flowers, dark green leathery leaves. Sun, semidry between waterings. *Color:* white.

CONTAINER PLANTS

COMMON NAME SCIENTIFIC NAME	KEY	HEIGHT	COMMENTS
Streptocarpus Cape Primrose *Streptocarpus rexii*	B	To 10″	Open-faced flower, long narrow quilted basal leaves. Moist, 14–16 hours of light a day for continuous bloom. Some varieties have dormant period. Also dwarf and variegated varieties. *Color:* white, pink, red, purple.
Swedish Ivy *Plectranthus australis*	F	vine	Waxy dark green leaves on square stems. Bright indirect light, barely moist; pinch for bushiness. Good in hanging baskets. *Color:* insignificant white flower.
Ti *Cordyline terminalis*	F	2½′	Long drooping leathery leaves grow palmlike at top of stems. Very humid, sun. Used for roof thatching and hula skirts.
Umbrella plant *See* Paper plant			
Umbrella tree *See* Schefflera			
Wandering Jew *Tradescantia fluminensis*	F	trailer	Smooth leaves and stems, insignificant lavender flower. Sun, moist. Good for hanging baskets; easy to grow. *Color:* green, red and green, green and purple foliage.
Wax Plant *See* Hoya			
Yesterday-today-and-tomorrow *Brunfelsia australis*	B	2′	Fragrant flowers change from purple to white over three-day period. Half-day direct sun, moist, bloom best when pot bound. *Color:* purple, lavender, white.
Zebra plant *Aphelandra squarrosa*	B	12″–18″	Large flower cluster of bracts, ovate leaves with veins marked with white. Sun, moist. Fall bloom, occasionally other seasons. *Color:* yellow.

BONSAI

Bonsai (pronounced bone-sigh), literally translated, means "tray planting." Simply, it is the Japanese art of keeping a tree or shrub dwarfed by confining it to a small pot. Horticulturally speaking, it is the highest art form of all, blending artistic ability and horticultural expertise. Controlling the size of any bonsai is done by pruning the roots and branches at the time of planting. During its lifetime, it will periodically be unpotted, root-pruned, and repotted with new soil so as to retain its size and shape. It will also demand constant pruning and pinching of new growth.

These plants are basically outdoor plants, although bonsai can be tropicals and kept indoors. They must have protection when temperatures drop below 28° and be protected from wind and continuous freezing and thawing. Water is an important factor in growing bonsai. They must never be allowed to dry out as it will kill them instantly. In most places, this means watering them every day in the summer. If the drainage is correct, they can never be overwatered.

There are five basic styles of bonsai: formal upright, informal upright, slanting, cascade, and semicascade. There are variations to these basic styles including forest and clump style.

Here are some brief guidelines to follow for making a bonsai. First, in the spring before the leaf buds begin to swell, find a hardy conifer such as a juniper or any plant with an interesting trunk and small foliage. Look at the rootage and decide which is the most interesting side. That becomes the front of the plant. The formal upright style, for instance, requires that the bottom third of the branches be removed in most cases. This not only reveals the trunk, but gives the look of age. The lowest, longest, and thickest remaining branch should be the first branch. Wire it to reach slightly forward and lean either to the left or right of the trunk. Now, a back branch should be wired either to the left or right to give depth. The third branch should be slightly higher on the opposite side of the first branch. Continue this alternating of branches, pruning to make them smaller, and then wire the apex of the tree. Each branch should form a triangle and the finished tree will be a triangle with the trunk tapering from bottom to top.

Use aluminum wire as it is easier to manipulate. Since it comes in various sizes use a size that is one-third the size of the branch being wired. Always wrap the wire toward the front and keep a constant distance between each wrap, bending the branch to the desired curve. As the tree grows, watch for wire damage and remove when damage shows, as the tree can be rewired at any time.

Bonsai pots come in all sizes and shapes. Each tree is styled and shaped and a bonsai pot is selected for that individual tree. The pots are unglazed inside and have large drainage holes which should be covered with one-eighth inch hardware cloth cut slightly larger than the holes and wired down. This keeps the slugs from coming into the pot and the soil from coming out. Unglazed pots in brown, gray, or terracotta are generally used for evergreen while glazed pots are used for deciduous trees. The length or breadth of the pot should be approximately two-thirds the height of the tree. Straight trunks are better in a rectangular pot while curved trunks look better in round or oval pots. Cascade pots are deep and usually tall.

Always use new clean soil. A good average mix is equal parts commercial potting soil (sterilized), peat moss, and a large to medium type aggregate. A rule of thumb is that the equal amounts of roots and foliage should be removed. Leave the small hairlike surface roots on the ball. Loosen the root ball and rake away most of the soil, then cut away one-fourth, one-third or one-half the root system, depending on how much has been cut off the top of the tree. If it has a tap root, cut it out and also remove old clumps of dirt under the root. Place soil in the bottom of the container and fit the tree into the container, cutting the roots to the size and shape of the pot. Straighten all roots and finish potting making certain soil is in, under, and around all roots with no air pockets remaining. Use a chop stick or a pencil to achieve this. The plant should be tied down with a length of wire going through the bottom holes and around the plant to secure it. Place the bonsai in a tub of water or sink filling to brim of container. When soil is entirely wet, remove and place in a semishaded area for a week to ten days. Do not fertilize for a month or two. If new growth appears, pinch back continuously. The plant should eventually be placed in full sun and watered daily. If the sun gets too hot, filtered sun is favored. Fertilize with bonsai fertilizer or any organic fertilizer. Water and protect it in the winter from 28° or colder. Bonsai can be wintered by burying the pots in the compost bin to keep pots from cracking.

Some classic plants used for bonsai are: *Evergreen*—camellia, five-needle pine, cedar, Japanese holly, San Jose juniper, Norway spruce, Shimpaku juniper, boxwood, chamaecyparis cypress, Japanese juniper, Japanese black pine, dwarf Alberta spruce, podocarpus, Satsuki azalea, and pyracantha. *Deciduous*—Japanese maple, trident maple, red maple, hornbeam, barberry, flowering quince, hackberry, beech, ginkgo, cotoneaster, hawthorn, crabapple, sweet gum, flowering apricot, bald cypress, elm, wisteria, and Zelkova elm. *Indoor bonsai*—Natal plum, gardenia, olive, camellia, jade plant, aralia, citrus, ficus, and myrtle.

There are excellent books on bonsai, such as The Brooklyn Botanic Garden's *Handbook on Bonsai* for beginners and John Naka's *Bonsai Techniques I* and *Bonsai Techniques II* for the student. Bonsai is a living art form that is constantly changing because of growth and change. Make one or buy one, but enjoy one.

FERNS

Selection

Buy from a reputable dealer who knows the fern's cultural requirements and size at maturity.

Buy only a healthy plant—(a) Clean with no dead or wilted foliage; (b) Free from bug or disease infestation; (c) Good color; (d) Adequately potted; should not be growing out of pot and need repotting.

Light

Most ferns grow best in shade or filtered light, as dense shade is not suitable. Inside supplemental artificial light is frequently required. Fluorescent lamps are best, but ordinary incandescent bulbs can be used. The fluorescent fixtures have a lower heat output which greatly reduces the chance of injury to the fern. Also, natural light from a window will vary from season to season with the rotation of the sun. Artificial light may have to be added at some season.

Watering

The majority of cultivated ferns prefer soil which is consistently moist, not soggy. Less active growing periods require less water. Interior heating greatly determines the amount of water required. The warmer it is inside, the more water is needed. Air conditioning causes ferns to dry out faster.

Ferns in small pots and clay pots require more frequent watering. If the soil is sandy or loose, the more frequent the need to water. Since overwatering can cause root damage, try to water when needed rather than by a set schedule.

Water thoroughly until water drains out of the bottom, remembering a crowded fern will require more time and water for the moisture to be absorbed into the interior of the root ball. Always try to water under the foliage as some of the finer fern foliage can be injured by water standing on their tips. It is best to water early in the day to let the leaves dry quickly.

Ferns will not tolerate standing in water. Place pebbles in the saucer to raise the pot out of the water. This also increases humidity around the plant.

Temperature

Ferns vary greatly in temperature requirements. Inside ferns tend to tolerate a 55°–70° temperature range. Do not place a fern too near the ceiling, on top of a TV, or in the flow of air from a heating duct. They need to be protected from hot air and drafts although a small amount of air circulation is desirable. If using artificial light, do not place too near light source.

Soil

Generally a well-drained soil is recommended. A combination of potting soil and perlite or sand makes a good mixture.

Fertilizing

Feeding is essential for all ferns. Container-grown ferns require frequent feedings as plant food is flushed out of containers and nourishment should be provided regularly.

Choose a fertilizer that indicates it is "low burn." It is advisable to use half strength and fertilize more often. Plants grown under artificial light require more frequent feedings.

Methods of Potting

1. Conventional potting
2. Baskets of wire with a spagnum moss lining
3. Plaquing for Staghorns

Reproducing

The most common way is by spores, but parts of the root, rhizome, or frond may produce new plants. Some ferns produce bulblets, others can be multiplied by dividing, while still others produce runners that start new plants. For more detailed information consult a fern grower's manual.

Pests and Diseases

Carefully check ferns periodically, looking on the underneath side of the fronds. Do not confuse the spore cases with insect scale.

The most common insects are aphids, scale, mealybug, and thrips. Biting insects such as slugs will leave holes. The best control method is prevention by keeping clean, well-kept containers and plants. Old fronds should be cut back to soil level for, if left intact, they harbor insects and disease and interfere with the development of new fronds. New ferns should be isolated for several weeks to make certain they are disease free. If insect infestation appears, isolate the plant and use a mild insecticide such as dipping in a 5% Sevin solution, since the ferns are very sensitive to chemicals. Adiantums are easily burned. Mildew fungus is prevalent on some ferns. Always read labels carefully and follow directions. If possible, reduce dosage.

FERNS

KEY

Information is listed under five headings, the first being CLASSIFICATION, where ten types are found. The second heading, SHADE, specifies one of three possible requirements using the code letters A, B, and C. Where two letters are given, considerable adaptability is indicated according to local growing conditions. The third heading, SOIL, indicates four possibilities using the code letters D, E, F, and G. D and E refer to types which may be grown in the ground, F refers to types which are usually grown in containers and G explains the limestone requirements. The fourth heading, WATERING, consists of five possible requirements using the code letters H, I, J, K, and L. The fifth heading, CULTURE, consists of the code letters M, N, O, and P indicating the relative difficulty of cultivation while specific cultural situations are designated by the code letters Q, R, S, T, U, V, and W.

CLASSIFICATION

1. Adiantum Ferns (Maidenhair)
2. Basket or Hanging Ferns
3. Basket Ferns, Footed (Rabbits Foot)
4. Low Growing Ferns
5. Medium Tall Ferns
6. Tall Ferns
7. Tree Ferns, Low Growing
8. Tree Ferns, Tall Growing
9. Climbing Ferns
10. Platyceriums (Staghorn)

SHADE

A. Filtered sunlight, early morning sun, late afternoon sun.
B. Sun not essential but requires strong light.
C. Best grown without sun, requires good light.

Ferns will not survive in dark, dense shade.

SOIL

D. Climbing; Suitable for wall plantings facing north or east. Grows well in containers.
E. Garden type in mild winter areas. Requires more acid type humus, more protection from sun, wind, and cold. Also suitable for container culture.

F. Container grown. No soil incorporated. Depending on areas, material such as leaf mold, redwood humus, planter mixes, etc.
G. Limestone: Planting areas near cement foundations, walks, etc. In garden areas incorporate small pieces of cement 2 to 3 inches deep around root area. Container grown, add lime to a 6-inch pot of potting mix.

WATERING

H. After thorough watering, allow to become nearly dry (damp).
I. Should be kept damp, not allowed to dry out. Suitable for garden planting with camellias, azaleas, begonias, etc. Mulching required.
J. Requires consistent moisture. When container grown, thorough watering is necessary to penetrate all root areas.
K. Heavy moisture on fronds should be avoided. Moisture on fronds results in decay on lower layers of fronds.
L. Must be kept very wet. Container grown requires heavy, thorough soakings.

Many people have a tendency to feel sprinkling is watering. Watering is penetrating all soil and root systems. Sprinkling is beneficial during hot weather to create humidity. Good drainage is essential in all cases.

CULTURE

M. Relatively easy to grow.
N. Not too difficult, requires some attention.
O. Difficult in some areas. Requires ideal conditions with protection from winds or air circulation which result in dry air in summer and cold air in winter. Needs good overhead protection from mild frosts and strong sun rays. Requires high humidity.
P. Very difficult if ideal conditions are not provided. Heated greenhouses and high humidity essential (similar to Cattleya orchid cultures). Will not survive dry air and cold.
Q. Deciduous. In some cases they retain a few old fronds. In the winter months ferns that become deciduous must not dry out. In their native habitat they have sufficient rains to keep them moist. In areas with limited rainfall, if not kept moist, they will not survive.
R. During the winter months keep barely damp, but do not let dry out. In the spring, when the new growth is noted, water heav-

ily with thorough soakings. With heavy watering after their rest period they will develop much faster.

S. Multiple crowns. Some ferns produce an abundance of crowns as they get older. Becoming heavily massed, they crowd and rise above the growing media. When these ferns reach this stage in the spring and at the same time good, strong new growth is noted, they should be divided. In some areas when unusual spells of a few warm days and nights encourage new growth, do not divide. Be certain the spring warmth is going to be consistent. When the proper period arrives, an abundance of new fiddle heads will be noted about ready to uncurl. Dividing at the wrong time will result in loss of plants unless they are in a heated greenhouse to provide warmth for constant growth.

T. Some ferns without crowns, having a creeping, spreading root system, also require the above treatment. They are divided in sections being certain each section has sufficient new growth. Some types become so matted that dead areas will be noted. Sections without good new growth should be removed. This is true of types grown in the ground also.

U. In mild climates or in greenhouses cut off old fronds in February and September. In colder areas cut back only in the spring.

V. In the spring of the year when new growth is noted, cut off all the old fronds. This should be done before the new fronds get too big to avoid bruising and damage. The time will vary with each fern. The large majority of the old fronds have gone through their reproduction stage and will die.

W. Groom throughout the year, removing spent fronds. The majority of these ferns put out consistent new growth year round. All ferns should be groomed when spent or damaged fronds are noted. Keep all pots clean.

FERNS

COMMON NAME SCIENTIFIC NAME	CLASSIFI- CATION	SHADE	SOIL	WATERING	CULTURE
Autumn Fern					
Dryopteris erythrosora	4	A	D	I	M, W
D. filix-mas	5	A	D, F	I	N, S, V
D. filix-mas cv.					
'Cristata'	4	B	F	J	N, T
Humata tyermannii	3	A, B	F	J	M, V
Lygodium japonicum	9	A	F	J	M, V

FERNS

COMMON NAME SCIENTIFIC NAME	CLASSIFI-CATION	SHADE	SOIL	WATERING	CULTURE
Bear's Paw					
Polypodium angustifolium	2	B	F	J	O, W
P. aureum	3	A, B	D, F	I, J	M, V
P. aureum cv. 'Mandaianum'	3	A, B	E, F	I, J	M, V
Bird's Nest Fern					
Asplenium nidus	6	C	F	L	N, W
Boston					
Nephrolepis biserata cv. 'Furcans'	2	C	F	H	P, W
N. cordifolia	5	A	D, F	I	M, W
N. cordifolia cv. 'Duffii'	4	C	F	H	O, T
N. exaltata cv. 'Anna Foster'	2	B	F	H, K	O, W
Nephrolepis exaltata cv. 'Fluffy Ruffles'	4	A, B	F	H, K	M, T
N. exaltata cv. 'Norwoodii'	2	B	F	H, K	O, W
N. exaltata cv. 'Rooseveltii'	2	B	F	H, K	O, W
N. exaltata cv. 'Smithii'	2	C	F	H, K	O, W
N. exaltata cv. 'Trevillian'	2	B	F	H, K	O, W
N. exaltata cv. 'Verona'	2	B	F	H, K	O, W
N. exaltata cv. 'Whitmannii'	2	B	F	H, K	O, W
Osmunda regalis	4	B	D, F	I	N, W
Pellaea falcata	4	A, B	G	I	N, W
Brazilian Form					
Polypodium polycarpon cv. 'Grandiceps'	2	B	F	J	O, W
P. scolopendria	3	A, B	E, F	J	N, W
P. subauriculatum cv. 'Knightiae'	2	A, B	F	J	N, R, V
P. vacciniifolium	3	C	F	L	P, W
Polystichum munitum	5	A	D	I	M, V
P. setosum	4	A	D	I	M, V
P. tsus-simense	4	A	D	I	N, W

FERNS

COMMON NAME SCIENTIFIC NAME	CLASSIFI- CATION	SHADE	SOIL	WATERING	CULTURE
Button Fern					
Pellaea rotundifolia	4	A, B	G	I	N, W
P. viridis	5	B	F	J	N, W
Phyllitis scolopendrium cvs.	4	C	G	J	N, S
Pityrogramma calomelanos (Silverback)	4	A, B	F	J	O, W
P. chrysophylla (Goldback)	4	A, B	F	J	O, W
Climbing Bird's-nest					
Polypodium polycarpon integrifolium	2	C	F	J	P, W
Crested Bird's-nest					
Polypodium polycarpon cv. 'Cristatum'	2	C	F	J	P, W
Felt Fern					
Leatherleaf					
Pyrrosia lingua	3	A, B	E, F	I, J	N, W
Rumohra adiantiformis	5	A	D	I	M, W
Stenochlaena palustris	9	B	F	J	M, W
Tectaria gemmifera	5	A, B	E	I	M, W
Todea barbara	7	A	D	J	M, W
Woodwardia orientalis	2	A, B	F	J	M, W
Lady Fern					
Japanese Painted					
Athyrium filix-femina	5	A	D	L	M, S, Q
A. goeringianum pictum	4	A, B	D, F	J	N, Q
Blechnum brasiliense	7	B	E	I	O, S, W
B. gibbum	7	C	F	J	O, S, W
Cibotium glaucum	8	A	D	I	M, W
Cyrtomium falcatum	5	A	D	I	M, V
Maidenhair					
Adiantum anceps	1	C	F, G	J, K	P, W
A. bellum	1	C	F, G	J	O, W
A. capillus veneris	1	A, B	D, G	I	M, R, U
A. capillus-veneris cv. 'Imbricatum' (Green Petticoats)	1	C	F, G	J, K	P, W
A. caudatum	1	C	F, G	J	O
A. hispidulum	1	A, B	D, G	J	N, V
A. microphyllum	1	C	F, G	J, K	P, W
A. pedatum	1	C	E, F, G	L	O, W
A. peruvianum	1	C	F, G	J, K	P, W

FERNS

COMMON NAME SCIENTIFIC NAME	CLASSIFI- CATION	SHADE	SOIL	WATERING	CULTURE
A. raddianum cv. 'Fritz-Luthii'	1	A, B	D, G	J	N, V
A. raddianum cv. gracillimum	1	A, B	F, G	J	M, T, U
A. raddianum cv. 'Grandiceps'	1	C	F, G	J	O, W
A. raddianum cv. 'Lady Geneva'	1	C	F, G	J	O, W
A. raddianum cv. 'Pacific Maid'	1	C	F, G	J	O, W
A. raddianum cv. 'Pacottii'	1	C	F, G	J	O, W
A. tenerum	1	A, B	D, G	I	M, T, U
A. tenerum cv. 'Farleyense'	1	C	F, G	J, K	P, W
A. trapeziforme	1	C	F, G	J, K	P, W
Aglaomorpha meyeniana	3	B	F	J	O, W
Alsophila cooperi	8	A	D	I	M, W
Mother Fern					
Asplenium bulbiferum	5	A, B	D, F	L	M, W
A. daucifolium	4	B	E, F	J	N, W
Rabbit's Paw or Squirrel Foot					
Davallia fijeensis cv. 'Plumosa'	3	A, B	F	J	O, V
D. solida	3	B	F	J	O, V
D. trichomanoides	3	A, B	F	J	M, V
Dicksonia antartica	8	A	D	I	M, W
Dryopteris pedata	4	C	G	J	O, W
Staghorn					
Platycerium bifurcatum	10	A, B	F	J	M
P. grande	10	C	F	H	N
Table Ferns					
Pteris cretica cv. 'Albo-lineata'	4	A	D	I	N, W
P. cretica cv. 'Parkeri'	5	A	D	I	M, V
P. cretica cv. 'Rivertoniana'	4	A	D, F	I	M, V
P. cretica cv. 'Wilsonii'	4	A	D, F	I	M, V
P. cretica cv. 'Wimsetti'	4	A	D, F	I	M, V
P. ensiformis cv. 'Victoriae'	4	C	F	J	P, W
P. quadriaurita cv. 'Argyrea'	6	C	E	I	N, S, W
P. vittata	6	A	D	I	M, S, W

ORCHIDS

The orchid family is the most extraordinary, exotic, and vast of all plant life. It is the largest family in the world with 25,000 known species. They come in dazzling colors, fanciful shapes, and many fragrances. They grow from the Equator to Greenland; from sea level to 14,000 feet; in swamps, forests, deserts, and meadows.

The texture and substance of the orchid tissue is remarkable. It is fleshy, thick, and waxy which explains the lasting quality of the blooms. Some look as though they have been lacquered. Their shapes are unlike any other flower, both spectacular and unique. In some, their foliage and roots are not attractive, but others are grown for their interesting foliage alone. The flowers range in size from less than 1″ to 8″ across.

There are two types of orchids: 1) *Epiphytic*—which means that they grow on trees in nature, their roots clinging to the bark. They get nourishment from the air, debris, and rain. Their thickened leaves and stems store water, and they can tolerate periods of dryness; 2) *Terrestrial*—which means that they grow in the ground, and must have more water.

The best place to obtain orchids is from a professional grower. Choose a plant while it is in bloom to see the color and type.

Culture

All orchids have most of the same cultural requirements: the correct potting mix, perfect drainage, proper amount of water, frequent fertilizing, correct amount of light, correct temperature, and proper ventilation. Special pots for orchids have larger drainage holes.

Potting mix for Epiphytes—tree fern fiber, which does not disintegrate, and/or fir bark. Add 3 or 4 pieces of pot shard for drainage and nylon screen over draining hole to prevent slugs.

Potting mix for Terrestrials—1 part gravel, 1 part leaf mold or compost, 1 part tree fiber or fir bark (available at garden centers).

Temperature—**Cool,** 50° night; 60°-70° days.

Intermediate—55°-50° night; 65°-70° days.

Warm—60°-65° nights; 70°-85° days.

Fertilizing— When buds appear and during blooming period, use an 18-18-18 orchid fertilizer such as Peters, every two weeks. After blooming use a 30–10–10 orchid fertilizer every two weeks. These are the general rules for fertilizing. For more details check with a grower. Plants require less fertilizer when light intensity is low and when they are not actively making new growth.

Greenhouse Aids—Cool water and mister for summer, evaporative cooler with thermostatic control. Fan not necessary but helpful. Automatic opening and closing control for vents.

Pests—Orchids are surprisingly pest and disease free. Most pests can be removed with soap and water. For heavy infestations, see below.

Aphids—Leave a black fungus. Wash off with water and detergent or spray with an insecticide such as Malathion or Diazinon.

Mealy Bugs—Leave a cottony mass. Remove with cotton swabs dipped in alcohol. Rinse with water.

Scale—Leaves hard-shelled bumps. Pick or scrape off or swab with rubbing alcohol. Spray with oil based insecticide.

Slugs and Snails—Chewed holes in leaves and flower and damaged roots. Put cotton wool around stem to protect flowers. Trap with commercial slug bait or saucer of beer at night.

Spider Mites—Stippled leaves or white webbing on underside of leaf. Scrub and rinse with warm water. Spray heavy infestation with an insecticide such as Diazinon or Malathion.

Diseases—A combination fungicide-bactericide such as Natriphene (available from orchid growers) will control most diseases.

Black Rot—Brown blotches with yellow edges on leaves caused by fungus and too much water or humidity. Destroy badly diseased plants.

Petal Blight—Small brown dots on the flowers (a fungus). Cut off and destroy infected flowers.

Virus—Yellow brown streaking and malformation in leaves and flowers. No cure. Destroy infected plants. Avoid by sterilizing pots and tools. Dip potting sticks in household bleach.

Orchids are not difficult to grow, provided their cultural needs are met. However, they can stand some neglect. They do not require long hours of work, can survive if watered once a week and repotted every year or two. They give more pleasure for less work. One orchid grower once said, "It takes a genius to kill them!"

ORCHIDS

KEY
*D.G.S.—During Growing Season
E—Epiphytic
T—Terrestrial

Orchid Genera		a. Light b. Temperature	a. Humidity b. Water	Colors	Bloom Time	Description
Brassavola	E	a. 4 hrs. sun daily. *D.G.S. b. Intermediate	a. Medium b. Keep moist, not wet	White and Greenish white	Spring Summer Winter	Easy to grow. Tough leathery green leaves from pseudobulbs and shiny oval pointed leaves. Large spiderlike flowers. Fringed lips. Reduce water for two weeks when new pseudobulbs appear.
Cattleya	E	a. Bright b. Intermediate	a. High b. Once a week, nearly dry between waterings.	Clear purple, pink, yellow, orange, white	All 12 months depending on species	Flower stalks, 2″ to 8″ across of 2 to 6 flowers each. All are fragrant. Important commercially, good for beginners. Do not fertilize in winter.
Cymbidium	T	Difficult in hot climates. Should have cool nights in Aug.—50° to set blooms	a. High b. Keep damp at all times	Solid and combinations of green, yellow, rose, maroon, bronze, and white	Late fall to spring. Blooms last 6 wks. to 2 mo.	Use ice cubes on roots in August. Flowers borne on spikes. 2 to 40 flowers. Narrow grasslike foliage. Like to be pot bound.

ORCHIDS

Orchid Genera		a. Light b. Temperature	a. Humidity b. Water	Colors	Bloom Time	Description
Cypripedium or *Paphioipedilum* "Lady Slipper"	T	a. Bright filtered b. Intermediate	a. Medium humidity b. Medium water. Moist, not soggy.	White, green, yellow, orange, pink, brown, plus multicolors	Spring-summer. Blooms last 1 to 2 mos.	Mottled leaf varieties are good house plants. "Lady Slipper" from ballet-shoe shape of lip. Native.
Dendrobium	E	a. Bright filtered b. Intermediate	Needs cool, dry period from Nov. 1 to Jan. 15	Golden yellow, white, pink, violet, purple, fuschia	Early spring. Last 2 to 3 wks.	Can be grown like a cattleya. 1" to 2" flowers borne on drooping spikes. Good for home growing. Direct sunlight will burn leaves.
Epidendrum "Dancing Ladies"	E	a. Bright b. Intermediate	a. Medium b. D.G.S.* allow to become almost dry between waterings	White, green, yellow, pink & multi-colors	Spring, Summer. Long lasting flowers	Three wide, leathery leaves and reedlike stems. Waxy single or clusters of blooms. Tiny to 3" on long spike. Fragrant.
Laelia	E	a. Sun 4 to 8 hrs. a day. b. Intermediate to warm	a. Medium b. D.G.S.* allow to become moderately dry.	Vivid and fiery yellows, and red orange, rich violets	All seasons. Long bloom time, flowers lasting more than 2 mo.	1 or 2 evergreen, bladelike leaves. Flowers 1½" to 4" on various length sprays from pseudobulbs. Similar to Cattleya, but with narrower petals. Genus used to produce brilliant hybrid colors.

Oncidium "Yellow Bee" "Dancing Ladies"	E	a. Bright sun except at noon b. Intermediate	a. 40% to 60% b. Adjust plant to growing cycle. More water while growing.	White, green, yellow, orange, pink, red, multi-colored	Flowers last about 2 to 6 weeks	Tips look like flaring skirt. Generally grown like Cattleyas. Most have showers of up to 100 bright yellow blossoms on long, arching stalks. Other varieties have large flowers.
Phalaenopsis "Butterfly Orchid" "Moth Orchid" Also miniatures	E	a. Filtered b. Warm	a. 50% to 70% b. They do not have pseudobulbs for water storage. Must be kept moist—not soggy.	White, soft pink, lavender, purple, green, yellow, brown.	Bloom once a year. Jan–Mar. Bloom spray lasts 2 mos. After bloom cut back to third node for another bloom spike.	Good house plant. Flowers resemble tropical moths on long, generally flat, sprays of 10–20 1" blooms. Some have wide, flat, leathery yellow green leaves, long roots. Should be protected from excessive heat.
Vanda	E	a. 6 hrs. bright sun. Shield from noon sun. b. Warm	a. 40% to 60% b. Keep constantly moist but not soggy. Water less D.G.S.*	Blue, salmony pink, red, purple, and multi-colored. Used in many hybrid crosses	May & June. Flowers last 3 to 6 wks.	Erect plant with opposite leaves. Open-faced flowers on long fluttering stalks that emerge from evergreen leaves, either cylindrical, strap, or V-shape. Stem may need support. 5 to 80 blooms. Repot as little as possible. Easy to grow.

PALMS

Palms are mostly tropical. Therefore, the only palms mentioned in this chapter are for the house or greenhouse. They should be kept moist, not wet, to avoid root rot. Good drainage is essential. Water all the way around the pot, not just in one spot. Though they tolerate neglect, they respond well to high nitrogen fertilizer. Some varieties tolerate low light. For cosmetic reasons, remove dead fronds with scissors.

Palms like to be pot bound. If necessary to repot, be very careful of the fragile roots and do not remove old soil. Be sure to match the firm consistency of the old soil with the new mix, otherwise the roots will not spread.

Palms are slow growers, so purchase desired size. Palm leaves should be deep green in a healthy plant. Do not purchase a plant with yellow fronds.

PALMS

COMMON NAME SCIENTIFIC NAME	COMMENTS
Areca or Butterfly Palm *Chrysalidocarpus lutescens*	Arching featherlike fronds, yellowish stalks. Bright indirect light; moist, do not let stand in water. Suckers can be rooted.
Chinese Fan Palm *Livistona chinensis*	Open, fan-shaped leaves on long thin stalks; a tough plant. Keep moist; slow grower.
European Fan Palm *Chamaerops humilis*	5′ stiff fan-shaped dark green leaves. Needs good light, cooler room than most house plants.
Fishtail Palm *Caryota mitis*	Leaves shaped like fish tail; tolerates being pot bound. Culture same as Butterfly Palm; likes humidity, place well away from air conditioner.
Lady Palm *Rhapis excelsa*	Shiny fan-shaped leaves grow intermittently along fibrous trunk. Tolerates cool or warm conditions; keep soil dryer than other palms. Heavy feeder.
Miniature Date Palm *Phoenix roebeleni*	Graceful, arching leaves consisting of many leaflets, rarely exceeds 2 feet; culture same as Butterfly Palm.

PALMS

COMMON NAME SCIENTIFIC NAME	COMMENTS
Miniature Japanese Palm *Rhapis excelsa*	Many varieties. Dark green, pleated leaf. Tolerates low light; requires little water.
Parlor Palm *Chamaedorea elegans*	Featherlike arching fronds; dwarf, to 18″, often used in terrariums. Does best in north exposure; tolerant of neglect, low light, and air conditioning.
Pony Tail *Beaucarnea recurvata*	Not a true palm; bulbous at base of trunk for water storage; wrinkled ball of bark, leaves forms a tuft at top of trunk. Let dry between waterings, do not overwater; fertilize in spring only.
Sago Palm *Cycas revoluta*	Not a true palm but a cycad; shiny dark green leathery leaves resembling fern fronds; slow grower. Semidry between thorough watering; fertilize every two months spring, to midsummer only.
Sentry Palm *Howea forsterana*	Feathery, arching leaves with many slender leaflets; slow grower. Barely moist, use several plants in container. Tolerates cooler temperature than other palms.

SUCCULENTS AND CACTI

These plants usually are native to arid or semiarid regions. They have fleshy leaves, stems, or both, in which needed moisture is stored. Succulents (including the cacti) can be grown most successfully as house plants, especially in window gardens, and they offer much in beauty and interest.

They like porous soil, plenty of sunshine, very little water during the resting season and, most important of all, they *must* have perfect drainage.

Succulents are more effective when planted to themselves. Up to three may be grown in a single container; but if more than one are used, choose plants of complementary colors. The varieties available are numerous and of many intriguing forms. They provide the truly unusual in house plants.

The Preparation of Cut Materials for Flower Arrangements

To prolong the life of cut flowers and foliage, certain steps should be followed. Conditioning is the process of soaking flowers or foliage in solutions for about two hours or burning the stem ends. Hardening is the process of soaking flowers or foliage overnight in deep tepid water. Most flowers are conditioned and then hardened.

THREE STEPS IN PREPARATION OF FRESH FLOWERS FOR ARRANGEMENTS

Cutting

DO'S

Use garden flowers if possible. However, these suggestions apply also to florist's flowers.
Use sharp clippers.
Place cut flowers immediately in a bucket of tepid water.
Remove leaves to the water level of bucket.
Clip off about 2 inches of stem under water.
Cut flowers very late on the day before arranging (not in sun), then condition and harden.

DON'TS

Cut flowers in the sun.
Leave flowers in the sun or in a breeze.
Spray flowers after conditioning.
Use more than one chemical when conditioning flowers.
Soak white stemmed flowers (bulbs) in water over four inches deep.
Change the water of an arrangement if foliage has been removed below the water line. Just add fresh water.
Take a dead flower out of an arrangement. Simply clip the stem near the holder and put in the replacement.

Conditioning Ingredients

Refer to the alphabetical list below for directions to condition different flowers. All ingredients are obtainable from grocery or pharmacy.

Alcohol (rubbing)
Alum
Ammonia (household)
Boric Acid
Camphor (liquid)
Glycerine
Hydrocloric acid
Oil of Peppermint
Paraffin
Salt (rock)

Salt (table)
Sugar
Vinegar
Washing Soda (Sodium carbonate)

Hardening

Soak the flowers, "neck high," in tepid water overnight. (Delicate leaves, wild flowers and ferns should be completely covered.) This is known as hardening.

While hardening, a long leaf may be shaped by taping a wire on the back in a desired position.

After hardening, remove the wire and the tape. Shape lupine, stock, and snapdragon by placing at an angle while hardening.

FLOWERS AND SUGGESTED PROCESSES

African Violet—Burn ends—Harden
Ageratum—Dip the tip of the stem in boiling water—Harden
Almond—Crush ends—Dip in boiling water—Harden
Apple Blossoms—Cut in bud, crush ends of stem—Condition in 1 tbsp. household ammonia to 1 quart water—Harden
Alyssum—Condition in ½ tbsp. sugar to 1 quart water—Harden
Amaryllis—Condition in 1 tsp. peppermint oil in 1 quart water—Harden
Anemone—Scrape lower 2 inches of stem—condition in 1 pint of water to ½ cup vinegar—Harden
Aster—Condition in 1 tsp. sugar per quart of water—Harden
Azalea—Burn stem—Condition in 1 tbsp. alcohol per gallon of water—Harden
Baby's Breath—Condition in 1 tsp. alcohol to 1 pint water—Harden
Bamboo—Remove foliage. Use stalk only.
Begonia (tuberous)—Condition in 2 tbsp. salt to 2 quarts water—Do not harden
Bells of Ireland—Crush stems—Harden
Bird of Paradise—Condition in ½ cup vinegar to 1 quart of water—Harden
Bittersweet—Split stems—Harden
Bougainvillea—Dip tip of stems in peppermint oil 2 seconds—Harden
Broom—Dip tips of stems in boiling water—Harden
Buttercup—Harden

Caladium—Put salt on end of stems—Harden
Camellia—Place flower between layers of cool damp cotton
Calla Lilies and Leaves—Condition in ½ cup vinegar to 1 quart water—Harden for 24 hours
Canna—Condition in 7 drops hydrochloric acid to 2 quarts of water—Harden
Canterbury Bell—Burn ends—Condition in 2 quarts of water plus 2 tbsp. soda—Harden
Carnation—Cut below node—Condition in ⅛ tsp. boric acid to 1 quart water—Harden
Cherry Blossoms—Break stems—Plunge in boiling water—Harden
Christmas Rose—Do not cut leaves but split stems—Harden
Chrysanthemum—Burn stems—Condition in 2 quarts of water with 8 drops of oil of peppermint—Harden 25 hours
Clematis—Burn ends—Condition in 3 tbsp. of alcohol to 2 quarts of water—Harden
Coleus—Dip stem in alcohol for 2 minutes—Harden
Cosmos—Harden overnight.
Cyclamen—Put salt on end of the stem before hardening
Daffodils—Cut blooms with a sharp knife on an angle above the white part of the stem—Put in shallow warm water for 12 hours—Recut stems and immerse in tepid water—They can be refrigerated for several days; mist blooms often
Dahlias—Burn ends—Condition in ½ cup of vinegar per gallon of water—Harden
Daisies—Condition in water containing 8 drops of oil of peppermint per quart—Harden
Delphinium—Crush stems—Condition in 1 tbsp. of alcohol per pint of water—Harden
Dogwood—Split ends—Plunge in hot tap water—Harden
English Ivy—Split stems 3″—Harden completely covered by cool water.
Eucalyptus—Split ends—Plunge in hot tap water—Harden
Evergreens—Crush end of stem—Condition in 1 quart water and 1 tsp. glycerine—Harden
Fall Foliage—Burn tips of stems immediately—Condition in deep water with 1 cup of vinegar—Harden
Flax—Dip in peppermint oil about a second—Harden
Ferns—Harden completely covered with cold water; hardy ferns difficult
Freesia—Condition in ½ tsp. alcohol in 1 quart water—Harden

Funkia—Condition in 1 pint of cold water to ½ cup vinegar—Harden

Fuchsia—Burn stem tips—Harden

Galax—Wrap leaf in damp paper

Gaillardia—Condition in 1 pint of water with 2 tbsp. salt—Harden

Gardenia—Spray lightly with water

Geranium—Condition with 1 tsp. alum to 1 quart water—Harden

Gladiolus—Break stems—Condition in water containing 1 tbsp. alcohol per quart—Harden

Grape Hyacinth—Dip ends in hot tap water—Condition in 1 tsp. alcohol to 1 pint of cold water—Harden

Hyacinth—Squeeze fluid from stem—Harden in cold water

Hollyhock—Remove all leaves, split the stems, and burn the tips—Condition in 2 quarts water with one handful of rock salt—Harden

Hydrangea—Crush the stems—Burn tips—Harden overnight

Heliotrope—Split the stem, plunge in hot tap water—Harden—This can be repeated if need be

Iris—Burn the tip of the stem—Harden

Iris, Bulbous—Condition in 3 tbsp. of salt to 1 quart of water—Harden

Larkspur—Condition in 2 quarts of cold water with ½ tsp. of alcohol—Harden

Lantana—Dip in hot water—Harden

Lilies (all)—Turn them upside down and allow cool water to flow over them—Harden

Lily-of-the-Valley—Plunge the tips of stems into boiling water—Harden in cold water

Lily (Water)—Pump water into the stems with a syringe—A drop of paraffin in the center will keep flowers open—Harden

Lilac—Leave only the leaves near the head—Split the stems—Spray the flower heads with tepid water—Harden in tepid water

Lupine—Harden

Magnolia—Split the stems—Dip in boiling water—Harden

Maple—Split the stems—Dip in boiling water—Harden

Marigolds—Same as Daisies

Marguerites—Condition 2 hours in 1 quart of water and 1 tsp. of oil of peppermint—Harden

Nasturtium—Condition in 3 tsp. of sugar to 1 quart of cold water—Harden

Pansy—Harden

Peony—Split the ends—Condition in 1 quart of water with 3 tsp. of sugar—Harden

Petunias—Condition in cold water with 1 tbsp. of alcohol per pint—Harden

Pine—Condition in 1 part water and 1 part alcohol for 10 minutes—Harden

Pinks—Condition in 3 tbsp. of table salt to 1 quart of water—Harden

Peach Blossoms—Dip the stem tips in boiling water—Harden in cold water overnight

Poinsettias—Burn the stem—Rub salt into the burned end and harden in cold water

Poppies—Same as Poinsettias

Primrose—Dip the stems in boiling water—then harden

Rose—Burn the stem—Condition in cold water with 1 tbsp. of powdered alum to 1 quart of water—Harden

Snapdragon—Scrape the ends—Condition in 3 tbsp. of salt to 1 pint water—Harden overnight

Statice—Condition in 3 tbsp. of sugar to 1 pint of water—Harden

Spirea—Split the ends—Condition in hot water—Harden

Stock—Split the stems—Condition overnight in cold water with 1 tbsp. sugar and 2 tbsp. of white vinegar per quart of water

Shasta Daisy—Burn the ends—Harden

Sunflower—Burn the ends—Harden overnight

Sweet Pea—Condition in 1 tbsp. of alcohol per quart of water—Harden in water with 1 tbsp. of sugar to each quart of water

Sweet William—Condition in 1 tbsp. of alcohol to 1 pint of water—Harden

Thistle—Condition in 3 tsp. of alcohol to 1 quart of water—Harden overnight

Tulip—Harden in cold water overnight, wrap petals with wet tissue.

Verbena—Split the stems—Harden

Violet—Let stand in ice water up to neck

Wild Flowers—Condition in water with ¼ cup of sugar to 1 gallon of water—Harden

Willow—Dip split stems in boiling water—Harden

Wisteria—Cut after sundown—Split the stems—Condition in ¼ cup of vinegar to 1 quart of water—Harden

Zinnia—Condition in 2 tbsp. of alcohol to 1 quart of water—Harden

Helpful Hints

To force blooms on cut flowers or plants, put a little ammonia in the water. Cover container tightly with a plastic bag. Flowers will open the next day.

To force a spray of flowers, such as gladiolus or dendrobium orchid, to open slowly, pinch off the very top tiny buds.

To make gladiolus show more color in a flower arrangement, strip off green sheath on all upper flowerlets.

To keep blooms open longer, add a small amount of a clear, sugared soft drink.

THE DRYING OF FLOWERS AND PLANT CUTTINGS

The peak of maturity is the best time to collect and dry flowers and foliage. Do not gather material when damp because it will mold. One of the four methods below should be selected depending upon the general character of the plant.

Pressing

Flowers, leaves, and small branches can be pressed between layers of newspaper. Open and lay out a section of newspaper, placing the material on the lower half of the inside sheet. Fold a loose sheet of newspaper in half horizontally and place on top of material. Next, fold over the upper half of the first section of newspaper. Place on top of the whole stack any proper weight such a board, bricks, or books. Twenty-four hours later remove the horizontally folded sheet from the top of the flowers. The absorbed moisture will lessen the chance of discoloring or molding. Replace the weight and leave for ten days or longer until thoroughly crisp and dry. Any number of flowers can be pressed this way by stacking layers of paper under increased weights. Clean leaves or small branches with a cloth dampened with mineral oil, then proceed as above. Clean ferns gently with a light brush. Fall leaves retain their color when pressed between two sheets of wax paper with an iron at low heat. Then press between newspaper under weight for two days.

Non-floral Materials for Pressing

Autumn foliage, Beech foliage, Chestnut foliage, Forsythia foliage, Oak foliage, Rose foliage, Scotch broom

Hanging

Flowers and leaves which do not contain a great deal of moisture can be hung in the air to dry. Tie several cuttings together loosely for good air circulation. Hang in a warm, dry place but out of sunlight to preserve color. Fine textured grasses, feathery weeds, and flowers with small blossoms along the stem dry well this way. They should be crisp in less than a month.

Plants Which Can Be Dried by Hanging

Ageratum
Bittersweet
Bluegrass
Bramble
Buckeye
Catalpa pods
Chinese Lantern
Cockscomb
Dock
Dollar plant (Honesty)
Feather grass
Goldenrod
Gourds
Herbs
Hickory
Honey Locust pods
Hydrangea
Iris seed pods
Japanese Iris
Lavender
Magnolia cones
Milkweed pods
Mimosa pods
Oats
Onion bloom
Palm
Pepper pods
Pomegranate
Poppy pods
Princess-feather
Pussy Willow
Pyracantha
Red Bud
Sage
Strawflower
Summer Seed Pods
Wheat
Yarrow
Yucca

Covering

When a flower is heavy with moisture and less delicate it must be covered with one of the following drying substances.

A. Sand and borax—one part fine dry sand, two parts borax with one tablespoon of table salt per quart of mix.

B. Half and Half—yellow corn meal and borax.

C. Commercial products containing silicagel. An effective but expensive method. The chemical keeps indefinitely and can be reactivated by warming in the oven.

To dry by covering line flat containers with waxed paper and fill with at least one inch of the drying mixture. Individually place flowers with two-inch stems on the mixture. Sift more drying mixture gently through and around petals until each bloom is completely covered. Place flowers with curved petals, like lilies, stem down to preserve their shape; place flat flowers, like daisies, face down. Do not make two layers. Do not put a cover on top. Let flowers remain in the mixture until crisp and dry but not long enough to crumble. Varying lengths of time are required for drying depending on flower texture. Remove flowers gingerly. Remove small clinging particles with a soft brush. The foliage must be dried separately according to its type. Later attach the dried flowers to their stems with florist wire.

Materials Which Can Be Dried by Covering

Apple blossom	Larkspur
Aster	Lilac
Bachelor's button	Lily
Bells-of-Ireland	Marguerite
Black-Eyed Susan	Marigold
Calendula	Narcissus
Carnation	Pansy
Chrysanthemum	Peony
Daffodil	Queen-Anne's-lace
Dahlia	Rose
Daisy	Snapdragon
Dogwood	Sunflower
Forsythia	Tulip
Hollyhock	Thistle
Lantana	Zinnia

Glycerine

Glycerine treatment is good for plants with smooth leaves like the magnolia. Crush and split stems for 2″ or 3″. Clean leaves with cold water. Immerse in hot water for a short while then place in a solution of two parts water and one part glycerine. Stem should extend at least 6″ into the solution. Leaves turn golden, bronze, or dark brown depending on the type of foliage. Make sure there is enough solution in the container at all times. To hasten absorption recut stems one-half inch once a week. The process takes 2 to 3 weeks, a little longer for thick leathery leaves. When desired color is reached, remove material, and store in a dust free place until used. Submerge galax and

English ivy completely in half water, half glycerine. Late spring to midsummer is the best time to treat these plants. Late summer is best for magnolia and beech. Glycerine-treated foliage will last for years. It can be used dry or combined with fresh flowers. Water does not injure treated stems.

Materials for Glycerine Treatment

Castor Bean
Beech foliage
Chestnut foliage
Cleyera
Dogwood foliage
Forsythia foliage
Galax foliage
Ivy
Magnolia foliage
Oak foliage
Periwinkle
Photinia
Rhododendron

Poisonous Plants

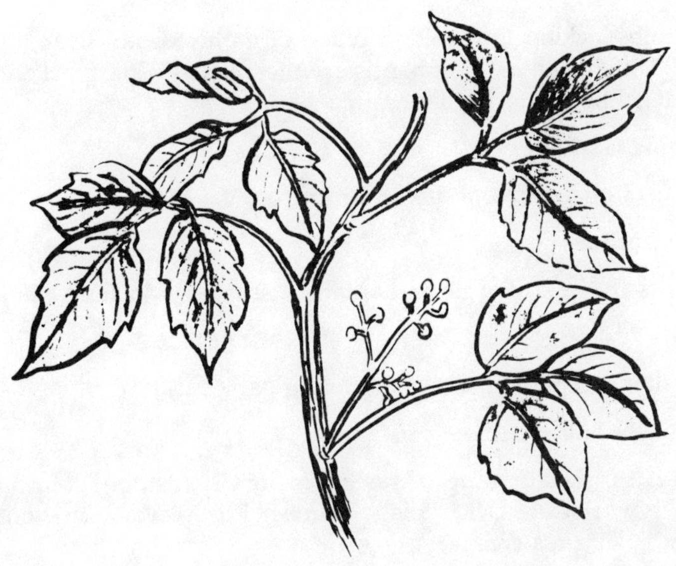

Fortunately, relatively large amounts of most plants are necessary to produce serious or fatal poisoning in adults. However, much smaller amounts of the toxin can cause very severe or fatal results in children. One or two seeds could cause death in some instances.

Become familiar with dangerous plants in the home and garden and know them by name.

Teach young children to keep plants and plant parts out of their mouths.

Keep all plants, seeds, fruits, and bulbs away from infants.

Do not eat wild plants, including mushrooms, unless positive of identification.

Be careful of jewelry made from seeds or beans.

As a general precaution, avoid plants with milky or colored juices, all unknown red or white berries, all bulbs lacking the smell of onion or garlic.

If plant poisoning occurs, or is suspected, immediately call a poison control center, physician, or hospital. Be prepared to identify any suspect plant. Save evidence, such as plant parts, which may help identify the plant involved, and take samples to the hospital.

Shown below is a listing of poisonous plants.

House Plants

All bulbs lacking the smell of onion or garlic, Castor Bean, Dumb cane (Dieffenbachia), Elephant's-ear, Jerusalem Cherry, Lantana, Oleander, Philodendron, Poinsettia.

Vegetable Garden

Potato (all parts except tuber), Rhubarb.

Flower Garden

Angel's-trumpet, Foxglove, Lantana, Larkspur, Morning-glory.

Bulbs

All bulbs lacking the smell of onion or garlic.

Field Plants and Wildflowers

Buttercup, Death Cup (Mushroom or Toadstool), Mayapple, Poison Ivy, Poison Oak, Poison Sumac, Pokeweed, Snow-on-the-mountain, Virginia creeper.

Vines, Shrubs and Trees

Azalea, Boxwood, Buckeye, Carolina Jasmine (Yellow Jasmine), Dogwood, Elderberry (Black Elder), English Ivy, Golden-chain tree, Holly, Morning-glory, Privet, Trumpet creeper, Wisteria, Yew.

Fruit Trees (seeds)

Apple, Apricot, Cherry, Peach, Plum.

Glossary of Botanical Terms

acanth (ak-anth): spiny, spiky or thorny
aceae (*ay*-se-ee): family
acu (ak-yew): sharply pointed
aden (ad-en): sticky
adsurgens (ad-*ser*-jens): pushing straight upward
aeneus (*ee*-neus): of a bronze color
aggregatus (ag-greg-*ay*-tus): clustered
alatus (al-*ay*-tus): winged
alb-, albi-, albo-, albus: white
albiplenus (al-bee-*plee*-nus): double white flowered
alpinus (al-*pi*-nus): above timberline
alternifolius (al-ter-ni-*fo*-lius): with alternate leaves
altus (*al*-tus): tall
americanus (am-er-ik-*ay*-nus): American
amurensis (am-oor-*en*-sis): of Amur River area in eastern Asia
angustifolius (an-gus-ti-*fo*-lius): narrow-leaved
anosmus (an-*os*-mus): lacking scent
apodus (*ap*-o-dus): having flowers without a stalk
aquaticus (ak-*wat*-ik-us): growing in or near water
arenarius (a-ren-*air*-ius): growing in sandy places
argenteus (ar-*jen*-teus): silvery
ater-, atra-, atrum- (*ay*-ter): dead, black
atlanticus (at-*lan*-tik-us): of Atlantic regions
atro- (at-ro): dark
aurantiacus (aw-ran-*ty*-ak-us): orange colored
aureo- (aw-reo): golden
australis (aw-*straw*-lis): southern
baccatus (bak-*ay*-tus): fleshy, berried
bellus (bell-us): handsome

biennis (by-*enn*-is): biennial, living two years
botryoides (bot-ri-*oy*-deez): resembling a bunch of grapes
brachy (brack-i): short
bullatus (bul-*ay*-tus): puckered
caeruleus (see-*rool*-eus): dark blue
calcicola (kal-kik-*o*-la): growing in limey soil
Calla (kal-la): beautiful
callicarpus (kal-i-*karp*-us): with beautiful fruit
Camellia (kam-*ell*-ia): pronunciation preferred
campanulatus (kam-pan-ew-*lay*-tus): bell-shaped
canadensis (kan-ad-*en*-sis): of North America or Canada
canescens (kan-*ess*-ens): downy gray
cardiopetalus (kar-dio-pet-*al*-us): with heart-shaped petals
cernuus (see-*new*-us): nodding, drooping
chinensis (chy-*nen*-sis): Chinese
Chrysanthus (kris-*anth*-us): golden flowered
ciliatus (sil-i-*ay*-tus): hairy fringed or margined
coccineus (kok-*sin*-eus): scarlet
columnaris (kol-um-*nay*-ris): columnar
compactus (kom-*pak*-tus): compact
coniferous (ko-*niff*-er-us): cone-bearing
contortus (kon-*tort*-us): twisted
cornutus (kor-*new*-tus): horned
crenatus (kree-*nay*-tus): scalloped
dasy- (das-i-): thick
deciduus (de-*sid*-yew-us): with parts falling (as leaves), deciduous
dentatus (den-*tay*-tus): toothed
dioicus (dy-*o*-ik-us): having male and female flowers on separate plants
diurnus (dy-urn-us): day-flowering
divaricatus (dy-va-rik-*ay*-tus): straggling or spreading
echinatus (ek-in-*ay*-tus): covered with prickles
elatus (el-*ay*-tus): tall
erythro-: red
exoticus (ex-*ot*-ik-us): foreign, not native
fastigiatus (fas-tij-i-*ay*-tus): growing like a column
fili-: thread-like
flavus (*flay*-vus): yellow
flore-pleno (flor-e-*plee*-no): with double flowers
floribundus (flor-i-*bund*-us): flowering profusely
florida: flowering

foetidus (*fee*-tid-us): bad smelling
formosus (form-*o*-sus): handsome, beautiful
Forsythia: popularly (for-*sith*-ia), preferably (for-*sy*-thia)
fragrans (*fray*-grans): fragrant
fructescens (fruk-*tess*-ens): fruit-bearing
frutescens (frew-*tess*-ens): shrubby or bushy
fulvus (*ful*-vus): tawny orange
glaber, glabra, glabrum (*glay*-ber): smooth
glaucus (*glaw*-kus): covered with grayish, powdery coating
gloriosus (glow-ri-*o*-sus): superb
gracilis (*gras*-ill-is): slender, graceful
grandis (*grand*-is): big, showy
guttatus (gut-*ay*-tus): spotted, speckled
gypsophila (jip-*soff*-ill-a): baby's breath
haemanthus (hee-*man*-thus): with blood red flowers
helix, properly (*hell*-is), often (*he*-lix): twining
herbaceus (her-*bay*-see-us): not woody
heter-, hetero: diverse
hirsutus (her-*su*-tus): hairy
humilis (*hew*-mil-is): low-growing, dwarf
hyacinthus (hy-a-*sin*-thus): dark, purplish blue
ibericus (eye-*ber*-ik-us): Spanish, Portuguese
ilicifolius (eye-liss-i-*fo*-lius): holly-leaved
imperialis (im-peer-i-*ay*-lis): fine or showy
indicus (in-*dik*-us): of India
insignis (in-*sig*-nis): remarkable, outstanding
japonicus (jap-*on*-ik-us): Japanese
kaempferi (*kamp*-fer-eye): varietal name of azalea
Kalanchoë (kal-an-*ko*-ee): Chinese succulent
kousa (*kow*-sa): Japanese name for *Cornus kousa*
labiautus (lab-i-*ay*-tus): lipped
lactatus (lak-*tay*-tus): milky
lancifolius (lan-see-*fo*-lius): lance-leaved
latifolius (lat-i-*fo*-lius): broad-leaved
leuc-: signifies white
longifolius (lon-ji-*fo*-lius): long-leaved
luteus (*lew*-teus): yellow
macro-: large or long
maculatus (mak-yew-*lay*-tus): spotted
majalis (ma-*jay*-lis): May flowering
mega-: big

micro-: small
mollis (*moll*-is): soft or with soft hairs
nanus (*nay*-nus): small, dwarf
Narcissus (nar-*sis*-us): daffodil
niger (*ny*-jer): black
nivalis (niv-*ay*-lis): snow white or growing near snow
nudus (*new*-dus): naked, bare
obtusus (ob-*tew*-sus): blunt
occidentalis (ox-id-ent-*tay*-lis): western
odoratus (o-do-*ray*-tus): fragrant
officinalis (o-fiss-in-*ay*-lis): medicinal or useful
ornithogalum (or-nith-*og*-al-um): Star-of-Bethlehem
ortho-: upright, straight
packy-: thick
pallens (*pal*-ens): pale
palustris (pal-*us*-tris): marsh-loving
paniculatus (pan-ik-yew-*lay*-tus): with flowers arranged in panicles
parvus (*par*-vus): small
patens (*pay*-tens): spreading
pedatus (pee-*day*-tus): like a bird's foot
pennatus (pen-*ay*-tus): feathered
penta-: five
phlogiflorus (flog-i-*flo*-rus): flame-colored flowers or phloxlike flowers
pilosus (py-*lo*-sus): covered with long soft hairs
platy-: flat or broad
plenus (*plee*-nus): full, double
poly-: many
praecox (*pree*-cos): very early
Pteris (*tee*-ris): feathery fronds
pubens (pew-bens): downy
pugens (*pun*-jens): sharp pointed
quercifolius (kwer-si-*fo*-lius): with leaves like an oak
racemosus (ras-see-*mo*-sus): bearing flowers on a short stem connected to a longer stem
radicans (*rad*-ik-ans): having rooted stem
recurvus (ree-*ker*-vus): curved backward
repens (*ree*-pens): creeping
reptans (*rep*-tans): creeping
reticulatus (ree-tik-yew-*lay*-tus): netted, net-veined
rotundus (ro-*tun*-dus): rounded

rubens (*roo*-bens): red or ruddy
sanguineus (sang-*qwin*-eus): blood red
sativus (sat-*ty*-vus): cultivated
scandens (*skan*-dens): climbing
sempervirens (sem-per-*vy*-rens): evergreen
sept-: seven
serratus (ser-*ray*-tus): saw-toothed
sessilis (*sess*-il-is): stalkless
silvestris (sil-*vest*-ris): growing in woods
sinensis (sin-*nen*-sis): of China
speciosus (spess-i-*o*-sus): showy
spectabilis (spek-*tab*-il-is): spectacular
splendens (*splen*-dens): splendid
stellaris (stell-*ay*-ris): starry
steno-: narrow
strepto-: twisted
striatus (stry-*ay*-tus): striped
suffrutescens (suf-froo-*tess*-ens): somewhat shrubby
sylvaticus (sil-*vat*-ik-us): of woods and forests
tenuis (*ten*-yew-is): slender, thin
tetra-: four
tinctorius (tink-*tor*-ius): used in dying
tomentosus (to-men-*to*-sus): densely wooly
tri-: three
tuberosus (tew-ber-*o*-sus): tuberous
umbellatus (um-bell-*ay*-tus): umbrellalike
variegatus (vair-ree-*gay*-tus): irregularly colored
vegetatus (vej-et-*tay*-tus): vigorous
vernus (*ver*-nus): of spring
versicolor (ver-*si*-kol-or): variously colored
virens (*vy*-rens): green
vulgaris (vul-*gay*-ris): common
xanthinus (zan-*thy*-nus): yellow

References

American Daffodil Society. 1980. *Daffodils to show and grow*. Tyner, NC: The American Daffodil Society.

American Iris Society. 1969. *What every iris grower should know*. n.p.: The American Iris Society.

Baumgardt, J. P. 1968. *How to prune almost everything*. New York: Wm. Morrow.

Beatty, V. 1975. *Consumer Guide rating and raising indoor plants*. Skokie, IL: Consumer Guide/Publications.

Brooklyn Botanic Gardens. 1959. *Handbook on dwarfed potted trees*. Brooklyn: Brooklyn Botanic Gardens.

Bush-Brown, L. and Bush-Brown, J. 1955. *America's garden book*. New York: Scribners.

Cobb, Broughton. 1956. *The field guide to the fern*. Boston: Houghton Mifflin.

Crockett, J. U. 1978. *The Time-Life encyclopedia of gardening*. New York: Time-Life Books.

Dean, B. E. 1968. *Trees and shrubs in the heart of Dixie*. Birmingham: Southern University Press.

Free, Montague. 1961. *Plant pruning in pictures*. New York: Doubleday.

Hawkes, A. D. 1961. *Orchids*. New York: Harper & Row.

Johnson, H. 1973. *The international book of trees*. New York: Bonanza Books.

H. L. Bailey Hortorium, Cornell University. 1976. *Hortus Third*. New York: Macmillan.

Lee, F. P. 1965. *The azalea book*. New York: Van Nostrand.

Naka, J. K. vol. I, 1975; vol. II, 1982. *Bonsai techniques I and II*. Santa Monica: Dennis-Landman.

Peterson, Roger Tory, and McKenny, M. 1968. *A field guide to wildflowers*. Boston: Houghton Mifflin.

Petrides, G. A. 1958. *A field guide to trees and shrubs*. Boston: Houghton Mifflin.

Reader's Digest. 1979. *Complete book of the garden*. Pleasantville, NY: Reader's Digest Association.

Rickett, Harold William. n.d. *Wildflowers of the United States*. New York: McGraw-Hill.

Seymour, E. L. D. 1970. *The Wise garden encyclopedia*. Union City, NJ: W. H. Wise & Co.

Shaver, J. M. 1954. *Ferns of Tennessee*. Nashville: George Peabody College.

Smith, A. W. 1963. *A gardener's book of plant names*. New York: Harper & Row.

Steffek, E. M. n.d. *Complete book of houseplants and indoor gardening*. New York: Crown Publishers.

Sunset Books. 1979. *How to grow orchids*. Menlo Park, CA: Lane Publishing.

Taylor, N. 1948. *Taylor's encyclopedia of gardening*. Boston: Houghton Mifflin.

Tyson, R. 1962. *Growing home orchids*. New York: Van Nostrand.

Wigginton, B. E. 1963. *Trees and shrubs for the Southeast*. Athens: University of Georgia Press.

Index

NOTE: Page numbers in bold italic are where charts are to be found.

NOTE: Page numbers in bold italic are where charts are to be found.

NOTE: Page numbers in bold italic are where charts are to be found.

NOTE: Page numbers in bold italic are where charts are to be found.

NOTE: Page numbers in bold italic are where charts are to be found.

NOTE: Page numbers in bold italic are where charts are to be found.

NOTE: Page numbers in bold italic are where charts are to be found.

NOTE: Page numbers in bold italic are where charts are to be found.

NOTE: Page numbers in bold italic are where charts are to be found.

NOTE: Page numbers in bold italic are where charts are to be found.

NOTE: Page numbers in bold italic are where charts are to be found.

Notes

Notes

Notes

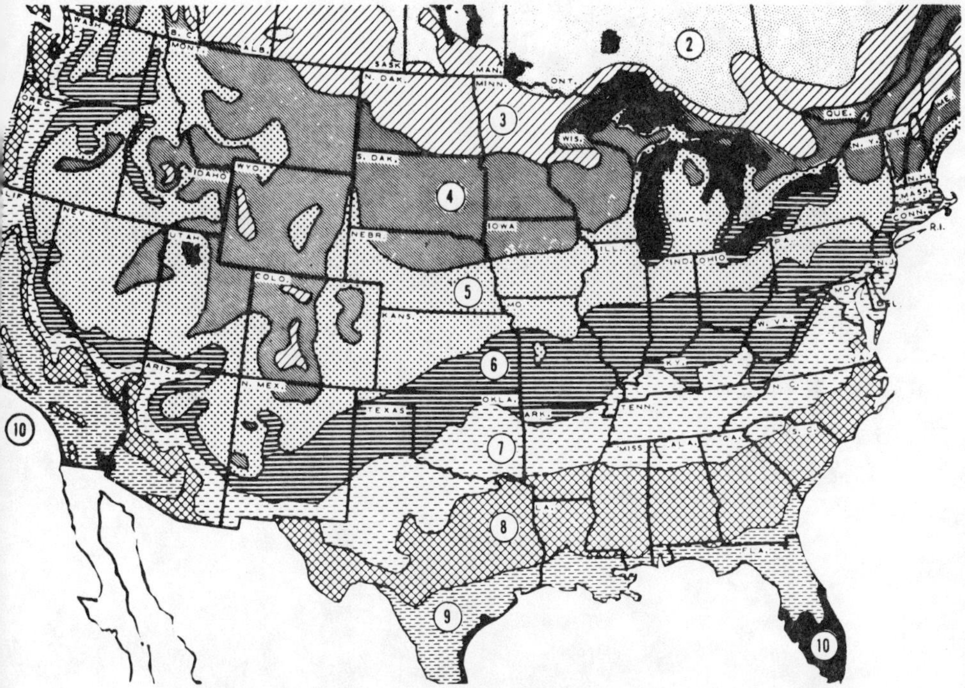

HARDINESS ZONES

The above hardiness map was developed by the Agricultural Research Service of the U. S. Dept. of Agriculture. The hardiness zones 1 - 10 are based on the average annual minimum temperature for each zone and divide the United States and Canada into areas that indicate the winter hardiness for certain plants. Many factors such as altitude, length of growing season, exposure, moisture, soil types, etc., can create variations within zones, but adhering to your specific zone will generally give you the best results. Often, however, inhabitants of the southern-most portions of one zone may safely use plants suited for the northern-most portion of the next zone.

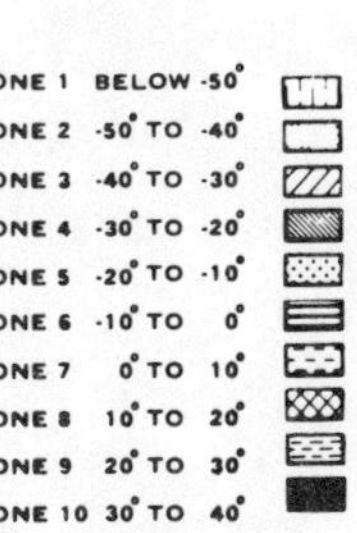

Notes

Notes

Need Additional Copies? Use this handy order form. Please Send _____ copy/copies of *The Mid-South Garden Guide* at $16.95 each, plus $2.50 in postage ($19.45) for each book. TN residents add $1.40 tax ($20.85) for each book.

$ Amount of order _____ My check or money order is enclosed.

Payable to:
Memphis Garden Club

Signature ____

Name ____

Address ____

City/State/Zip ____

Send order to:
Memphis Garden Club
Dixon Gallery & Gardens
4339 Park Avenue
Memphis, TN 38117-9886

Need Additional Copies? Use this handy order form. Please Send _____ copy/copies of *The Mid-South Garden Guide* at $16.95 each, plus $2.50 in postage ($19.45) for each book. TN residents add $1.40 tax ($20.85) for each book.

$ Amount of order _____ My check or money order is enclosed.

Payable to:
Memphis Garden Club

Signature ____

Name ____

Address ____

City/State/Zip ____

Send order to:
Memphis Garden Club
Dixon Gallery & Gardens
4339 Park Avenue
Memphis, TN 38117-9886